ALSO BY AGATA TUSZYŃSKA

Lost Landscapes: In Search of Isaac Bashevis Singer and the Jews of Poland

VERA GRAN
The Accused

VERA GRAN
The Accused

Agata Tuszyńska

TRANSLATED BY CHARLES RUAS
FROM THE FRENCH OF
ISABELLE JANNÈS-KALINOWSKI

 ALFRED A. KNOPF NEW YORK 2013

Library of Congress Cataloging-in-Publication Data
Tuszyńska, Agata, author.
[Oskarzona Wiera Gran. English]
Vera Gran : the accused / by Agata Tuszyńska ; translated by Charles Ruas from the French of Isabelle Jannès-Kalinowski.
pages   cm
ISBN 978-0-307-26912-6
1. Gran, Wiera.   2. Women singers—Poland—Biography.
3. Actresses—Poland—Biography.   4. Jews—Poland—Warsaw—Biography.
5 World War, 1939–1945—Jews—Poland—Warsaw.
6. Warsaw (Poland)—Biography.   I. Title.
ML420.G81T8713 2013
782.1092—dc23
[B]   2012036281

Jacket photograph courtesy of the Archives of Vera Gran
Jacket design by Kelly Blair

Manufactured in the United States of America

First American Edition

for those who know the taste of ashes

What is fate?
It's the traps we set for ourselves.

—I. B. SINGER

Contents

CONTENTS

Illustrations

ILLUSTRATIONS

**VERA GRAN
The Accused**

1

She picked up the receiver
but didn't speak

She picked up the receiver but didn't speak at first. She breathed—with increasing difficulty, and more loudly—as time passed. She was expecting curses and insults. She waited; they will track her down, they will find her, they'll finish her off. She won't give in. She concentrated all her energy on that.

"I'd like to see you, Vera."

"I can't leave the house."

"I can come to you."

"It's not possible."

"Please."

"Out of the question."

"Why?"

"They'll break in and steal everything."

"Who will?"

"Are you crazy or what? Do I have to explain it to you? Who am I dealing with? Shhhh . . . keep quiet, please! They're listening in, and we're being taped. You know very well who I'm talking about. They're spying on me, they want to get rid of me. I'm followed everywhere. The concierge is in cahoots with them. They are always breaking in, when I'm in the bathroom or when I fall asleep. They carry off what they can, what is most valuable, what is dearest to me. They steal, they ransack, they burglarize me. Without any scruples. There's no question of my leaving the apartment. They are always watching me."

HE is the most dangerous, whose name she never mentions. Sometimes she calls him the Brute.

"I want to write a book about you."

"I'm not afraid. They've already made up so many lies about me. You have to think of me as Mister K., the one from Kafka . . ."

"Madame K. . . ."

"Madame, Madame . . . !!! It's my skin we are talking about! You still don't understand, you can't understand anything. You numbskull!"

Shortly afterward:

"Vera is sorry. Very, very. Please . . . please excuse me. When I'm having a fit, I become an unbearable old lady!"

After weeks of negotiation, in the spring of 2003 I was granted the honor of meeting her at the door of her apartment.

It was an elegant neighborhood of Paris, the sixteenth, around the Eiffel Tower. After climbing up one flight, I knocked. An inscription, in French, on the door: *Knock Loudly!* An old woman, not very tall, in a pink dressing gown, opened the door a crack. She didn't trust herself, nor me. A gray chignon coming undone with protruding wisps, a gleam in her eyes, and her right hand leaning on a crutch.

She opened the door a little more. She blocked the dark interior with her body. A chair had already been placed on the landing. She looked at me with suspicion. Her soft hands moved nimbly. "I am casting a spell. I love casting spells." With these

This is how I saw her for the first time: the meeting with the star at the threshold of her Paris apartment in the spring of 2003. She was eighty-seven.

gestures she didn't arouse pity. She tried to bring out a second chair by opening the door as little as possible. The inside of her bunker, dark and disturbing. A hideout. On the right, I could see written on the wall, also in French: *Thief, thief, put back everything you took, especially the blue poncho . . .* I couldn't manage to make out any more at first glance. Her hair, parts of her dressing gown, and her hands quivered. She sat down. We both sat down.

She handed me a tape recorder, even though I had mine. She would keep warning me: "Record it, or else you will forget what they are saying—or worse, what you yourself have said! RECORD IT!"

Her confidences were dull gray, like ashes. Periodically the lights went out in the stairwell. Then my feelings of compassion grew until the lights came back on. A moment of light—the harshest words, the most biting, the most sinister and revealing, until the poignant moment when the lights dimmed. There were several encounters like this, on the edges of darkness.

"You want to reach right into my soul. Just like that. You think it's normal, and that I should agree completely. Just because you feel like it. Because you thought of it. You have no conscience, no heart, you scribblers. Not a penny's worth of consideration. Contemptible!

"You Polish girls, you are so insolent, it's in your nature. You are odiously arrogant. Here she shows up, she wants an interview. And she's not the only one.

"I don't ask anyone in. I see nobody. You are the only one, and afterward, I always regret it. I regret that you've seen what you saw. I don't have any confidence. You have a strange professional bias: cruelty, no compassion."

"That's what you think?"

"Yes, insolent. Insensitive, and not an ounce of compassion for your milk cow. You want to milk me, you take my milk. I can't even kick over the pail. Give it a good kick to spill everything out. Or take back my treasures. I would have liked that, but it's already too late. I've already spoken. Why did I allow this to happen? I don't know. Out of loneliness, perhaps."

We spent a week on the landing. White chairs. Uncomfortable. Tiles on the floor and faded paint on the walls.

It was a place of passage. We were on the threshold of trust. A preface to a relationship.

And then one day I knocked, as usual, and she cracked open the door. Timidly, almost excusing herself, but with a determined gesture, she pulled me inside. I squeezed through a narrow hallway to a room difficult to describe. She made an impatient gesture, pointing to a chair. I can't recall much beyond the darkness, the stifling and oppressive air.

"I've made a pact with the dust. I won't disturb it and it won't trouble me. It's capable of feeling pity. It really is. My enemies work tirelessly. I recently heard a radio program about the Stasi. That's my life."

She moved around cautiously, she navigated between the furniture and piles of cardboard boxes and stacks of newspapers. Barely fifty centimeters from the bed to the table, the chair to the refrigerator; a little farther, a path worn through columns of stacked papers (newspaper clippings, reviews, manuscripts . . .) led up to the hallway, crowded with suitcases, clothing, dried-up house plants, piles of accessories either useless or indispensable. Her home was the size of an average bunker in the ghetto (when does it stop, calculating everything in terms of cost—for her hideout, the price of survival, the money extorted by blackmailers?); if this place were emptied out, several people could hide here. The books were falling off the shelves, squeezed together, amassing in the stagnant air.

I had trouble staying there even for a few hours. For months she hadn't left this hideout. For years, if you believed her distorted view of time and reality.

"It's not about you. You are a tool. The ear and the pen, the extension of my hand and my eyes—you are keeping a record of my past. The role doesn't please you, I can see from the face that you are making. But we don't have any time. We don't have any choice. Either it's me on my terms, or else it's silence."

Hanging over the table was a lamp, the shade like a flower with translucent petals of a tree from Israel. Fragile like fragments of parchment, looking like shells. Moneysworth, that's what she called them; that's how she wanted to remember them after lugging them from the desert through Ben Gurion Airport to Orly. She fell in love with the lamp. She fell in love easily with

The interior of Vera Gran's apartment on rue Chardon-Lagache, in the elegant 16th arrondissement of Paris. After her death, the windows were opened for the first time in years.

anything that didn't feel human. She painstakingly arranged the little sprigs in a crown. The lamp was a light. Apparently she once saw no danger in it.

Today it's always dark, the shutters are closed.

How is it possible for a person who has spent half her life on stage not to turn the lights on at home? She willingly lived in twilight.

"It's because of them, it's them. Because they installed everything here, I had to get rid of all the lights. The twilight came, I had to get used to it. Their light is stronger. It's special—to enable them to record and film. I can't always stay in the light of a movie camera. Do you understand?"

· · ·

"What was the most important thing about singing for you?"

"I wanted to stir emotions. I sang for other people, not for myself. I gave, but I also received from the public an outpouring of emotion and involvement.

"I must have been conceited. That goes with the unthinking nature of youth. I wanted to give, share, I had everything in abundance. I also wanted—and I can't deny it—to be admired. I had been singing since I was very little. It made me feel good, people paid attention to me. I was in a hurry to go on stage. To work. They were waiting for me. The public. Who were they? What, are you also going to throw that up at me? The rich people in the ghetto, the black marketers, guys from the Jewish police, all those to whom fate had given a second chance, who had struggled for it and won, who refused to end up as victims, or as a bar of soap. I didn't want to become soap. I had to sing. To show my worth, so that they would know it, so the game of life could continue. We lacked for nothing, it's true, but do I have to justify myself forever? I worked in order to eat. I received nothing for free. I worked hard."

"Under my pillow I keep a knife, a hammer, and a screwdriver. They press their shapes into my back and the nape of my neck. I have never sold myself cheap. Never! Should I feel guilty? Guilt, always this Jewish guilt. I am guilty of nothing! What were we talking about?"

"That you can't stand journalists."

"Can't stand? That's an understatement."

"What was the most important thing in life for you?"

"Mother. Always. I did everything so as not to hurt her feelings. I know that she was always afraid that someone would harm me. Take advantage of her child. She was smart enough never to say it to me, but she died of fear. I can't remember any longer when I promised her that I would never change my faith. She was a believer. Which I could tolerate. I watched her with emotion as she lit the candles on Fridays, cupping her hands, and praying in a low voice. I will always picture her with her arms folded and her hands open above the flames. A long time ago, I rebelled, I screamed at her, and I was angry. The Jews, the language, the religion! It's only now that it awakens a tenderness in me. I kept my promise even though there's not an ounce of faith in me."

"Is your life fulfilled?"

"I don't understand what that means, a life that's fulfilled.

"There was no time for dreams. I was carried by a wave, it swept me along, it began with a success that I wasn't prepared for. Then it went further, carried me higher. I crashed many times, but I always recovered from my fall. I don't know why I picked myself up again. What's the use of such a long life? I didn't find any relief with the Liberation. They wouldn't let me forget. They have all forgotten, but me, I don't have the right. They reproach me, they want to bury me alive, because I know something that threatens them. I know. They are on tenterhooks. It's a relay race of slanderers that has lasted sixty years already. Now everything is distorted. The merchandise is rotten. You would think that I have descended into Alzheimer's.

"I know a psychologist in America who asked me one day, 'What do you feel, when you come from the stage back to your dressing room and nobody is waiting for you?' That was the first time that someone realized, understood that there could be an open grave dug there. The hole into which I fall once the dressing-room door is closed. Most people have someone with whom they can share their lives; they are mirrored in the eyes of the other person. For a long time my mother played that role. But she is no longer there. She hasn't been there for years. I remain alone. I take off my dress, my makeup. I cast aside my

boa. I sit without moving in the easy chair. After the thunder-
ous applause, the bravos and encores, the silence prevails. I am
not reflected in admiring eyes—I cease to exist. The difference
is brutal. The top and the bottom. The euphoria is the height
I fall from. It's painful. I'm afraid of ending the performance,
because I know what is waiting for me.

"I have had so many joys. I knew how to appreciate them. I
am humble concerning destiny. I know how to say thank you.
I don't know whom to thank because I believe in nothing, but
I say thank you. It seems that I was pretty, but I wasn't aware
of it. It's only now on rereading the old reviews that I notice it.
It's repeated often: 'She is beautiful, beautiful.' But was I intelligent or not? I believed that I wasn't stupid."

She was seated on her bed, leaning over. As if keeping vigil over
her fear, her hands clasped around her knees. The television
screen threw an intermittent light on her face.

She was at home. In her hiding place. Still in the ghetto, fifty
years later. She knew very well that she had to hide. The danger
was lying in wait, behind every step. Everybody was suspect.

" 'You are not dead!?' I heard the astonishment and the dread
in this voice. I had just arrived from Babice near Warsaw, where
I had been hiding after getting out of the ghetto. 'You are not
dead . . .' That's how I was received a few days after Liberation,
in January 1945, by Szpilman, my accompanist during my time
in the ghetto, my colleague from the Café Sztuka. He categorically refused to employ me on the radio. *They say that you were
working for the Gestapo!'*

"For days on end I don't open my mouth. I've forgotten that
I even had a voice. I can't manage to drag myself out of this
place. Curious Jewish women ask me how I manage. How do
I manage? I cut myself in half. The sick half stays in bed, the
healthy half gets up and takes care of the sick one. It's difficult
for one to follow the other. I tried having some help, but they

never stopped stealing from me. It's a miracle that I'm still alive. But that's what fate decreed. I've lived a long time, too long."

"Vera, what do you think about the most often?"

Silence.

"That people are bad and I hate them, that I am alone.

"I have to record, and then when I have the time, I will TRANSCRIBE everything . . . I still don't know how to use a recording machine."

She turns it on and clicks it off, then turns it on again. Some background noises. A voice.

"For moths, lemons are best. Lemons cut in halves, piles of lemons. They have to be cut in quarters with a sharp knife and placed on shelves in closets, in drawers. Acid lemons, juicy and as yellow as the sand on the shores of the Świder. Unbearable taste. Guaranteed to kill.

"Newspapers also can kill moths, old newspapers. They kill more slowly than acid lemons, but just as effectively. The dried-up ink has a deterrent power. The emanation from the old type can paralyze. The moths can't move, they become rigid, they are plunged into sleep.

"The larvae are no more than two millimeters long, they don't need to eat, the sustenance they obtain from their mothers is enough for them. (Milk—I couldn't produce enough, a wet nurse, a peasant woman, fed my son, there wasn't enough from me. You take in hatred and fear with mother's milk.) The larvae destroy us, produced by mature individuals nonstop, nonstop; they lay millions of eggs. In one season there can be three generations. Vermin, they are all over the place. Cockroaches, waterbugs, ticks. Those, over there. THEM! My enemies are multiplying, they proliferate with their insults, their accusations, spinning their webs of deceit. Moths eat clothes. Thieves. There were lice in the ghetto, many children with lice. I collected money for bread for the children. Nobody believes me. For moths, lemons are best. You cut them in quarters and you put them everywhere, on shelves, in drawers. For moths, lemons are best."

"If I were you, I would write everything down. How about lighting the lamp, Vera?"

"There is no light. I am the light!!

"My story is a tragedy without end. It's the story of Dreyfus. A concierge is worse than a policeman. They turn all the people who come up to see me into enemies. I can't accept it, but I have no solution. No one understands. My virtues? Less than nothing. Even a prisoner leaves his cell, he breathes fresh air for a moment, he fills his lungs, he airs out his thoughts and lightens his conscience. A brief but reviving moment! I am not complaining. I want you to be aware of something that's inconceivable."

"I have bad thoughts. Even yesterday, I was still crying. Everything that's happened to me here, it annihilates me completely, it reduces my brains to jelly. There's no other word for it. I become crazy. Can you imagine being in prison, in complete isolation for four and a half years? For a crime that you never committed! Unable to go for a walk, get some fresh air. Without sky or light. It's inhuman, even for the worst of crimes."

Four years, that makes four times twelve months, four Decembers and four Aprils, forty-eight monthly cycles of useless bleeding, and as an echo, four months of March and trees in bloom, the anniversary of the death of her little boy, and the battles she had to fight, and yet, and yet, more than a thousand dawns and sunsets at the very least she never experienced, without light, and without world, condemned and isolated.

"I am not afraid of solitude. The only thing that terrifies me is other people. I have the instincts of an animal. Also the thinking of an animal. Animals are scared of people, they flee from them, they know how to defend themselves, but they also love them as much. They struggle to become familiar with this other being that is man. I am like that. I have a passion for films about animals. I believe that you can't live without knowing about the world of animals. Therein lies the essential truth about the world. Animals don't know jealousy. They kill because they are hungry, not for the fun of it. They are exceptional, these films. Very far from Poland, Germans, and Jews.

"I am going to throw myself in the Seine. That thought eases my pain. Or I'm going to set myself on fire and burn up with all my papers."

Vera's doctor makes her do exercises for her memory, they consist of her learning something every day—no matter what. She has clutched at this straw, and tried to remember the songs she sang for years. Impossible. The weakness of her body, and her heart, and especially her brain, is stronger than she is. She had to give up.

"Thirty-two songs? I recorded as many as that? In more than ten languages . . . It's not surprising that I'm in the process of dying. I was at the end of my strength. And because of you, I am bringing up to the surface memories that no longer existed at all. Why do this? Why do I let myself be manipulated? A hole has opened up, the abyss of memory. I am falling into it. I don't know how to get out of it. I don't know! Now I am going to take up my pen and dip it in my blood. And you are going to listen."

2

She had promised me her dress

She had promised me her dress after she died—the little black dress in which she sang so seductively. She didn't give it to me. Perhaps she left it for me to find in the empty apartment, but I am not sure that she even thought of me then.

The dress was curled up, as if in a defensive position. As if it were impregnated with the reactions of the person who had always owned it. I couldn't even get into it, although I would love to. I can't even try it on.

The table in her Paris apartment didn't look like anything anymore. For years it had been foundering under papers, scattered newspapers, clippings of articles, telephone bills and bank statements, advertising, musical scores, the lyrics of songs, heaped up day in, day out, in successive layers, like a massive tottering fortress. Between the list of errands dating from spring 2007 (coffee, marzipan, lemons, honey, garlic . . .) and an empty Wedel chocolate box now filled with buttons, I found a piece of notebook paper. A firm but nervous handwriting. In green ink.

She was photographed by many, including
Benedykt Jerzy Dorys, a postwar society
photographer in Warsaw.

*I would request your opening an inquiry into the accusations
made publicly against me for crimes of collaboration with the Germans,* she wrote in a request to the state prosecutor at the Ministry of Justice, addressed to Adolf Dąb, October 23, 1947. To
set out her case with precision, she enclosed the necessary documents: the verdict of the Special Court, the testimonies from
the Association of Polish Stage Artists and the Association of
Professional Musicians. All these organizations affirmed the fact
that her behavior during the Occupation had been irreproachable, and she had never sullied her honor as a Polish woman.

The following paragraph: *A campaign of slander on a large
scale has been put in motion, with the resulting consequence of
making me lose every chance of finding employment, and has*

caused my financial ruin. If the national authorities to whom I am addressing this appeal do not take action, I will be condemned to be socially blacklisted.

She was accused of the following: *During the German Occupation, over a period starting in 1941 up to August 1942 in the Warsaw Ghetto, and from August 1942 on the Aryan side, she had maintained friendly relations with persons who were known agents of the Gestapo . . . which constitutes a crime according to article 1 of the Regulations of the People's Tribunal (Sąd Obywatelski). According to these regulations, this infraction can be brought before the People's Tribunal for the Central Committee of the Jews of Poland.*

She was considered a person to avoid because her behavior could legitimately raise suspicions of collaboration with the people she frequented.

She had recopied by hand hundreds of documents from the courts concerning "the case," which she filed in enormous cardboard boxes with the private and official correspondence related to the trial. I have the impression that in her lifetime she had written more petitions than letters, she produced more documentation than her personal wishes, that she had justified herself more than she ever expressed herself.

She could never find in her apartment the few tapes she recorded for Steven Spielberg's USC Shoah Foundation Institute in 1995. They were given to me ten years later in New York, when I visited an acquaintance of Vera's, in whose home the recording had taken place.

She was seated in an easy chair. She struggled against the striped oval chair back she was leaning against, she relaxed, then straightened up. I suspected her of having told this story numerous times, with slight alterations appropriate to the situation, the place, and the hour. A half-century had passed since the events described.

The years superimposed on one another. Memory with its long work to correct itself.

She wore a blue blouse and black sweater. Her hair was pulled back. A loose strand fell on her forehead, interrupting her narration. She looked through glasses with heavy trapezoid frames, fashionable in the seventies. She turned her head to the right and to the left like a chicken, swinging the chain that held her glasses.

It began badly. The questioner's Polish was rusty and coarse.

"Please state your first and last name."

"My given name is Vera, my last name is Gran."

"Please spell it."

"G—R—A—N (N as in 'Natalie')."

"Have you assumed any other name or carried false papers?"

(She looked at the woman defiantly, with condescension and disgust. *What does she want from me, that one? I am my name.* She stared a little too long. She shook her head.) "No."

She was not telling the truth. She had taken more than one name. Thanks to them, and to Aryan papers, her life was spared. Wanda Czajkowska, Weronika Gacka, Tomaszewska, Jezierska . . . these were the ones that come up most often, even if her papers from the period of the Occupation have been lost. But Vera was proud of being Gran(de). She never wanted to acknowledge that she had to give up her name. That necessity humiliated her. Like having to hide in this city where before the war she was applauded. "I will not forsake my legend. I am and have only been a singer."

"Date of birth?"

"April 20, 1918."

(She didn't blink. This is also the date on her identity papers, which she had until the end: the French residency card for a stateless person of Polish origin. I was never able to find her birth certificate. I assume that Vera Grynberg, the youngest child of the Grynberg couple, was in reality two years older. In biographical notices written in Poland after the war, several times the year given was 1916.)

"Place of birth?"

"Warsaw."

(She would never again confirm this. She fiercely kept her secret. She guarded this last bastion of intimacy in a life exposed to the light like a film strip. Everything indicates that she was born in Russia.)

"Where is it?"

(Where is—what? Warsaw? She makes a face, she doesn't understand, she has the impression that she didn't hear correctly. Her contempt is mixed with disgust. Instead of answering, she gives a brief and dry grunt, as if she were giving a slap.)

"In Poland."

The questions continue.

"Given name of the father, given name of the mother . . ."

"Liba Kaplan, daughter of Pejsach and Fajga."

Dark hair, dark eyes, corpulent. In the only photo I have seen of her mother, which must date from the thirties, she is standing very straight in a photographer's studio. The décor is old-fashioned (on the right a wooden column, on the left a low wall, in the background the frame of a painting). She wears a long, ample dress, low cut, with three-quarter sleeves, a pendant around her neck and a bracelet on her right hand. She doesn't look natural in the pose, as if someone had suggested she should act bravely. Her face is very pale.

The more the years passed, the more Vera loved her. On her own deathbed, more than half a century after the death of Liba, she still wept for her, repeating that she had to avenge her. *Mother, Mamochka,* she cried, *I saw him drag you by the hair. I saw who did it.*

Her mother had not wanted her. She was approaching her forties. Perhaps she didn't want any more children, and certainly not another girl. She warned the midwife that if it was not a boy, she would not even look at it. But the midwife was shrieking with admiration at the sight of the beauty of the little one. It motivated Liba, already the mother of Helena (Hinda), eleven years old, and of Maryla (Marjem), six years old. She took the newborn in her arms—and never gave her back. Vera has the name of this midwife.

In the family, all the same, they called her the little runt.

She spoke less about her father than about her mother.

Eljasz Grynberg. He was one of the five sons of Moszek Hersz and Ester Perła of Łomża. He was the second-born, but he was treated as if he were the eldest.

He smelled of blood. He came back from hunting all heated from vodka and emotions. He wanted absolutely to take her on his knees. She fought back. She didn't know what revolted her more: the fact that just a little earlier he had taken a life— against mankind, she was always on the side of animals—or that he was hand in glove with fellow hunters. He was neither protective nor affectionate.

In time this smell disappeared little by little, and he with it.

She was three years old when she last saw him.

According to family lore, he was a trafficker, first in the sales of forest and lands, then in that of buttons, and who knows what else besides. He bet often and a great deal at the races. On his documents he wrote under "Profession," "manufacturer." He was registered as a merchant in Warsaw. He had a notions shop at number 9 Przejazd Street.

Liba was his second wife; from his first he had a son, Abram. Vera doesn't know why Eljasz left them also. Nor when—still in Russia, in Kiev, or after, in Poland? For a time his name appeared in the directory of Mława.

His second wife perhaps disappointed his expectations, was not as attractive, became tiresome? Vera spoke of her goodness, but also about her demanding side, her piety and perfectionism for Friday prayers. One of Vera's friends from ballet school, for whom Liba faithfully made steaming hot soup, appreciated her biting sense of humor. Nothing more.

Vera did not remember any distant members of the family.

She said she didn't have any. She didn't remember any reunions, celebrations, or holidays. She was still playing with dolls when they fled pogroms in the East. They lived then in Wołomin, a little town among the suburbs of Warsaw with its Jewish glass manufacturer and bedding factory. It's not known how long they had been there. No documents mentioning a common address for the Grynbergs in Wołomin have survived.

After coming from Russia, Liba Grynberg had to fend for herself with three children. All she had brought with her were her Russian accent, her fear of pogroms, and a samovar.

Vera found Wołomin ordinary. It smelled of pork—a non-kosher town that nevertheless had been filled with Jews since the beginning of the nineteenth century. The name did not make you want to linger there. Wołomin—*Wolę-omiń,* "I'd

The house on Warsaw Street near the train station in Wołomin, where Vera lived with her mother and two sisters until 1931. From there they moved to Warsaw.

rather avoid it" in Polish. That's the derivation of the name of this village in the Mazovia district, lost between forest and swamps. In the innumerable volumes in the library of a local landowner, there's a much more refined origin for this name.

In her youth, books didn't interest Vera, people did.

She spent a lot of time under the table. "Where is Vera?" the neighbors would ask. Her mother would point to the ground with her finger to indicate that she was hiding underneath and that they should act as if she weren't there.

"Mother used to say in Russian: '*Vierochka, kem ty khochech byt?*' What would you like to be?"

She was five years old.

"*Ia khochou byt artistka.* An artist!" she answered.

"*No kak, artistka, ty nechevo nekogda nie khochech govorit.* An artist? But you never say anything."

"*Ia skazhu.* I will talk, I will talk, I will say something, I will sing. But you can't look at me."

She was terribly shy with everyone and everything.

Once the guests had left, in their kitchen in Wołomin, the real show could then begin.

She would put on a clown's outfit, as she did years later. She told me all this several times. With the skill of a real wizard, she managed to "reproduce" the stories she had heard. She stuttered with the declaration of love, like the suitor of the shoemaker's wife on the second floor. She reenacted the scene where a snake strangles an operetta star in Warsaw. She spoke to it softly so that it would release its grip. Her mother would heat up the samovar and watch the stories come alive before her eyes. Vera gave them a second life.

On a poster for a variety show at the Teatr Nowości in Warsaw, there was a black man playing the saxophone. She found a cane, blackened her face with shoe polish. She tried to imitate the voice of Josephine Baker. She knew how to imitate perfectly the tone of Jewish jokes. A used-clothes salesman actually asked the prima donna of the Warsaw Operetta, "Where can I find another fat floozy like Madame Messal?" (She was in fact very stout.)

Vera was all ears when the schoolteacher who lived across the way described the funeral of the singing star Wiktoria Kawecka. Her husband had ordered a monument that showed her standing with all her diamonds; you could swear she was alive. In front of her was a marble angel, lifting a curtain of marble.

"And do you know what?" the schoolteacher cried excitedly. "From the window of the jeweler Turczyński, on Ossoliński Street, they stole a 'butterfly' of forty-four carats that she had donated to charity years ago . . ."

Perhaps Vera should have become an actress? But she was always singing romantic songs, which over time became second nature to her.

What did they live on? She didn't know. They were poor.

A family of four could live on ten zlotys, but they didn't even have that much. On Fridays they had to have carp, and that cost as much as seven loaves of bread. Her mother kept meticulous accounts, each day adding up the sugar (1 zloty a kilo), milk (45 groszy a liter), and eggs (20 groszy apiece).

Liba Grynberg went to work in Warsaw, it seems. At the local Ilusja factory, manufacturing thread, lace, and other textiles, the pay was very low. She liked to sew. She liked talking with the customers. Corsets were an important item in their femininity. The walking stick factory, also managed by a Jew, offered the same salary. She gave it up.

The limited generosity of Aunt Morgenstern, a millionaire, owner of well-established banks, prevented her from offering the Grynbergs an easy life. Neither she nor any other of the rich relatives—Vera gave names difficult to verify—took an interest in their poor relations. Neither the bankers named Sołowiejczyk, nor the businessmen Szeryszewski, the Lewin cousins, owner of the Sunburst Shoe Polish and Floor Wax factory, nor the rich relative known as the King of Astrakhan from Leipzig. To the single mother their occasional financial help was in fact charity.

Liba Kaplan was invited to spend some time in France at the end of the twenties, but she returned at the first opportunity and out of gratitude fell to kiss the Polish soil she had hardly stepped on. Whether out of patriotism or because of the host family's lack of hospitality, I don't know. She never ventured abroad again.

Vera was eight, at most nine years old when she decided to help her mother. She could catch the missed stitches in sweaters at the knitting factory. She mended stockings. She could reproduce the designs deftly and speedily with a needle. And to pass the time, she would sing to herself. She wanted to earn money for her school books. For a pencil case, a school compass, notebooks that she filled carefully with the simple words from her reading primer. She was proud of herself.

Vera remembered the wooden stairs of the tenement building in Wołomin. The stairs, steep for a child, went straight up to the third floor, and they continued on to the fourth floor. Thirteen Warszawska Street, on the corner of Chopin Street. I walked up those stairs eighty years later, looking in vain for traces of her on those steps covered with several layers of industrial paint. Mud-colored. On the balcony from which she could see the train station, new generations of night-blooming wallflowers were growing.

School No. 3 for Jewish children doesn't exist anymore. There she learned to read, and there her music teacher predicted that she would become a singer. In the courtyard on the other side of the apartment building there were still the same garbage containers. Not really in better condition than in the past.

Vera used to climb up on the wooden lids of these containers, straighten out her dress, pull back her hair, and begin her performances. She would occasionally hear her sisters coming home from a musical revue given at the Morskie Oko, or at the Alkazar; that's where her repertory came from. The latest hit of Hanka Ordonówna: "Love Will Forgive You Everything" or "At the First Sign" . . . Sometimes she would be holding in her hands a bunch of feathers found in a henhouse, her sister's scarf, or gloves. She sang for her friends songs that spoke of love, lessons of the heart, and separation, when they had no idea of what any of this meant. In a low, subdued, deep voice. She ended up performing her numbers at school, during the breaks. They were so popular that the audience wouldn't let her return to her classes.

She had music in her blood. Liba used to hum to herself in the kitchen, in an untrained soprano voice, fragments from *The Merry Widow* or *Orpheus in the Underworld*. Vera's sister Helena earned a living teaching piano sonatas and polonaises. She was also a teacher of Esperanto.

For years Vera believed that her mother could not bear her voice. She couldn't understand how she could have given birth to a little girl with such a deep alto voice. To punish her, Vera would telephone home pretending to be a male friend. She would then fly into a rage and reproach Liba for not recognizing her own child.

Vera collected photographs of famous performers, and in her classroom as in the salons of Warsaw, the admirers of Eugeniusz Bodo argued with the worshipers of Adolf Dymsza. These two stars had country houses in Wołomin, which excited their admirers' imaginations all the more. "I Kiss Your Hand, Madame," sang Bodo, this gallant dandy—"king of the stage and king of fashion"—and his fans had the illusion that he was singing to them. Each fan wanted to be the one with whom he had "a rendezvous at nine o'clock" and they "wanted it so much and yet they were afraid."

She never discussed these interests with either her mother

or her sisters. Warsaw and its stars seemed inaccessible. But there was a movie theater at Wołomin, which had a name full of charm and attraction—as appropriate for all creators of illusions—the Oasis. It was there that Vera became intoxicated for the first time. Usually so obedient to her mother, reporting on every hour spent outside the house, she let herself be carried away without resisting into the depth of the espionage intrigues of *The Masked Spy* with Hanka Ordonówna, Jerzy Leszczyński, and the irresistible Igo Sym. She and one of her friends did not stir from their seats during two consecutive showings. She identified with the fate of the magnificent singer and spy, and the passion that cost her her life.

Two of the songs that caused Vera's success in the backyards in Wołomin were taken from this film. She had not only a voice, but an extraordinary memory.

On Vera's return home, her mother greeted her on the threshold of the apartment with a slap. She would remember it for a long time. It was the price of her platonic love.

She ascribed her move to Warsaw to the plot of the latest film by Marlene Dietrich. She remembered the words "liberated woman" and "aggressive eroticism" as well as several stanzas from the songs of *The Blue Angel.* The fate of the cabaret singer could touch the lives of others, and the feelings of millions of spectators. It made her think.

In the year 1931 she lived with her mother and sisters in a large building at 8 Elektoralna Street at the corner of Orla Street. It was a neighborhood in the center of town, not one of the best. Near a marketplace and the slaughterhouse. One sitting room, and the toilets down the hall. The cooking was done on an alcohol stove. The windows faced Elektoralna Street. It was very high up.

"I often sat on the window ledge to look at the street. A little to get some air, a little to watch the theater of the street. Below there was a coach stop. Do you remember?" She often asked me that, only to add immediately after, "No, obviously you don't remember. Excuse me, when I speak to someone, I sometimes think that it's to a normal person, from before the war. There were horses, gray, black, all sorts of horses, and some had an . . . enormous, horrible . . . that hung down almost to the ground."

Vera, more than eighty years old, always became excited at this narrative:

"The first time that I noticed it, I was panicked. I thought that the horse must be suffering monstrously. I called out to the coachman, 'But mister, this horse is sick! It's going to die!' It was horrible. It marked me for the rest of my life. And then I understood . . . It was not a disease. Delight? Well, bravo."

To reach the bedroom where all four were crowded, they had to cross a long, narrow hallway, and absorb the smell of others—laundry, sweat, cabbage, decay, stale scent of lily of the valley. You could let your thoughts drift away from the spilt milk, hang on to other people's hopes of a better life, or avoid the sorrows of others. She felt humiliated by this poverty.

Elektoralna Street in Warsaw's Jewish district, a neighborhood of mixed poverty and bourgeois prosperity. The four of them occupied one room in the attic, with no kitchen and with a common toilet down the hall.

Vera remembered fighting with her middle sister, Maryla. It was she, according to her, who broke her nose. Years later, the pain wore away and only the memory remained of the tender presence of her sister. Like the memory of Helena, the eldest, the blonde, the loveliest of the three, the intellectual, who hit her on her fingers with a ruler if she didn't wash behind her ears, or if she didn't practice the piano.

Was it an upright or a grand piano? Rather an upright, if you go by the narrowness of the rooms. "A Bechstein: it survived the war," she wrote years later on the corner of an envelope.

Vera would have loved to play, but without making the effort to learn. "I didn't like learning!" She watched her sister. She watched how she played, how she glanced at the score, and then where she placed her fingers. She tried to imitate her.

"I respected my mother, and I insisted that she be respected. I remember one day two admirers, Catholic students, came to the house to fetch me. I must have been fifteen years old. Both of them greeted me by kissing my hand. On leaving I gave a little demonstration. I went up to my mother, and I bowed down to her hand. The next time they kissed the hand of this old Jewish woman, even if it was not to their taste."

Vera spoke Russian fluently, with that lovely melodious intonation of the Confines region. She spoke with verve and jovial high spirits. Her mother preferred speaking Yiddish. Vera could, and did, understand, but sometimes pretended she didn't understand. One day she pounded on the table with her fist: "Enough of that! We live in Poland and we speak Polish." Besides, Liba Grynberg got along well in Polish. She read *Our Review*, a popular Jewish newspaper.

"Not another word of Yiddish. About that, if in nothing else, I was tyrannical."

She attended secondary school at the Professors' Union, nearby on Rymarska Street, right next to Bank Square. Later, she succeeded in being admitted to the dance school run by Irena Prusicka, a student of the celebrated German choreographer Mary Wigman. Both of them preached "free dance," incorporating elements of acrobatics and modern individualism. Vera entered the school at the recommendation of an older friend, Stefania Grodzieńska. Stefa knew that Vera, her mother, and her sisters barely managed to stay afloat. She remembered this household of women where the traditions of kosher cooking were strictly observed. That's where she ate a cholent for the first time, for the Sabbath meal, even though it was only a substitute—she called it a pseudo-cholent—made from the leftovers of yesterday's meal: vegetables, potatoes, coated with sauce.

Vera remembered fasting for Yom Kippur, the most difficult day for Jews—the day of reconciliation, penitence, and forgiveness. She claimed that's where she experienced real hunger for the first time, and for the rest of her life, real hunger—orthodoxy—was a duty to be accomplished.

"Prusicka never asked me for money. I tried to earn a few pennies. I massacred other people's fingers doing manicures. I was paid fifty groszy for both hands. I could even afford to have a cake from Lardelli's."

Lardelli, an Italian Swiss, came to Poland as a child. He opened his first bakery shop on Krucza Street. It created a sensation: the cakes were elegantly arranged behind the window, under the emblem of the firm, a picture of Milan Cathedral.

Vera remembered the special taste of his éclairs, different from those made anywhere else in town, filled with a yellow custard of egg yolks beaten with chocolate, thicker and less dry. She loved his pastries. For a long time, they were the height of luxury.

"My husband and I looked after Vera a little," Stefania Grodzieńska said; the wife of Jerzy Jurandot, the satirical writer and lyricist, she herself was a comedian on the popular stage. "When she was late for her lesson, or she didn't go at all, Prusicka would telephone us, not her mother, to complain. Vera

Irena Prusicka created a school of modern dance in Warsaw, teaching the style of German choreographer Mary Wigman. The young Vera studied there for several years until an automobile accident changed her aspiration from dancing to singing.

often came to visit; we had a piano dating from my childhood in Łódź. We spent long hours singing. That's why I remember so well the songs that were popular before the war. I found her voice unique—warm, gritty, deep. She also knew how to sing a cappella. She had perfect pitch. Young and small, she was as cute as can be, a little cuddly. You couldn't help loving her. Our director and teacher liked her immediately."

Vera remembered the visit of a photographer during the free-dance class, but not the photo. He talked a lot and explained at length how they should hold themselves to better display their charms. She felt ill at ease in the nude, and in the seductive poses that he wanted and that he approved afterward. She never saw this photograph. Half a century later I gained access to it, torn in half, through the son of the dance teacher.

Vera is the first one on the left, slender, dark haired, smiling. A white silk leotard, and short pants. The girls are fifteen years old at the most. There is a mischievous look in their eyes. The knees are bent amusingly, and the arms folded, a double gesture of seduction. "The feeling expressed by the body," according to the precepts of German expressionism.

"Irena looked after me like a mother. For a year, perhaps two. At home things went from bad to worse, we needed money. I learned that they were hiring young women at a cabaret."

It was Prusicka who took her to the Adria, the most elegant, most expensive cabaret in Warsaw.

"Cactus plants, parrots, cakes, and marzipan," Vera listed in evoking the Adria.

The owner was Franciszek Moszkowicz, bald, round glasses, in smoking jacket, with a chimpanzee hanging on to his neck. Originally from Lwów, former tobacco salesman, page, waiter, this joker and omnipresent owner of one of the capital's most exclusive clubs was held in deservedly high esteem in Warsaw society. An avid devotee of the waltz and Viennese music, in the Adria he not only had a movable dance floor, spinning crystal light fixtures, and two bars, but also the best orchestra and the most attractive dancers and singers. He always started off the evening with a Polish national dance: an oberek or a kujawiak.

Vera had to present herself to Moszkowicz. She danced. She curtsied. He followed her into the dressing room. "You will

The most elegant prewar Warsaw nightclub, the Adria. Vera
tried without success to get a job there as a dancer. This is a
scene from the New Year's Eve ball in 1935. (Tickets had to
be reserved in the fall!) The eccentric proprietor, Franciszek
Moszkowicz, welcomed guests with a chimpanzee in his arms.

come to see me? This evening at my place on the sixth floor, my
little lady? We'll see if you are well built. Then we will sign you
up with a contract." (People talked about a private elevator that
stopped at his floor right in front of his private office.)

She answered that she had danced half-naked, in panties
and bra. "That doesn't count, I want to see more than that,"
he insisted.

She burst into tears. Thus ended the career of Vera Gryn-berg, fifteen years old, at the Adria.

She tried her luck at the Paradis. This small club on Nowy Świat Street right by the Square of Three Crosses hadn't yet become popular. It was one of the dance halls on this Warsaw thoroughfare known for its night life. Paradis, Bodega, Cardinal, Gastronomie . . . At first they offered her a very modest fee. She was the opening number.

"Waksmacher, the manager and owner of the club (married and father of a daughter my age), fell head over heels in love with me. He liked Lolitas! Did I tell you that he had chocolates delivered to me every Friday? The delivery man from the Wedel chocolate factory with his red cap knocked on the door and handed me a box weighing a kilo. I couldn't eat it all even though I love chocolate. Waksmacher would stand for hours under a gate across the street waiting for me to come out, to see where I was going."

Stefania Grodzieńska remembered that Vera always was incredibly popular with men, but also that she was very proper. There was always an admirer in the wings, but Vera never showed much interest.

She grew up and matured. In the streets, men turned around to get a second look at her. But her mother continued to treat her like a little girl. Every evening she accompanied her to the cabaret and would accompany her home again. She had a really embarrassing conversation with Julian Front, the orchestra leader, in which she explained to him that Vera was very naïve. She asked him to be understanding with her daughter, who had no father, and to look after her. He promised to do so.

One night he proposed an excursion to Wilanów. It was an adventure after work, champagne, followed by an early breakfast. They finished their performance around two in the morning. Usually very cautious, she followed his decision. His age, and seriousness, impressed her.

Four of them went, he and a friend, she and another young

Vera was still a minor when she began performing in clubs. She quickly gained a group of devoted admirers. Some remained faithful even after the outbreak of war.

woman. The men started drinking seriously. They included the taxi driver, served him abundantly so that he would not get tired of waiting for them. One glass, two glasses, three glasses. She started to complain, she got scared of their lustful way of looking at her and became hysterical. They had had enough, finally.

Returning to Warsaw, they turned at a high speed into the Square of Three Crosses onto Książęca Street, as a streetcar came head on. They all woke up in the hospital.

The glass pane separating the driver from the passengers disfigured her friend's face. Vera was diagnosed with a broken pelvis. The former would never again look pretty. The latter would never again be able to dance.

"I wanted to be an acrobatic dancer, but they broke my bones. I was worthless even for the ballet."

Sometime earlier, it happened that Vera, hidden in a corner beneath the staircase, was singing the songs the orchestra was playing. Perhaps "Only the Heart of a Mother," or else "Nobody Knows How to Love Like You." One day when the café was nearly empty, a client noticed her. "Who is this boy singing?" he asked. They told him that it was a young woman. He was taken with her voice.

Waksmacher proposed that she sing in his cabaret. She accepted because she had no choice, she had to earn a living. But she could not overcome her shyness. "I'll never come out in front of a crowd, even for all the gold in the world!" she kept saying. When her accompanist threatened to no longer work with her ("I am not going to accompany a shadow!"), she finally decided to stop hiding.

The Paradis was entered directly from the street; small tables were crowded together behind the door, and there were separate boxes from which you could watch the performances below. The cabaret was known for hits from films played by an orchestra made up of several musicians. That's where "Tango Notturno" was played for the first time. Leon Wyrwicz put on his satiric monologues, and Vera sang.

She was fifteen, or eighteen—these figures always irritated her. She couldn't remember if it was "Brazilian Tango" or maybe "The Dance Swept Us Up in Its Whirl." Was it important in taking stock of her fate? By the end of spring 1934, she made her first two records. Under the name Sylvia Green, she sang tangos with an "orchestra of Hawaiian guitars." Her collaboration with the Syrena-Electro Company proved productive.

"They tried to make me go on stage. I resisted for a long time. They aged me according to the conventions of the times. They styled my hair in accordance with the fashion of the day, hair pulled back high from the forehead; they put on makeup and gave me a long dress. They layered on the years I lacked. Perhaps I wasn't fully of age," she laughed, "but I was fully mature!"

Another time, she told me, she didn't have any appropriate dresses. As a consequence she had to appear in her school uniform. A young girl with her hair down. No accessories. She would later call this the Juliette Gréco style.

At the Paradis they served sausages with mustard and jellied fruit. The atmosphere made up for the lack of culinary refinement: a dark basement with ambient lighting, sweet melodies. It was a place primarily frequented by young people who came to dance, close to each other, and drink a glass of orange liqueur. The modest club was becoming fashionable. It was not—as in the memory of Vera Gran—the most elegant cabaret in Warsaw, but it had a certain sex appeal.

She chose her favorite hits and sang others by audience request. They brought the scores and asked her to sing them. More and more people came out of curiosity to see the little Gran. Stefania Grodzieńska called her a "revelation."

As a young girl, Vera was in love with Stefania. She wanted to be like her. She envied her red coat. But even more, her charm.

Show her face. Use her voice. Play, seduce, captivate, at any cost. Conquer. What was she trying to accomplish onstage? What kind of fulfillment? What was the cost of taking on this new role in the spotlight? To what extent did the applause help her? All of this required a different concentration, a new outlook. Change her rhythm, live during the night, keep her energy for the evening, for the performances. Once you go on stage you can't do without mirrors. There is a perpetual need for affirmation. A double existence begins, and the one in the reflection seems to be more important.

She was conscious of her beauty. She knew that she was attractive. She often verified it in her own mirrors and other people's glances. She enjoyed looking at photos of herself. Décolleté dress with a small fur hat, or a sleeveless dress, or a small, fashionable coat with a collar. She liked listing the admirers of each part of her face: so-and-so for the nose, another for her dimples, a third for her mouth. And finally her eyes. She always made them up in the same way, black mascara and black eyeliner, very simple, very effective.

She seduced with her voice, as if coming from a depth of sorrow. She was radiant with an inner light.

"Bolesław Wieniawa-Długoszowski was one of my great admirers, the last true cavalry officer of the twentieth century. They still speak of how one day he arrived on horseback at the Adria's dance floor. He drank constantly, and, dead drunk, he always wanted to sing with me. As with all drunkards, his was a lament more than a song. I remember once, I couldn't stand it anymore, I stopped singing my song and I said to him: 'My general, it's you or me.' He stopped. He sat down next to me at the foot of the podium. He was quiet for a moment, and then he began again. From time to time I had to kick him to calm him down again."

Others approached her with greater respect.

"It warmed my heart to see officers salute me straight and stiff on entering the Paradis. They did the same on leaving. These very handsome boys would turn around, doing a dance step to say good night."

In 1936, she moved into a big apartment at number 40 Hoża Street. She was listed as a performer in the Warsaw city directory at this address until 1940. Telephone number: 701 83. For a long time she walked home from the Paradis to save the twenty-five-groszy price of the streetcar ticket. She crossed the Square of Three Crosses, going down Hoża Street, crossed Krucza Street, and it was just a bit farther. During the summer it was a lovely stroll.

Warsaw Courier, evening edition, November 5, 1936:
The Paradis, 3 Nowy Świat Street. Along with Greta Gordon, "extraordinary foreign performer," and Del Rio, "dancer from

the Spanish Review"; Vera Gran, Polish singer; "the idols of War-
saw," Messalka, Gold, and Peterburski. New show: reduced prices
for food and drinks, 1.30 instead of 2.50, for customers arriving
between 10:00 and 11:00, ticket valid all night.

"I remember the first time I received roses. My God, ROSES!
It was unimaginable, me, the daughter of Liba, from Wołomin,
across from the train station, me, the flowers of a queen—for
me! I didn't know what to do, how to react. So I caressed their
petals. That was afterward, long afterward. For a long time I
didn't understand, I had no idea of what I was doing, and what
was expected of me.

"In prewar Warsaw, a Jew could not become a star, I had
no illusions about it. But the nationalist gangs didn't touch
the windows where my posters were displayed; there were even
some who came to applaud me."

She later learned the identity of the beautiful member of the
audience who every now and then came to the Paradis toward
the end of the evening. She would sit high up, at a certain distance, with a glass of wine. She listened to two or three songs
and then left. Distinguished, silent. She looked alone and
unhappy. Vera was told that it was Nina Andrycz, an actress in
the Polish Theater.

"This was a true artist, who had played Solange in *A Summer in Nohant* and Alexandrine in *Masquerade* by Jarosław
Iwaszkiewicz, Joanna in *The Night in November* by Stanisław
Wyspiański, who came to see me . . . What could I give her? I
didn't know her personally. It wasn't then that we were introduced," Vera remembered.

I met Nina Andrycz during the summer of 2006. She told
me the story of her great, unique love that she was grieving
then: "The moment I heard the words 'Every separation leaves
room for tears,' I wept into my wine glass to avoid distressing
the man who accompanied me."

Stefania Grodzieńska recalled that she and Jerzy Jurandot

had recommended Vera to Andrzej Włast, poet and theater producer. At the time Włast was directing *The Great Revue* on Karowa Street.

"He listened to her, and he nodded and hired her for a trial period of three months. But—he added—with her own repertory. She was scared. No one had ever written a song for her. If Jurandot was so interested, let him arrange it himself.

"It had to be sad, a tango or a waltz. I thought and I thought, and then I found it: the fog . . . the fog so close, spreading (or waiting for me, I can't remember anymore) . . . the streets, the houses in a gray fog . . . We started singing until something came out of it. We wrote a sketch. Vera complained that the beginning was difficult, and her tongue slipped, but I told her, so be it, and to stop making faces, or else she could just go somewhere else.

"I told her to sing it until she knew it down to her fingertips. Jerzy had called one of his composer friends to write the melody. She went to see Włast with all that.

"He didn't let her finish. He said to Jurandot: 'It's not a pearl, it's a diamond.' "

In March 1937, in the *Spring Revue of Stars*, Vera appeared beside Mira Zimińska, Loda Halama, Kazimierz Krukowski, Ludwik Sempoliński . . .

Her fee went from 25 to 150 zlotys a day, sometimes double that on tours. She toured all of Poland: from Lwów to Gdynia, from Brest to Katowice, passing through Radom, Poznań, Białystok, Wilno. In Łódź, at the European Café, she was paid 200 zlotys, and they gave her a suite in the very elegant Grand Hotel, her travel and incidental expenses. During Carnaval, she earned 500 zlotys each performance. She appeared at least once a week on Polish Radio, which in addition to the fee offered her a wide audience. *Tea Time by the Microphone,* broadcast live from the Bristol Hotel, brought her 300 zlotys each time.

"I was earning a good living and had all the work I could

handle. On top of it I earned big fees making short advertising films (lotions, creams, soaps, colognes) . . . I made records, and not only for Syrena-Electro, but also for the international studio Odeon."

I know that poverty had humiliated her. I don't know if wealth had ennobled her. I think perhaps yes. No more unknown people's stockings to darn; collecting old newspapers from which she liked to cut out advertisements for cosmetics; an end to looking enviously, covetously, planted in front of window displays of fashionable clothes; and the need to count every grosz if she wanted to treat herself to something.

A quick transition to luxury:

Two gold watches, a Patek Philippe and a Schaffhausen, three gold bracelets, precious stones mounted on solid gold chains, a pearl necklace that went three times around her neck, rings set with diamonds . . .

On her table, overflowing with souvenirs from the past, I found several lists of her belongings from before the war. After the war, in Paris, she had made a complete inventory to send on to German organizations established to compensate Jews for war damages. Out of pride? For the memory? To recover a lost treasure? And why was it always so crucial after everything that had happened?

All this jewelry—an elaborate work of goldsmiths—at the time she appraised them at 60,000 zlotys, her mother's at half the value, which still came to a considerable amount. In those days a housemaid earned 10 zlotys a month. A worker, a little more . . . a clerk . . .

Plus a car: an eight-cylinder Buick (valued at 12,000 zlotys). Plus the luxuriously furnished apartment on Hoża Street.

The revenues from the tenant farmers on her father's estate (Kozienice) near Mława (approximately eight hundred hectares of forests, an orchard, as well as a house that could accommodate eight people): 15,000 a year. A rental building in Otwock:

The Grosz Library of Hits. Subsequent books of hits sold at 95 groszy and included music and lyrics of favorite songs along with photographs of their performers (Tango: "Over the Cradle").

5,000 a year. And if she was to be believed, she also had a magnificent villa of seven rooms with a large garden in Wiśniowa near Warsaw (valued at 30,000 zlotys). In addition, she received revenues from a café (at 11 Sienkiewicz Street), which she owned half with her sister.

She still had two fur coats: a mink and a Persian lamb estimated at 20,000 zlotys.

What was the use of these detailed accounts? Did it come from a need to reconstruct past splendors, if only for herself? Or a need for money, and the desire to make the Germans pay, who were responsible for her misfortune? I don't know. It has never been established to what extent those records corresponded with reality.

In a small handbag of gold, with her monogram in diamonds, she had a gold cigarette case (encrusted on an enameled ground), a gold Dunhill lighter, a platinum compact with clasp encrusted with diamonds, and a platinum comb in a case with her monogram.

In the course of the conversation, she recalled a café on Piłsudski Square where she was considered the equal of Polish stars such as Mira Zimińska, a great artist.

She couldn't tell if it was at the Institute for the Advancement of the Arts (IPS), with its colored parasols, or rather at the Arts and Fashion with its orangery and delicacies; in any case, the snobbishness of these places seemed to perfectly satisfy her dreams and true ambitions. On the program, in addition to the entertainment, were added fashion shows, exhibitions, and even dog shows. She scrupulously cut out the least mention of her name in the press.

No one can say when, or by whom, her stage name was chosen. She had tried several: Sylvia Green, Vera Green, or Mariol, none of which stuck. Shortly before the war in the little Theater of Thirteen Rows, a marionette with dark hair neatly pulled back, in a black dress with a high neckline, sang a song by Janusz Minkiewicz and Światopełk Karpiński about Café Vogue at number 7 Złota Street, "where Vera Gran, the Marlene Dietrich born Grynberg, is the brightest star and projects her voice with such ease." It was all sung on the melody of her hit "I Have a Locked Drawer" by Eddy Courts. "Her deep and sensual voice makes you shiver . . ."

Without hesitation she abandoned Grynberg for Gran; there was no harm in her changing her last name for a more resonant one, full of charm and promising greatness in the future. She loved being compared to Garbo or Dietrich.

For Vera Gran, people would always take the trouble to go and see her. One day in a rage, she explained, "They wouldn't come to see a Vera Kugelszwanc in the same way."

She performed at the Café Vogue for two years in a row until war broke out.

And all this entirely in Polish.

Vera Gran always insisted that she did not know Yiddish. But in 1939 she appeared in Aleksander Marten's film *The Homeless,* the last Yiddish film produced in Poland before the war. In it she played a femme fatale, the singer Bessie, who devoured the hearts of men while singing her seductive songs in a New York café. *"Libe Mameniu, Niszt Wajn"* ("My Darling Little Mother, Don't Cry") drew tears while they were filming and in the theaters. A modest fisherman from the old continent succumbs to her charms. From Vera's lips Yiddish had a sad and languorous quality, as it should.

An exclusive Warsaw café of the 1930s, a favorite haunt of painters and poets, run by the Art Propaganda Institute. Vera aspired to perform in similar places in the capital.

She appeared beside the famous Ida Kamińska, an extraordinary artist who played the role of the poor wife of the enamored immigrant. As was fitting for her role as an American diva, Vera changed costumes several times, paraded in lavish outfits. Lovely, though perhaps a bit plump, imperfect in her acting, she could still chalk up this role among her successes.

Nothing of the sort.

Years later, she speaks of her experience in the role only as a nightmare: "But what a nightmare!"

What did she find to complain about in this role? Ridiculous, dangerous, unsuitable, in the sense of alien. Had she accepted the role only for the considerable fee? For this role she received the sum of 6,000 zlotys, an amount that tailors, professors, or clerks took years to earn.

I never really understood what she found so revolting in this episode of her past. Nor why it did not correspond to her idea of the status of a star. Was it only because of the language that she had to speak, when she had vehemently vowed to distance herself from it? She could have gained affirmation as a performer playing beside Ida Kamińska, personifying a seductress on the screen. But the experience would never repeat itself.

Perhaps this was when she had finally come to define her identity?

Or perhaps it was the role that opened the path to the ghetto for her?

3

It was a massive building

It was a massive building several stories high, elaborately decorated, like Paris during the Belle Époque. She said that it was full of "amenities," because in the drawing room she could enjoy a rounded bay with enormous windows.

She lived in the apartment on the top floor. It was spacious, comfortable, and furnished with care because she finally had the means. She spoke of antiques; perhaps they were Louis-something furniture, or in the Biedermeier or Empire style.

It had to be spacious. It had to be different from when she was poor.

So, a china cabinet filled with Rosenthal porcelain?

A chest of drawers? A secretary?

Photographs, a gramophone. Paintings. She had a Roman Kramsztyk, but it has disappeared. It must have been a landscape of the south of France or a portrait. I don't think that she would have dared to hang a nude in her drawing room.

In the sideboard there remained some food. Bags of biscotti, and some dark chocolate.

At that time, light did not frighten her. But I can imagine that while she was waiting that day for her mother and her sisters, she must have drawn the heavy drapes across the windows.

From this apartment on the top floor, there was a view of a corner of the sky. Everything was shattered, masked, blanketed with smoke, torn by the impact of shells.

September 1939, another day of bombing. The Royal Castle was destroyed.

Mayor Starzyński, on Radio Warsaw II, described in a hoarse voice the "heroic resistance" of the city.

The lack of coffins.

They were late, and the tea had gotten cold.

It was Helena who came in first. Her mother was still painfully climbing up the stairs. Maryla rushed in a little later. She threw a large package tied up with string on the table.

That was her whole fortune! Her husband, a jeweler, had already left Warsaw for the east, but he wanted to provide for his young wife.

Quickly tens of gold wedding bands made pretty little piles. Gold, twenty-four karat. Very fine gold. And besides them, rings of platinum set with little diamonds.

Their mother advised them to wear as many as they could. The sisters preferred to hide them all.

It was Vera who found the hiding place. At first she wanted to use the rings to hang the filmy curtains, but they were too small. It was impossible to pass the brass curtain rods through them. However, they did manage to unscrew the ball-shaped finials. She inserted the gold wedding bands one after the other. They stood on a ladder and extended her reach with a duster of ostrich feathers.

An hour later, she had put everything inside. For a short time, they felt a little safer.

"The beginning of the war is not the end of everything," Vera said, to reassure herself like many people her age. She didn't know how to be afraid.

"I was brazenly young," she acknowledged, "unaware of what threatened us in this situation. What could happen was beyond my imagination. I was dancing with death, but it was a graceful dance."

She was twenty-three years old, and life was swirling about her, carried by a natural flow that was only beginning to seduce her.

She had spent two weeks in Sopot at the Grand Hotel in a suite overlooking the sea. The strolls along the jetty became shorter and shorter, the conversations about the war more and more dramatic. A terrible sense of foreboding overcast the blazing month of August.

War? Nobody believed it.

The train was packed. The feeling of impending danger was heightened.

She was supposed to leave for Paris, at the invitation of the famous singer Yvette Guilbert, who was a friend of her wealthy aunt. The star of the Moulin Rouge with her long black gloves, as in the drawing by Toulouse-Lautrec, had heard Hanka Ordonówna years before. Vera was impressed by this sequence of connections.

All the formalities had been accomplished, and the contract with the ABC Theater signed. Her departure was set for the first of September.

Too late for Paris. She had a rendezvous with the war. She still didn't recognize the full weight of that word.

It was proposed that she flee to Italy. She refused.

At the famous Café Ziemiańska, the cakes with prunes and cream were selling out. The echoes of literary puns fell silent; no one brought flowers. She was still singing. Despite the limitations of the blackout, she gave a concert at the Café Vogue on the first of September 1939 and another the following week.

Of these days she remembers only the flames and the chaos. The interminable errands in town; maybe things were better elsewhere. The search for family, friends, and loved ones.

Many had fled. She had neither anyone to go with nor anywhere to go.

Standing in line for bread, for water, for potatoes, for coal. The streets strewn with barricades. The houses pockmarked with exploded shells, the roofs blown off, on fire. The traces of life in the interiors of apartments, the bed still unmade, the pot of soup, tomato soup, a piece of knitting in green wool, a sleeve, a book open in the middle of a chapter . . . on what would turn out to be a last sentence.

The first wave of bombing spared Hoża Street. By chance. Then, nothing had been planned. It was one of the good streets among those around Marszałkowska Street. The buildings in this section of Warsaw appealed to civil servants and to German officials. That's where they started settling progressively. Across the way in the little Theater Victoria, replacing the old movie house Hollywood, they would soon stage shows for the Wehrmacht. In the city, flags with swastikas and German insignias would start appearing everywhere.

The corner of Krucza and Hoża streets, downtown Warsaw, after German bombings and the surrender of the capital on September 28, 1939. Vera's apartment was nearby.

One afternoon, her mother had spent a moment alone at Vera's on Hoża Street. She had first gone to fetch shoes at the shoemaker and had stopped for a word with Kajetan, the hairdresser. She tried to maintain the routines of everyday life. She had washed half the plates and glasses. She watered the plants, but really drowned the cactus and the pansies. Neither she nor Vera had a green thumb.

They were banging on the door. She hesitated, but she couldn't just not open up.

The screaming Germans chased her out. She fled as she was, in her slippers.

She ran to her eldest daughter's, where she and Maryla had moved recently. Because together they could better face things. Because the lower floors were safer.

Vera came home from the bank, tired and angry; she had to line up several times, because they would give out only fifty zlotys at each window. She bought herself some valerian, just in time. Immediately she had decided they had to save their belongings. She had always been the courageous one, even if she was the youngest. Her sisters were screaming that she was crazy. Her mother held on to her by her sleeve. Vera didn't listen to them and ran to Hoża Street.

She had turned the key in the lock when her neighbor cracked open her door—she was Polish, Catholic. She knew that the Germans had gone through there. "I am going into my home, I am not going there to *steal*. Nobody can forbid my doing that," Vera said with determination.

For the first time she saw someone had devastated her home. A violation. That's how she experienced it. The wreckage had taken on the theatrical appearance of the apocalypse. They had opened the armoires, the drawers, the hiding places. They overturned the furniture, ripped open the sofa and easy chairs, broken the plates. They must have been looking for valuables.

She rushed up and down, losing her head completely. She looked for photographs, scores, records, here and there. Like a child saving her toys. She carefully wrapped an ugly, cheap Ćmielów porcelain vase filled with dried flowers that her mother had given her after her first performance. (It survived until her death more than fifty years later.) Shoes, a fan, some books, she fled with a full bag, satisfied. She had the feeling of having fooled the Germans.

"And the rings? Where are the rings, you recovered how many of them?" Those were the words with which her sisters greeted her.

"The rings? I forgot. But wait . . . I'm going back. It's not so complicated. It's not far. The front door, the stairs, the key, the door. The window, the ladder. Unscrew. Recover, and wrap it all up. I'm going."

The guards with their blue caps and high shoes. She knew that the concierges were the most dangerous. They were always snitches working for the stronger side, whether Jew or German, depending on circumstances.

"I'll manage . . ." She decided to rush there right away. Liba showed herself the more determined. "Not as long as I'm alive."

Vera gave in, even if she didn't understand the danger. Nor her mother's anguish. The anguish frightened her.

The end of September, or perhaps a little later. The ban on dance halls and balls was in full force. They instituted a system of ration cards; food rationing was particularly meager. They forbade posting notices of death services on the walls of churches, on houses, or even the walls of cemeteries. On the other hand, there appeared small notices posted by resistance organizations: *We want to inform women who have intimate relations with Germans that there are still openings in private whorehouses.*

At 15 Hoża Street a fortuneteller had an office. *I read rare cards, water, palms, photographs and manuscripts. Clairvoyant for finding missing persons.* Serious work. *Every day except Sunday.*

Vera's mother had been sick for years. She was in the care of Dr. Jezierski and later his son, Kazimierz. A dark, handsome medical student, a little coarse, but attentive and cordial, he made home visits, gave her medications and injections. Sometimes he spoke of the military hospital of Druskienniki, where he was an intern. He also spoke of Buda and Pest in Hungary, where he had interned in surgery. For Vera it all sounded like Hans and Fritz, the Katzenjammer Kids; it was idiotic, but sounded logical. She tried to be nice to him.

He knew who she was. He had perhaps even been once or twice to the Paradis. She felt that he was attracted to her. She was even inclined to like him a little. He brought comfort to her mother. She had never given him a second thought, and yet when one afternoon he came to say goodbye, she found it painful. He was leaving for the east, like everyone else. She was worried about who was going to take care of her mother.

A few weeks later, Kazimierz Jezierski stood again in the doorway of their apartment in Warsaw. Impatient; his eyes looked somber.

He had come to fetch her, to save her. She had to live! She had to sing! He had gone up to the Polish-Lithuanian border in the north of the country. He went to the hospital in the village of Druja on the Dźwina River beyond Wilno, in the district of Witebsk. They needed a doctor. He immediately received the appointment from the administration. Now that he had a base, he decided to come and fetch Vera.

He said that from Druja they could reach Latvia or Sweden. She wanted to believe him. She wanted to believe everything.

She was not thinking of love. Neither at this period nor later.

Her mother wept as she put in her hand her gold wedding band, which she had taken off her finger. A moment later, she removed another one that she kept in a little bag at her breast. "Leave," she said. Vera had the impression that she was casting her out. She gave in to the panic of flight. Perhaps her mother

Thanks to him Vera survived: a notebook belonging to Kazimierz Jezierski, then a medical student at Warsaw University in 1933. His father was the doctor treating Vera's mother, Liba Grynberg. A few years later Kazimierz planned Vera's escape from occupied Warsaw. He protected her throughout the war.

knew something that she did not. She does not remember their words of farewell.

Liba Grynberg remained in Warsaw with her two elder daughters. The youngest, the only one who mattered, the beloved, she wanted to spare her at any price. She probably would have turned her over to the devil himself so that she could survive. To keep her far from the Germans and the war.

In mid-November the first snow began to fall. In December, Jews were ordered to wear an armband with the Star of David. They followed regulations.

Vera was not prepared for the wandering life of the war.

When she left the city center of Warsaw, she was wearing flat shoes, a brown herringbone suit, gloves, and a little fur hat. She carried a bag containing a change of underwear, the remaining music. Cigarettes. She smoked a lot, to cut her hunger.

They were traveling on foot, catching trains or any other means of transport. Soon they had to cross the river Boug. On one side the Germans, and on the other, the Russians. On an autumn night they crossed the frozen river, their feet numbed and burning from frostbite, even though they had borrowed rubber boots. Or perhaps because of these rubber boots. They didn't have the money to rent a cart. Walking exhausted her to a degree where she lost touch with reality.

She renewed her spirits in a cottage, they didn't know where. She couldn't remember much. People spoke to her and gave her something to eat, potatoes, pork bits, an unfamiliar smell. She could not remember what happened afterward. She woke up in Druja, in a clean bed, in the home of the village doctor, who everyone believed was her husband. Kazimierz, called Kazik. It was because of him that she survived, but she never even said thank you.

"My first night with a man . . . With good will, I gave myself over to a ritual that was totally strange to me. It's hard to imagine how ignorant I was about the subject, a real goose."

She no longer remembered the pain, rather the humiliation.

"We remained in Druja and in Nowy Pohost in the district of Wilno from October 1939 until March 1940," Jezierski wrote in official documents after the war.

The village of Druja was in the district of Brasław, with its Orthodox churches and cloister, as well as a synagogue and Jewish cemetery, near the estate of Sapieha with Witebsk on the horizon. Nowy Pohost was the neighboring village, part of Nowogródek district. She had heard about its fields filled with lupins in bloom. She saved a photograph of the place, with a handwritten inscription: two men and three women wearing white aprons standing in front of a snow-covered wooden hut. A fragment of a label: PRZ . . .

Kazimierz worked in the hospital, and she nursed her frost-bite. He saw patients in his consulting room and performed operations. She wanted to sing. But for that she needed a club, a cabaret, a theater; that is, to be in a city. She contacted her uncle Nathan, her father's brother, who lived in Lwów. He wanted to convince her to come, he proposed to lodge her and promised that he would find work for her. He repeated that her friends wanted news about her.

She left first.

She had remembered Lwów from before the war. She had sung at the Bagatela and Chez Georges. A majestic city of Galicia, modern, with its musical revues, and jazz bands, and dances imported from America: shimmy, fox-trot, and Charleston. Large, welcoming streets, bright lights.

Now, cars and tanks. Bolsheviks in rags, or in costumes as if straight out of a theater wardrobe. Craggy faces. A cacophony of Russian, increasingly elusive. More and more people leaving, more and more questions: How to reach Romania? Which is the safest road to Hungary?

Since September 1939, the city had been under Soviet rule. The Polish Ensemble Company was henceforth called "Polish Soviet Theater," whose function was to put in practice "Soviet political culture." I don't know to what extent she paid any attention to this sort of detail, nor how she understood this new political order of daily life. She was young. But did her youth prevent her from understanding, or wanting to under-stand, the traps into which Polish artists risked falling in their profession, that is, by serving a foreign flag? I have never had any explanations on this subject.

The citizens' command ordered a boycott of the occupational forces. Not everyone obeyed this command. Fear reigned. And in time, hunger. Even if only the presentiment of it.

A great fear and a great unknown, wrote Ola Watowa, the

wife of Alexander Wat, a Polish poet, who also found herself there during this period.

I think that it was another sort of fear than the one felt toward the Germans in the first months of the Occupation of Warsaw. There, from the beginning, and a long time after, there was an opposition of anger, rebellion, and resistance. Here it was different. People tried to melt into the masses, to be useful, to please and to participate in the creation of "the tomorrow that sings." Fear was transformed into abject servility, more efficient for survival. To win what, a medal?

The Artists' Club at 39 Jagiellońska Street was a preferred meeting place for refugees—actors, singers, musicians who the war, in dealing out a new hand, had landed in Lwów. Runaways, the homeless, all in need and looking for work and shelter. And Vera also went there.

She stood on the threshold. A scarf on her head, in an enormous coat and man's boots taken off a corpse, very far from looking like the Warsaw star of the Paradis. But she was recognized right away. Before she could say a word, her friends threw themselves upon her to kiss her. They removed her disguise of clothing, made her sit down, and served her some tea.

She wanted to sing; she asked for help and protection.

"You are lucky," said Tadeusz Hollender, satirist and poet, "just today the administrators of our Ministry of Culture are here, those who hire us, the Russians."

They introduced her as a famous artist from Warsaw, popular and a guaranteed success. She sang "Krasiva Devochka" ("Pretty Girl"), they said. Right away she signed a contract. She remembered that the other women in the group detested her because she had her own dressing room. She told me that she performed in many places. The group from the Stylowy Theater Revue, reinforced with talent that had fled Poland, came to about twenty people. Well-loved Bodo played out his charming fantasies, Feliks Konarski (stage name Ref-Ren) was the master of ceremonies, who fought for "a little luck in love" for everyone. Their biggest hit was the song interpreted by Andrzej Bogucki, "I Already Miss Summer" . . .

Vera didn't mention any women in starring roles aside from herself.

"The performances . . . I had to be dressed—because I had nothing: I was naked from head to toe. I received a lot of money as an advance. The censors questioned the lyrics of the songs, even those of 'The Letter'—because under a proletariat regime, songs aren't about gold chains—but I knew how to defend myself. I explained that the song was in fact a satire of the relationships of bourgeois Americans. And as a tribute, or maybe an alibi, I sang one Ukrainian song. I came to enjoy it. They offered to have me perform in another theater, the Marysieńka. Then at the Splendid. I was earning about two thousand rubles a month, which was a fortune."

She no longer needed help from her family. She rented a room in Lwów. Even the revenues from Druja were no longer needed. Kazik, whom she does not call her husband in her narrative but her friend, often without even mentioning his first name, came to join her. In May he passed his final examinations at the medical school of the Jan Kazimierz University in Lwów—he received a pass in his examinations on forensic surgery, laryngology, and hygiene and an excellent in obstetrics and gynecology. His diploma proudly displayed the seal of the Institute of Medicine.

Pencils and graph-paper notebooks obtained or stolen from somewhere. Doctor's notes: laryngeal dyspnea, pachydermia, nodules on the vocal cords. Internship, work on the actual problem. Vera's notes on her music: refrains, chromatic and clef signs.

Both wanted to distract their attention from the recent news from the front that announced Allied defeats.

The Stylowy Theater Revue drew crowds. This light confection of tears and laughter in the gross reality of Lwów, overpopulated at the time, gave a breath of fresh air to these exiles' renewed memories of the recent past. It became a reference point.

The theater was frequented by Russian dignitaries accompanied by "their extraordinarily ugly wives"—I am quoting memoirs of the period—in their baggy silk nightgowns that they thought were evening dresses. The men never took off their coats, nor their hats, while the wives put finishing touches to their "distinguished" wardrobes without knowing exactly what they were doing. The inhabitants of Lwów perceived this as the occupiers' native costumes. Russians did not know about the usage of handkerchiefs, nor of toilet bowls.

"I want my mother to come, I don't want to wait any longer," she told Kazik. She wrote her mother letters in purple ink, which was the only kind available, in which she tried to persuade her that the place was less dangerous and that she had organized her life. She used every argument, even tried to coerce her. Without success.

Her mother refused categorically. She was sick and didn't have the strength. A voyage into the unknown frightened her; she didn't want to leave behind the remains of what she called her worldly goods.

She wrote briefly on postcards, as required by the Germans. She was careful not to use the words deleted from the official vocabulary of war: walls, raids, the Forced Labor Program . . .

I wish that Vera had received other letters.

Her sister Helena would have written her without mincing words. That the thermometer was reading below minus twenty degrees Celsius, and there was no means of heating: with coal at 300 zlotys a ton, people were cutting down trees in the city parks for firewood. They were all living in a single room, like everyone else. That they were fearful of going into the streets because Jews were being beaten, made to dance, or else to clean

In September 1939 Russians entered the Polish city of Lwów. On May 1, 1940, the city's International Workers' Day parade took place. Vera performed in a theater there for several months.

out toilets using their underwear. Stores were being looted. Everything was very expensive.

The Germans forbade the raising of homing pigeons so that information of this sort would not get out into the world.

Vera remembered the bitter winter of 1940 in Lwów, the unheated dressing rooms, hands stiff from the cold, vapor coming from her mouth when she sang. She caught a urinary-tract infection then, but she didn't stop working. In the market behind the Skarbek Theater you could find everything: blankets and curtains, keys, needles and buttons, and the most saleable item—mechanical toys. She bought a small amount of virgin wool, the remains of a red shawl and a navy blue vest. She unraveled the shawl and vest during the show. Then she busied herself making a sweater for Kazik. She knit her work according to the contrasting events of the Occupation. She linked the stitches one after the other—the questions about the future, longing for her mother (the colors of absence), the fear of the unknown—into an exotic rough design, knit two, purl two, one row going and one row coming, blue, red. Good/ bad. Cold/hot. For you/for me . . .

One evening someone threw something onto the stage. No, not a rock or a rotten egg, not yet at that time.

It was a jar of cream. Nivea, a luxury in those days.

Nivea, in Latin, "white as snow." She remembered the gentle perfumed soap of the brand, then the cream, a round blue container inscribed with white letters. For years it was advertised in the newspapers next to the weather forecast. *Nivea at home, and for sports.* Details from a time free of constant worries. The same German Jew had invented toothpaste and lipstick. During the thirties he was driven from his country.

Her colleagues listened to the radio. They were shooting people in Cracow, they sent the professors from Jagiellonian University into camps. Paris had fallen. Hope gave way to anxiety.

All the same, Vera wanted to return.

Shortly afterward, the last performance was staged.

They rebuilt the dressing rooms on the stage so each person was seated in front of his mirror. In the middle, in the light of the projectors, Ref-Ren's enormous mastiff was warming himself. Vera started the last song, joined in by the others . . .

Let us promise that whatever happens
Each of us will keep a hiding place in our hearts.
Let us promise that these hiding places will always be full
Of memories gathered starting today . . .

People didn't hide their tears, the audience as well as those on stage.

The Soviet administration clearly wanted the continuation of the Polish theaters in Lwów, because it created a semblance of normal life in the city. On the one hand the administration was fully aware of the provisional nature of these Polish centers; on the other hand they made them undergo an accelerated program of Soviet indoctrination. On the stage of the Marysieńka Cine-Theater on Smolka Square, every performance was preceded by Soviet propaganda films. Acrobatic dancing was showcased as the specialty of the troupe. The songs and acts had to display a "high-minded social goal."

This type of troupe spent many months on tour. They had started in July 1940. They toured the provinces as well as major cities such as Kiev or Moscow, to perform their own repertory but also to "cement the relationship of Soviet society." They crossed seven republics to bring to Polish citizens scattered here and there throughout the country "the fundamentals of the new ideology through humor and songs." The performers were responsible for "familiarizing themselves with the culture of the Soviet state, the tenets of the working class, which would permit in time a strengthening of mutual bonds."

The language of these goals, as well as of the programs, was totally foreign to Vera. Like the reinterpretation of the Polish classics with the purpose of "stigmatizing the Polish bourgeoisie, willing subjects of the scheming of the prewar capitalist elite" (in the tragicomedy of Gabriela Zapolska's *Madame Dulska's Morals*) or in order to "criticize the nobility" (with *The Vengeance,* a comedy by Aleksander Fredro), or to reveal the idleness, stupidity, and amorality of the bourgeoisie and the great landowners" (in Michal Bałucki, *The Open House*).

She had already left Lwów when they celebrated the eighty-fifth anniversary of the death of Adam Mickiewicz. I don't know if she could, or even would have wanted to, oppose the manipulations that were intended to give the author of *Forefathers* the "soul of a Soviet poet."

She had considered the possibility of going with her troupe

and the revue, but the final decision depended on the will of her mother. Would she agree to join her, would she allow herself to be saved from the Germans?

Vera faced the dilemma: the hammer and sickle or the swastika. Her parents had fled Russia years earlier. She did not know the Germans and was skeptical of the rumors and what was told by the refugees. Warsaw was always a familiar place, from which her mother sent imploring letters: *Come back, here everyone asks for news about you, and now they are opening cafés, there's work. You can put on shows again.*

She places events that unfolded on the border as happening during the days of late summer. Crowds of people wanted to pass toward the German side. She called that "defying fate." People tried to bribe the guards, they bargained, using tricks or pleading. There were screams and tears. Around sentry posts, there were duvets spread out, feathers flying from eiderdowns, and pillows ripped open, covering everything, people as well as baggage. The Germans were looking for objects of value. They found them: dollars, rubles, necklaces. A Russian let her pass, a German insisted on seeing her identity papers. She had forged papers, but she looked Jewish. The clerk decorated them with a Star of David.

The journey from Lwów to Cracow took over ten hours. She was with Kazik and the Czarnecki couple; she had worked with Maciej Czarnecki in a café before the war. With several partners a few months later, he would open a new club in Warsaw that would play a major role in Vera's story—the Café Sztuka (Café of the Arts).

At the station in Cracow, nobody asked any questions. They stopped off at a hotel across from the train station. For nearly an hour she examined her document with the Jewish star. She tried to erase it, to remove it, to scratch it out, to rub it off, to make it go away, a moment of panic, she wanted to make it vanish. She had nothing to do with this star. Not her.

They treated themselves to an extravagant dinner at the

Wierzynek Restaurant, on the market square. Slices of black bread spread with lard. It had been a long time since she enjoyed it so much. The next day they left for Warsaw.

Once she saw her mother she felt relieved and was certain that she had made the right choice. They wished one another happiness for Rosh Hashanah, the Jewish New Year.

Children were begging in the streets. Jews were being eliminated from the city center. Everyone was speaking of the ghetto, the limits of its boundaries, the dates of the forced move there. She considered it only a simple move, even if imposed; for reasons independent of her will she had to change her address. For a while. A new destiny, a different condition of war, perhaps worse, but still a comparable life.

She remembered having lived with Helena on Graniczna Street, near the Jewish quarter closed off on November 16, 1940. Not far from there, on Grzybowski Square, was one of the six gates leading to it. Guard stations were spread all around where the wall had not yet been built. The Germans considered that isolating the Jews was a "political and moral necessity."

Kazik corroborated that they had spent several months toward the end of the year 1940 in his father's apartment at 14 Próżna Street. After the Jewish ghetto was established, they left this address; they took some furniture and articles of clothing to a friend of the Jezierski family, Klemens Bednarski, who resided in the Mokotów neighborhood.

They still made the rounds of several spots in Warsaw, even if most places were henceforth off limits to them. The Adria had now become a club *reserved for Germans,* just like the grounds of the Royal Park of Łazienki, or Saski Park. For every trip by rail, taxi, or carriage, a special permission was required. They took a pedicab to Piłsudski Square, rebaptized Hitler Square. They left belongings with several friends. She took with her a favorite sculpture—a bronze statuette representing an expressive dancer—and a marble desk set. She never told anyone where she hid these objects, or how. A shame. She remembered custard tarts, pastries with roasted nuts and sugar, made and sold by the wives of the intelligentsia to feed their families. The sweet industry of the Occupation.

They went only to safe places and always tried to look good. She wore carmine lipstick.

Pregnancy. She remembered being stupefied, even years later, because she did not know where it could have come from. This was followed by fear, because a star cannot let herself be disfigured physically. And besides, what did it mean to give birth during the war. Birth? An abortion was the inevitable solution: no sentiment, no philosophy. The price of a few jewels.

A little afterward, another problem. Kazik believed that she had poisoned herself with the pork fat she had eaten so avidly in Cracow. She suffered pain, but also unbearable itching sensations that she could only relieve—momentarily—by taking very hot baths. She joked and said she could still afford to treat herself to such luxury.

"I was spared," she said, "because many rendezvous with death still awaited me. The devil, or else, fate, let me live to continue on my way."

They returned by train to Cracow again, without authorization. She had gone up to the ticket booth with effrontery, and did the same in the compartment. She succeeded. Until February 1941 she performed at the Café Polonia. A large, dark apartment transformed with ingenuity and handiwork into a nightclub. The need to hear songs was so strong. The audience, marked by the Star of David, still elegant, wearing family jewels, applauded her and consumed not-so-bad drinks.

But the stars on their sleeves caught her eyes and disturbed her. Sometimes she forgot the words of the song she was singing. She remembered that these emblems were different from those worn in Warsaw. Here they were patches, yellow and loud.

It was in Cracow, before a performance, that for the first time she witnessed a raid. She claimed that she was so absorbed in watching the sunset that she had avoided death. She was late; the spectators had been taken away before she arrived at the club.

A little later, in the spring, they also created a ghetto in Cracow, not yet sealed off. Her mother again summoned her to come back. She wrote Vera: *In the ghetto they are opening cafés where there are shows. The producers of these shows ask about you.*

She and Kazik returned to Warsaw at the end of March 1941. They were greeted by the posters of the *Stürmer,* the Nazi anti-Semitic newspaper, showing portraits of Jews with slogans in black lettering: *Jews–lice–typhus!* There was inflation again, black bread from now on cost six zlotys, with white bread even more expensive. Prices kept rising. Kazik insisted that she remain on the Aryan side. She categorically refused.

For their farewell dinner they went to the Mascotte, on Jasna Street, near the Philharmonic. Liver with onions and Fedora sponge cake. It cost a fortune, fifteen zlotys each course. For sixty you could buy a pair of shoes. They paid even more to the policeman who let her re-enter the ghetto.

4

What is the taste of hunger?

What is the taste of hunger? Stomach cramps, dreams of oranges, the smell of bread fresh from the oven, just beyond reach. The bread was burning, but there was no time to do anything about it. The need for immediate gratification rendered one powerless.

The ghetto.

The survivors say that they are the only ones who can understand life in a ghetto. Perhaps they are right. Then, why do I want to confront it once again?

Because for me, the ghetto remains a reference point. I want to survive and know the price of survival. I want to know. Perhaps it's because of that that I found Vera.

The ghetto. I try to enter it, I attempt to follow this path without hope.

Doctor Janusz Korczak used to say that the Jewish quarter resembled China, suddenly transplanted to the middle of Europe. Marked people, gray, dragging their feet, crowded together in the limited space of a few streets. Abnormally agitated, yet apathetic.

For me, the ghetto is mute . . . when I think of it, when I try to imagine it. And yet I hear coming from there the melody of a song about love. Indecent? Human.

The moment it was sealed off, the ghetto started searching for the resources for survival; it wanted to live. It was a closed city, but a city nevertheless, and a living, breathing organism that purchased, ate, dressed, and excreted. In the listing of ads in the daily *Jewish Gazette* (thirty groszy, twelve pages) you could read (sometimes on more than three pages) advertisements for tailors, dentists, and milliners. You could find hairdressing salons, and manicurists, shoemakers, engravers, variety shows, and symphony orchestras.

You can eat well at Café Gertner and at the Thorn Restaurant.
Pinuzan, the remedy for congested lungs.
Purchase false teeth, old dentures, even broken . . .

I buy, I sell, I buy. I invest, I spend. Perspectives of the future.

For many months people struggled to live. Then only "to stay afloat, to survive." To get by.

In every corner of everyday life dwelled destiny, in all its dimensions. An obsession to satisfy all needs. Hunger for bread and the hunger of emotions, the need for joy and tenderness. For dreams . . .

The ghetto must have been noisy in the mornings, the afternoons, noisy with its incessant commotion in the streets, its lamentations, its mendacity. The streets and the courtyards of buildings were bustling. The street music competed with opera melodies. A popular ballad—"Oj ta bona"—with Verdi or Moniuszko. In the street, the movies and the theaters, in the clubs. Vera Gran sang on one of these stages. Where, in this space threatened by typhus, could there be room for applause, spotlights, the sound of a piano? I can't imagine it.

At that time she did not understand why she should have stopped singing. That is not what she wanted. She clung ferociously to the idea of working. And work meant everything to her. The applause—that was life, acceptance, adoration. It can be felt in her every gesture, in each of her decisions. "I want to live, I want to be as I was before—admired, extraordinary, all-powerful.

"How could I have known what was going to happen?" She asked the question as if someone were accusing her. In the end, how could anyone have foreseen all that, even imagine such things? They promised that it wouldn't last long. Her instincts told her not to choose life on the other side of the wall, the Aryan side. Here, among her own, she was supposed to be safe.

She returned to Warsaw, crossed the barrier to the closed-off area. This must have occurred after the assassination of the celebrated movie actor Igo Sym, who had collaborated with the Occupiers. He was assassinated March 7, 1941. That afternoon, megaphones announced through all the streets the new ruling decreed and initiated by Governor Fischer, announcing the repercussions for the Polish people in the wake of this "atrocious crime." They put in place a curfew from eight P.M. to five in the morning. It made life more difficult. For the Passover holidays in April there was a shortage of matzo, the dollar was three times more expensive and went up to one hundred fifty zlotys. The beggars in front of the courthouse on the Jewish side painfully chanted verses from the Psalms.

The cafés were popular, therefore she immediately received several offers of work. She made a choice, which she could allow herself. She would proudly repeat that from the very beginning, Polish people would come secretly into the ghetto to treat themselves to the delicacies from Hirszfeld and Jagoda, do some business, and catch Vera Gran's act. She remembered that Bella Szwarc, on Sienna Street, offered her too little money, and the owner of the Club "By the Fountain" didn't seem exceptionally nice to her. She chose the Sztuka, located at 2 Leszno Street. Before the war it had been a hangout for coachmen, Gertner's Bar.

One of the few existing photographs of a café in the Warsaw Ghetto. There were about a hundred clubs and restaurants in the restricted zone.

"Vera, please sing something for us."

"Yes, but it will be in my café."

The café was located a few yards from a sentry box at the entrance to the ghetto, watched over by two Germans and a Jewish policeman. People would choose not to eat in order to spend an evening at the Sztuka with a glass of hot water and listen to the popular sentimental songs from before the war. This little restaurant in the ghetto became fashionable. The admirers of the place claimed that it was the most elegant, and the haven of the intelligentsia. It was frequented by Professor Ludwik Hirszfeld, Jerzy Jurandot, the young Marcel Reich Ranicki, critic for the *Jewish Gazette*. The café's enemies saw a nest of big spenders with bulging wallets.

Emanuel Ringelblum, tireless chronicler of the ghetto, depicts in his journal cafés sponsored by an association of several families, sometimes more than ten of them. That was the case for the Sztuka. The co-owners called it their home and spent a great deal of time there. Behind closed doors it was easier not to think about the ghetto.

Vera's first concert took place at the Melody Palace, on Rymarska Street. She probably didn't know that just before, a noisy celebration had taken place, with a beauty contest for the prettiest legs. The ghetto danced. The ghetto wanted to live. Ringelblum wrote that they tried to prevent these festivities from taking place, but one of the owners was one of "those people," and it was better not to offend her. That was the case with most of the places of entertainment. He unequivocally suggested that these people were conspiring with the Germans.

She remembered the preparations for the concert at the Melody Palace. It was the 20th of April, 1941, her birthday and that of the Führer. "The Germans were preparing 'a surprise' for Hitler," she said, "and what could have pleased him more than killing Jews?" She arrived in the dressing rooms around eleven o'clock. A moment later a woman rushed in to tell her that there was going to be a raid. Vera's immediate reaction was "what bad luck," rather than fear. By a quarter of an hour before the concert was scheduled to start, there was no one in the room. She understood that people were afraid; they remained cloistered at home. They were not coming. However, the room filled gradually, one, two, ten women. And that was all. The only men present were on stage—the master of ceremonies, Michał Znicz, and the pianist, Leon Boruński, winner of the Chopin Competition.

That's the evening she started singing in the ghetto. Because she was the draw, at that time they called her Vera the Magnet. She overcame her fear and her feeling of despair. She also performed several times in the theater for the Femina Theater Revue.

"The Sztuka started with me, and for me exclusively," she would repeat. "They came to hear me. Boys and girls came secretly from the Aryan side, they greased the palms of the policemen to come listen to me. There were so many of them. I took that for a great compliment. You have to be young and stupid to risk your life for some music. Every night I had some goyim like that in the room. They would check: Is Vera there?

"Over there the performances and songs were only in Polish. That's why for certain people the Sztuka was not kosher enough!" The biting, satiric cabaret was anchored in actual events in the form of a little spoken journal, by which laughter could render cruel reality bearable.

"In the beginning, there was only me," she liked to repeat.

"One day," she told me, "a pianist came up to me. It was Władysław Szpilman, the composer. He had accompanied me on the piano on occasions before the war. 'Help me, I have nothing to live on.' He was humble, and small . . . I tried."

She persuaded the manager to invite other talents, even if at the time she already had two female accompanists. That is how she remembered it. He took on Władysław Szlengel, the poet who called himself "the chronicler of those who are drowning." Pudgy, short, with American eyeglasses, he was the author of the overwhelming poem "Telephone." There came a time when there was nobody left to telephone on the Aryan side. They were joined by Józef Lipski, ugly, redheaded, frail, a marvelous writer. Leonid Fokszański and Andrzej Włast. Artur Goldfeder, the son of a banker, with a law degree, a conservatory graduate, also turned up. He fell madly in love with her, to die for. He looked like a Russian prince in exile. And he had a horror of lice.

She claims that she was the one who had the idea of having two pianists, Szpilman and Goldfeder, on a little stage. They moved two pianos, one facing the other, and she squeezed between the two. The audience was virtually sitting on the performers' laps. She told how the program was divided in two parts—the first with the participation of the writers, the second was just her.

Mina Tomkiewicz, a young lawyer, came often to the Sztuka. She admired Vera's costumes, especially a frivolous taffeta dress decorated with tiny buttons. The natural silk was iridescent with her every move. It reminded her of a ball. She remembered:

"The excitement gradually gave way to the applause, like a cake under its icing. Taking small steps, Vera Gran, the singer everyone adores, enters the little stage. Dimpled, her hair pulled back like a young girl's, wearing a light crinoline and a plunging neckline."

Vera Gran had her standard repertoire. Old lyrics or new ones set to music by Jurandot, or her young accompanist Janka Pruszycka. It sometimes happened that she sang "Three Letters" several times, because the audience would not let her leave. Songs about unhappy love, on the rustling of trees to the rhythm of a waltz, about golden bananas in a faraway island, about the brave sailors of the ship *Albatross*. This sort of emotion was what people sought out in cafés.

Vera was fully aware of it.

"It was an unbelievable feeling for an artist. So they could forget, and tear themselves away from the cruel reality of the ghetto, I would sing songs about mimosas and blue skies. I asked that a song be written about vast open spaces. In the ghetto we had a visceral craving for space. I sang: 'I believe that in this world somewhere far away, there is greenery, and grass and mist over the river, and the forest, and the immensity of the sky.' The audience demanded that I sing songs from before the war. It reminded them of another life, moments of happiness, a time when they were human beings, and not hunted animals. They wept, but those tears were a relief. They permitted them to hope, to think that there was more to life than the ghetto."

Irena Sendler, a legendary member of the clandestine organization Żegota (Council for Aid to Jews), who had saved many children, told about twice staying overnight in the sealed-off

The "Jewish residential district," as the Germans called the Warsaw Ghetto, was closed on November 16, 1940. The 400,000 Jewish residents of Warsaw were isolated behind a three-meter-high wall. They were identified by "bands of shame"—white armbands with a blue Star of David, which could be bought on the streets.

area. The people who brought her wanted to show her that life behind the wall was not only hunger and death. They invited her to the Café Sztuka, fashionable then. She couldn't believe her eyes. The people were elegant, there was food on the table, salmon, sweets, champagne. And tears, tears in the eyes of the spectators when Vera Gran was singing. She swore that everybody was crying.

Vera said that singing at that time was like acting in a mystery play. She came early, and waited for the public, and then she began her "Mass of Forgetting."

No, these words do not astonish me. It continues the trajectory of her thought. She had to do something in order not to go insane.

The ghetto was the central event, the principal stage of her destiny. The essential point of reference. Everything else would only gravitate around it.

She did not know that her life would be marked exactly by these days, fifteen months spent behind the wall, when she was not much more than twenty years old. What does one know about life at that age, how does one mature, and what does one have to do to protect oneself against the world?

Vera, a star before the war, wore an armband in the ghetto.

This small piece of white material with its blue star stigmatized thousands of people. Inferior people, condemned.

What could they do? And why should they have resisted from the beginning? They had not understood right away the perfidious nature of the diabolical plan; no one in their right mind could have believed it possible. Only the jester of the ghetto, Rubinstein, who didn't have all his wits, ran around in rags screaming in Yiddish, "Ale glajch, ale glajch"—all the same. He smelled death coming.

Someone called the armband the badge of suffering. I am against this comparison. I think that I would have been capable of seeing the progression from the signs *Forbidden to Jews and to Dogs* posted in the very elegant Saski Park, to the command to move behind the wall without the possibility of moving back, and finally to the transport toward the unknown.

In the streets they sold everything. Sodas and lollipops, clothing and underwear, housewares. Talmudic books and books of prayers were next to works by Feuchtwanger or by Zweig. Jewels were still being brought to the pawnbroker. The remains of an ancient splendor, relics of the family, everything that could be turned into money was exchanged for bread. Still they had to obtain those armbands.

In the first months of the ghetto, merchants suddenly sprang up on the sidewalks, like puppets rigged out with this piece of white material with a star.

There was a hierarchy of armbands, according to the level of wealth before the war. But only at the beginning, when life still gave the impression of being able to last. There were armbands of silk, delicate, having the shimmering echo of past elegance. Even the star was applied lightly, like a butterfly, and not like a cage. Those of cloth left fewer illusions; the roughness signified one thing that was certain: being marked. Never did they resemble a piece of jewelry, even for a moment. Nothing was ever decorative. They had to be washed and ironed. Those made of paper were a double curse. They had to be adjusted to the arm, often with a rubber band, or else they had to be sewn anew on each article of clothing worn. It was a unique Jewish craft of its kind, which never existed either before or after.

Vera had followed her family into the ghetto. Was that the only reason? It was the ghetto in its early days, no one could have known what would happen next. They all wanted to stay together, near each other. She wanted to work. Like everyone, like all the others, the musicians, the tailors, the teachers, the poets. She had to. She had a family to support. She also wanted to work because she loved singing. Perhaps even more; she couldn't imagine her life without the stage, and her public. To shine, to enjoy her success to the fullest. Some do not know how to live without that. They fall into dependence.

She saw nothing wrong with practicing her profession. She did not ask herself the question of whether this sort of activity could be inappropriate in this situation. Neither she nor her actress friends. Some theaters were open, and Vera agreed to perform here and there.

The Femina Theater was marginal for Vera, as well as for her friends from prewar dancing school, Stefania Grodzieńska and Franciszka Mannówna. There's no point dwelling on it. They certainly spent time together backstage—Vera, the cheerful Stefania, and the devil-may-care Franciszka, about whom it was said that she openly rode in pedicabs with men from the Gestapo. She was a little dark-haired girl like Vera, rather petite, more assertive with her little pointed nose, and she did not think anything of it. She didn't think "guilty, not guilty" about performing. She was living.

Three girlfriends in the ghetto. Not one evokes the memory of gossiping backstage. As if the weight of reality had taken their youth. But the theater existed. The admirers brought flowers. The girls would complain, "But how much bread can you buy for a bouquet of roses?" They would have to perform in skintight outfits or long dresses with bare backs. Stefania remembered a vermilion dress. They wanted to be elegant. "Besides, all the girls often went on stage half-naked. It wasn't an amateur performance, but a real production. For a moment we would forget that we were starving and numb with cold."

When the temperature dropped below zero, the people in the audience kept on their coats and gloves. You couldn't hear any applause. Precisely because of the gloves. In time, the audience learned to hold their arms up in the air so that the performers could "see their bravos."

She could not be responsible for her audience. She did not choose her admirers. It wasn't only those sitting with a glass of hot water, tinted or not, who applauded her. There were some, and they were numerous, who ordered champagne and grapes, Viennese coffee and cakes.

"The Group of Thirteen" (the name evokes dark memories)— that was what they called the Office to Combat Profiteering and Speculation—had its office right next door, at number 13 Leszno Street. The Thirteen was no doubt a Hitlerian agency directly under German orders and working for them. Several hundred functionaries (office workers, buyers, bookkeepers, engineers) wearing caps with a green band, therefore earning the name "forest rangers," had the daily task of struggling against speculation by practicing blackmail, denunciations, or demands for bribes. Who was trafficking in meat? Who was producing white bread and cake? How was sugar sold, and fish?

Abraham Gancwajch, the head of this office, was a regular at the Sztuka. "Patron" of Jewish literature and the arts, he had the knack of masking his dirty dealings behind great generosity.

Gancwajch liked to be called "editor." That's what Vera did. He had a diploma as rabbi, an extraordinary memory, and had made several trips to Africa from where he had sent numerous articles to the Jewish press. In the Warsaw Ghetto he administered more than a hundred houses, and he had become wealthy with the approval of the Germans. He was not required to wear the armband.

He believed in the victory of the Third Reich. He liked to say that hope would one day bring liberty to the Jews. He was in a position to arrange many things. He invited the always needy artists and effete writers to his home for copious dinners on Friday nights. In quoting Goethe, he said that his intention was "to do good," even if it was the devil who ordered him to do so.

It is difficult to understand what drove people to join this sort of service. Misery, or the desire to find the means to lead "the good life"? The need or the possibility to make money? The image of death in the mirror? The temptation to use what fate still offers even when knowing the daily threat?

It doesn't matter what the reason was, it provoked rejection by public opinion in the ghetto, which is probably the origin of the absurd expression "the Jewish Gestapo." Informers, Jewish Gestapo members? This expression was in current usage among the survivors after 1945.

They were "bad Jews," those from the Thirteen, those who denounced, or profited from the black market, traffickers who made their deals but only with those who could pay. They wrote denunciations and reports, made or confirmed accusations. Later those working for the Jewish police, the service to maintain order, were also called Jewish Gestapo.

Both collaborators of the Gestapo and their local informers frequented the Sztuka. It often happened that the commissioner of the Jewish quarter, Auerswald, would turn up in person. For the chief of the service to maintain order in the Jewish ghetto, Szeryński, and his followers, the staff would find the best tables. They were feared, but also their protection was solicited. Often one of the customers would treat them to a cognac or a serving of foie gras. The black marketers who had made a lot of money from the Occupation paraded themselves. They liked to show what they had. The music often disturbed them in the middle of trying to negotiate some new deals. The applause from the audience sounded the same to her ears, whether it came from those who gorged themselves or those who remained famished.

The bicycle squad of the Jewish police. Established in the ghetto at the very beginning of the war, the Jewish police fulfilled a variety of functions, primarily securing order and safety. After the war, those on duty until the end had to answer allegations that they participated in the Holocaust.

Vera could certainly differentiate the one from the other, but what for?

According to the historian Ringelblum, "It's an exaggeration to claim that we were more completely demoralized than others, especially if you consider that our difficult situation gave most people the following alternatives: either take the downward path, or die of hunger."

The Jewish police at the beginning had the task of ensuring order and security in the area behind the wall. The Judenrat, the Council of Elders, claimed it was well intentioned. Joining it were lawyers, doctors, engineers, like the unemployed, not always very honest. The work made certain people dream, and for others their dignity dictated avoiding such things at all cost.

I have verified: flat, rigid, navy-blue cap with shiny visor and blue band. Metal badge "Ordnungsdienst" and Star of David. On the arm, a yellow band. A leather belt, high shoes, and a white rubber truncheon. Others describe a wooden truncheon.

Afraid of them? In the semi-darkness of the café, when the lights had gone out again because they had not succeeded in bribing the employees of the electric company, and the flame from the carbide lamps hissed and smelled on burning? At times like these to be afraid, to avoid them? Demonstrate? They could still be considered old acquaintances who could turn out to be useful; they were not yet there to round up a specific number of "heads" to send to forced labor. Fear hadn't turned them cruelly intransigent. Not yet.

The ghetto survived. In the sequence of time as before, from spring to winter, from Passover to Chanukah, only Judgment Day came more often than before. Already by May 1941 bodies were being picked up from the streets. More than a hundred were buried every night, because at that time they were burying them, without shrouds, only covered with a piece of white paper that served another one the next day.

In October 1941, the first snow fell on Warsaw; in November, barefoot children froze to death in the streets of the ghetto. Was it at that moment that she had the idea of trying to help orphans? Perhaps later, when the cold became more intense, and the Germans ordered all furs to be handed over.

Fur. A luxury. How was it possible that it was left to the Jews for such a long time? Only a certain privileged few could wear fur. Furs were turned in, given away, or sold. But they were also being ruined with the help of scissors and knives, boiling water and acid. However, this was rare, because you could still get some money for them.

A dollar was now worth 200 zlotys, the value of ten kilos of semolina. And now there were furs. A long astrakhan could be sold for 150 zlotys, seal for 100, the price of four loaves of bread. And also there were muffs and collars, stoles. The haggling for them was pitiless. The furs, like the Jews, survived by being transferred. The Poles profited by it. Vera was not concerned about who they were, if they needed it, or were making a profit. They had greater possibilities and freedom than the Jews back then, they didn't refuse to buy; the police, their families and acquaintances. Bastards? Swine? It wasn't for her to judge.

Following orders, she turned in a black seal coat and a rabbit-fur lining. The Germans had already taken her other furs in 1939.

Why has no one ever mentioned Vera Gran's orphanage? Neither at the time—hundreds of diaries and narrative memoirs of the ghetto have been published—nor later. It is not even mentioned in the documentation about the ghetto.

According to a report from April 1942: *Orphaned children in the ghetto, homeless and suffering from hunger, numbered about 22,000, which corresponds to approximately 5 percent of the total population (450,000) of the area. In addition to the orphanages that existed, such as that of Dr. Korczak, a new orphanage, Dobra Wola—Good Will—had opened at 61 Dzielna Street. It num-*

*bered four hundred beds, a kitchen, and a warehouse. Children
from 6 to 12, a third of them in poor health. The monthly cost of
the orphanage was estimated at 25,000 zlotys.*

Could she have had at her disposal even a portion of such
an enormous sum of money? At the Sztuka, she earned a hundred zlotys a day. With shows given periodically at the Melody
Palace and at the Femina, her monthly income rose to four
thousand zlotys.

She said that she had had this project for a long time. She
started to put it into place when she was given (by whom?
how?) the use of a five-room apartment at 12 Nowolipki Street.
The baker Blajman (big, portly, heart on his sleeve), whom she
knew from before the war, would furnish her with bread, flour,
and semolina for free, and Henryk Fuks, proprietor of the Café
Modern and a partner in the pharmacological firm Spis, gave
her medicine, vitamins, and honey. She said that she took care
of everything all by herself. She collected money by giving
recitals. She remembered having given a performance for the
children in the presence of the lawyer Jerzy Lewiński, member
of the Jewish police of section 3 of the ghetto. He was supposed
to help her and write down the sums taken in.

"I wasn't mealy-mouthed when I was begging!" she told me
years later.

This project gave her a feeling of power. She went to see
whoever had some money—the Gestapo sympathizers of the
Thirteen, Moryc Kohn, Zelig Heller, and others. She would
have gone to see the devil himself. She was careful not to forget
anyone, to avoid putting herself into trouble. She feared that
Jonas Turkow, actor, director, in charge of entertainment in the
ghetto, would complain she never registered her fund-raising
galas with his office. By associating herself with the wealthy
people of the ghetto, she neutralized him. She shut him up.
Well, that's what she thought, in any case.

They didn't appreciate one another. Older than she was by at least twenty years, Turkow was a star of the Jewish stage before the war and a stage director in Wilno, Cracow, and Warsaw. He showed everyone what it meant to be the head of the Central Commission for Entertainment. He was influential in the ghetto, he could do a great deal, especially for performers.

Stefania Grodzieńska told me that he loved pretty young women. He tried to seduce all of them. She had firsthand experience, even though he knew that she was married. Perhaps Vera had rebuffed Turkow's advances a little too bluntly?

Rumors—in time they become all confused.

Vera called him the censor serving the Gestapo. His wife, Diana Blumenfeld, sang in Yiddish on stage in variety shows. She was said to have had a "minimal voice."

Emanuel Ringelblum jotted down on November 14, 1941, that the police were probably going to open a special shelter at 20 Nowolipie Street to house street children. It cannot be determined if this was related to the establishment that Vera directed.

She told me how she would by herself gather up children dying in the street.

She gathered them, that is to say, she found them, which was not difficult, because they were lying everywhere, on the sidewalks, in courtyards, in the corners of ruined houses. She had to choose, this one but not that one, this one and that other one. She herself used the word "selection." She stood them up, took them in her arms. One by one? She would lead them. No, she could not lead them, because they could barely stand up. Some, a dozen, several dozen exhausted little bodies; alone, without help, how could she pick them up, carry them, drag them along? She couldn't rely on their strength; they could hardly move. Their lives were being extinguished.

Several times she spoke of drawers fixed to the walls, of pallets as children's beds. She repeated that she had to have a cousin help her, a nurse, and several other people, also doctors. She claims categorically that she was the only performer, the only private individual in the ghetto to have put in place a shelter for children on such a large scale.

Why did so few people know about it? "I didn't want to be known, nor bring down retribution," she said.

She would have directed this shelter for one year. She claimed to have received from the wife of Adam Czerniakow, president of the Judenrat, a gift expressing gratitude: a sterling-silver compact with the inscription: *To Vera Gran—The Children of the Streets Shelter in Section III of the Service for Maintaining Order—January 1942.*

"It's my only memento of this dark period. I still have it," she would say.

She never showed it to me.

Charitable concerts she gave to benefit her orphans were often listed in the *Jewish Gazette*. After the war she herself would relate in her 1983 autobiography: *One winter I organized my own concert, which brought in 25,000 zlotys that I used for street children.* Later: *I was in charge of a shelter for a hundred children set up thanks to this sum until the liquidation of the ghetto.*

Marek Edelman, one of the leaders of the Warsaw Ghetto uprising, said in 2009 that Vera Gran was known in the ghetto for her social conscience and for the help she had given to orphans.

Jerzy Lewiński, in the ghetto's Jewish police, years earlier contradicted this statement. In a letter to the director of the Jewish Historical Institute written after reading Vera Gran's memoirs, he affirms that what she says about her work for the children of the ghetto and in particular the opening and the running of a shelter in section 3 is "an invention, pure and simple" and a "vicious lie," far from corresponding to the reality of the ghetto or even to simple logic or to specific names. "She would never have dared," he wrote, "proffer such wild imaginings after the war in Poland when a certain number of people who had survived the Warsaw Ghetto were still alive. She had nothing to do with the establishing of a shelter; she could not have run it as a private individual; hundreds of boarders—that's absurd." In the same way he refutes her statements that she collected funds for the children. "This was impossible for her to do, again, as a private individual. It's a story invented from beginning to end."

Here are extracts from Vera's monologues pieced together.

"I was rushing to the Sztuka after another raid, and having visited my mother. I wasn't paying attention, I was in such a hurry, I stumbled. I wasn't looking where I was going, my black flat shoes bumped into something. Something or someone, who was lying there. I caught my feet in a bundle of rags, my heels sank into it. I didn't fall. I just stumbled. A body, perhaps still alive. I was hurrying to arrive in time for the performance. To get to work. *Far a sztikélé brojt, guib far a sztikélé brojt:* 'A little piece of bread, give me a little piece of bread . . .' he begged in Yiddish.

"They were waiting for me, my public.

"I knew that if I sang, I was not one of these. One of the weak, the needy, hanging on to the hems of the wealthy in the ghetto. But then, who were they? I also was begging in front of them. I was begging for money, for alms, charity for the children, for my children, the children of the streets. Nobody believes me. It doesn't suit them. It doesn't fit the picture. Me, the lady in black, the star with two pianos, who took in—according to rumors—an unbelievable fortune, me, I had to go picking up these homeless victims? I had to cajole them? Swollen, ridden with lice? They could have dirtied my dress rented for the stage. The lace could have been ruined, wrinkled, curled up, wet by their drooling. They could have infected me with typhus, festering blisters, the despair of orphans.

"When one of them died, we went to find others. I tried to

save those I could. They were numerous, dozens, hundreds perhaps? So many children, you would think there'd be an unbelievable noise, conversations, screams, laughter, fights. There was only silence. Like lead. As if they were mute. They only looked at us with their large eyes.

"I keep in my mind's eye a picture engraved in my memory, that's anchored in me. A little child holds a small piece of bread, a small white roll, such as they dream about in the ghetto. 'Eat,' I say, 'eat. Taste it, suck on it, it's good, try.' He no longer had the strength to move his lips.

"I still dream of children who rip packages from passers-by and avidly devour them, including the paper. I dream of children who stretch out their hands toward bread they can never reach. Of mute children I didn't manage to help. I wasn't suffering from hunger.

"I took advantage of my position in the ghetto, asked for alms. I went to see everybody, as long as they gave something for the needy, for the sick, for the children. I didn't give a damn if it pleased them or if they found it unpleasant. If they gave too little, I said that I wouldn't leave until they increased their donation. And it worked."

June 28, 1942, Café Sztuka, 2 Leszno Street.

The *Jewish Gazette* announced a "matinée in honor of the pianist L. Boruński, who is seriously ill." Participating would be the Rubinstein Orchestra, Gran, Marysia Ajzensztadt, Szpilman, Goldfeder. Szlengel, who was master of ceremonies, originated a select committee with Vera Gran at the head. All the intelligentsia of the ghetto turned up. It was a program of the highest order.

She also gave her support to other causes.

"This world was magnificent—the color of chocolate and ebony, with the perfume of sweet almonds . . . I look out at the auditorium, filled with ashen gray faces, pale, wrinkled,

I can't see very well at a distance. I had to perform, whatever happened, sing. As long as we sing, it keeps everything going.

"I wasn't aware of any of this in Wołomin, nor later at dance school. I did not know that it was about flesh and meat, instinct and commerce. I didn't understand. I wasn't capable of it. Naïve to the highest degree."

"There will be room for everybody," Władysław Szlengel, the subtle chronicler of the ghetto, confirmed on the stage of the Sztuka. "Death opens wide its arms, there won't be a lack of space." Right after, the first convoys left Umschlagplatz.*

Szlengel, author of a magnificent poem about Jewish things—or should I say, formerly Jewish things—that remain and start wandering "until they gather on the platform above the black rails," wasn't much older than Vera. His short introductions talking about the Occupation enjoyed a great popularity at the Sztuka. He was also perhaps the originator of a sketch in which Pola Braun, poet and artist in the ghetto, held an egg at the end of a heavy chain as if on a leash. An invaluable treat offered to the voraciously hungry on the streets.

I admire Szlengel's imagination. It was highly colorful and full of bravery, bursting on a world of ashes. "Her First Ball," a great success for Vera Gran during this period, reveals the instinct for self-preservation and its mechanism: how one traveled in dreams so as not to sink into despair. Some knew how to describe this journey, others were happy simply listening. Szpilman wrote the music, Szlengel the words.

The idea for the song was inspired by a French film from before the war, *A Dance Card (Un Carnet de bal)*, by Julien Duvivier, and offered the singer an incredible opportunity vocally and in terms of interpretation. Its heroine goes through

---

* *Umschlagplatz* (German for "Place of Departure"): a place in the Warsaw Ghetto where Jews were rounded up for their deportation to the Treblinka camp.

her dance card from years ago, her unforgettable first ball. To the rhythm of the waltz from Ludomir Różycki's opera *Casanova,* she rekindles a "golden dream of love" with each of her five suitors.

Which one to follow, who will lead me
Enchant me, kiss me
Will console me when I'm sad?
Which one of you will be the one
Who among you will give me this happiness?
Who are we for, this waltz and me?

Not one of them changed her destiny, but these shades conjure up memories. She tried to tell what life has made of them.

The first, on a fox-trot rhythm, a bitter gigolo; the second, a sailor, happy and dashing, to the rhythm of a rumba: *I pick a flower, return on board, and in a hundred years will return* . . . His character is imbued with the blue of waves, wind, and the sea.

One day, probably during her second year in the ghetto, during winter, because they were always short of light, and despite the crowded room, Vera felt a cold draft in the middle of the tango for the portrait of the third suitor. She noticed a movement near the door straight in front of her. Two policemen holding rifles entered. She hesitated. Stop the performance? It would signify that she was afraid, or would maybe greet them. Besides, the audience didn't see anything. She continued singing.

The song lasted several minutes. *The fourth dancer loved wine, singing, and skiing* . . .

To be followed by Tyrolean yodeling . . . She tried. She succeeded. The concentration of the eyes of the audience scrutinizing her.

Free bird, agile bird, graceful bird . . .

She carried the audience's thoughts toward what was taken

A frame from a French film about the Warsaw Ghetto by Frédéric Rossif (*Le Temps du ghetto,* 1961). Vera spoke about her performances at the Café Sztuka and the role of music in the ghetto.

.

from them, what had become an impossible dream, which lived under the feathered duvet of everyday life that covered bodies in the street. It is not us, it's not yet us, it will never be us, but it's our place, our fate. We, we the Jews, we are in our ghetto, because it's here that we are supposed to survive. It was an illusion, and in time she understood.

A shout. "Stand up!" The presence of the Germans was no longer a secret.

"Stand up!" Everybody rose from their seats. "Sit down!" They seated themselves. And so on, several times.

And the fifth . . . the fifth dancer at the ball
The fifth and distinct from these gentlemen
Is today a sad composer
Who loves nothing but his piano.

At this point there should have been several bars of Chopin. It was forbidden to play him in the ghetto, but Szpilman inserted it in this piece. Invariably it made people's eyes well up with tears.

"I stuttered just like my accompanist. But we did not stop performing. The audience nicely followed the orders to the tune of the song. I don't remember if I felt fear. It was a game."

A few days before Vera's twenty-sixth birthday, during the night, the Germans killed Blajman, the baker, her benefactor. People came right up to the front of his house to weep for the "father of the ghetto," as they called him. That day and the following day, numerous men were killed. *And life goes on, gentlemen,* they sang, led by the poet Włast. April 19, to celebrate the first year of performances in the ghetto, she organized an evening for her friends. She made the traditional bigos, a cabbage stew.

When she celebrated Passover, when she sat down with her mother and her sisters for the seder dinner, something that she never mentioned neither during nor before the war, she didn't run errands and keep accounts. She gave her mother money, as I imagine it, and her mother took care of the housekeeping. Vera herself perhaps did not even notice the rising prices with the coming holidays. The Easter holiday on the Aryan side put a limit on the black market. Polish people shared the traditional eggs and drank vodka. Again the price of bread rose one zloty or even two. A loaf of bread now cost eleven zlotys, and a kilo of butter a hundred zlotys. The Passover holiday did not require bread; they made matzo, pies with unleavened flour in the ghetto, and everything else—the bitter herbs, the horseradish, the beets, the nuts and honey—came from the other side of the wall. Fish and beef both cost eighty to one hundred zlotys a kilo. And eggs, indispensable as on the Aryan side, except that here they were three zlotys apiece. Liba Kaplan, did she still keep a kosher kitchen?

The synagogues were crammed on the holidays. The theater and cafés equally. The performers were able to earn a better living then. Rumor had it that the Jewish Symphony Orchestra was being ordered to suspend all activities because despite the interdiction, they continued to play works by Jewish composers. The audiences were dejected by this news about the suspension of activities. Little by little, people allowed things to be cut from their lives, all the while saying, to justify it, that it could be worse.

For the whole month of May 1942, a German movie company was filming in the ghetto. "Orgies of films," as the head of the Judenrat, Czerniakow, called them in his journal—*loathsome, perverse, frightening*—which showed the Jewish inhabitants of the sealed-off quarters, reveling in luxury. Goebbels's technique of manipulating the truth. A shot of Schulz's restaurant at the corner of Leszno and Nowolipki Street—tables heaped copiously, drinks, meats, fish, liqueurs, white bread. Here is the Jewish paradise. Followed by the erotic rituals in the baths and in the dance halls.

Perhaps it was at that time there occurred the event of which Vera was to be ashamed. She couldn't remember the exact date.

She was in the street with a musician colleague when Szymonowicz suddenly appeared. Everybody in the ghetto knew about this personage. He was an officer of the infamous Thirteen and a nephew of Gancwajch, head of the organization, a smooth talker and a show-off agent of the Gestapo. I have no idea if Vera knew what was happening. He asked her if she wanted to appear at his place, right away, immediately, now in front of guests from the Aryan side. She didn't have the time to think, to answer, or even to invent an excuse. He had already called a pedicab. The colleague she was with said: "If you want to save your skin, accept." In her tentative attempt to justify herself, hurriedly, with confused words, she protested: how

could she sing without accompaniment? Her colleague suggested, without being asked, that he perform with her on the
concertino. This quick-thinking colleague, perhaps the only
reasonable person there, knew the thing you should never do:
contradict someone stronger than you.

Szymonowicz asked how much she charged. Or perhaps
"How much are you demanding?" She no longer remembered. Whatever you will give me, she thought. He promised
500 zlotys, that's what Diana Blumenfeld took. (Mrs. Turkow
had appeared in several musical revues in the ghetto—*Let the
Music Play, A Kiss in Front of the Mirror,* and *Five Happy Lads.*)

Five hundred zlotys, that's what a baker earned in one week!
It appeared that Gancwajch paid the same sum monthly to the
Yiddish writer Cejtlin. You could have a decent meal for one
zloty.

When they walked into the apartment, dinner was just over.
"I found her," the host announced.

Vera remembered a crowd of drunken people, songs screamed
hysterically, standing against the wall. And slimy gestures and
glances. Her excuse to leave: right after, she had a performance
in a café. Panic, flight.

The money she earned she gave to a charitable organization.
That's what she said.

What did she learn in mixing with the informers of the
ghetto, how did she behave with them, of what use were they
to her, and how and in what way did they help her? She doesn't
want to admit having had any close relationships, or intimacy,
or any contact other than professional, or when she was raising
money. She used her influence to the benefit of others—her
colleagues, children, those who asked her or who were in need.
She knew many of them. Had she been seen on the street with
a member of the Thirteen? It's possible. Stefania Grodzieńska
had been seen several times: they even tried to build a sordid
story about this sighting. Without success. She had a husband
who, after the war, foiled these false accusations.

Relationships in the artistic milieu of the ghetto don't allow for a careful selection of those you frequent, states Antoni Marianowicz in his book *The Strictly Forbidden Life.* When you are a famous diva it is impossible to isolate yourself from people in power.

Marianowicz met Vera in the ghetto as an enthusiastic member of the audience. He considered her his favorite singer, and also a very pretty woman. He sympathized with the fact she had to master all the nuances of the who's who of the ghetto.

I don't think that she understood the hierarchy of the ghetto, or that she saw the differences in the room among the caps and among the colors of the Star of David on the armbands. Gancwajch (small, wearing glasses) was very easy to spot. As an organizer of charitable evenings, he ended up losing his standing and was searching more and more nervously for alibis. Perhaps she had heard about a nocturnal banquet for which he had spent 25,000 zlotys, which would have compromised him even in the eyes of the officers of the Gestapo. It could have taken place in one of their favorite clubs, in the Hotel Britania, on Nowolipie Street. I don't know if she had personally met Stabenow, Gancwajch's superior, an officer of the Security Police in Warsaw. Or Żurawin, another Gestapo collaborator whom Czerniakow complains about in his journal: Żurawin and Gancwajch were blackmailing him.

I doubt that she had any knowledge of the tenor and end results of these relations among agents. However, it is possible. She maintained sporadic contact with some among them. It is difficult to imagine that she was linked to them by anything else.

That night they were ridding the ghetto of weeds, wrote Ringelblum. During the settling of accounts among agents, on May 24, 1942, the major leaders of the Thirteen were shot down, including Szymonowicz.

The ghetto was reduced several times. Vera changed addresses often, but she no longer could remember the names of the streets after all these years. Looking out the window didn't help her orient herself, either. The view usually came up against the wall.

She doesn't remember on which day of July 1942 she learned—on the telephone, from an acquaintance of Kazik's—they had organized her escape from the ghetto. She is not sure of having used the word "escape." Perhaps "leaving"? For months this piece of the city behind the walls was her world. The place where she woke up, she worked, she went to sleep, or she felt close to her family, and happy to sing for others. She never gave much thought to "tomorrow."

She had no philosophy other than the imperative need to survive. Each day she woke up to confront the inevitable daily life.

They closed the Sztuka. A place of work, of triumph, of satisfaction, had ceased to exist. What could she do in this dead city? Remain with her family? Perhaps if she had known that these were the last moments, the last cholent, the hands cupping the flame of the candle, the prayer that they would never again offer together? Stay with them, but what for? Besides, at that time, people knew nothing, there were no guarantees, not from anywhere. They were menaced with deportations and extermination, could you, should you, must you believe it?

She remembered the days of the heat wave at the beginning of July, and the rain. She remembered the music in the gardens recently opened and the ironic commentaries about this gesture of Czerniakow's. People said, "He is playing fanfares for a sinking ship." But she observed, and understood his pleasure. She went to performances for children who still managed to believe in the sun. Orchestras, choruses, ballets. She did everything to follow in the steps of the living.

She recalled the panic among her friends toward the 19th of July, when some spoke of forced displacements, and others of pogroms. And three days later she could read on the walls the posters announcing the deportations to the east. On the 21st, in an act of protest against this planned massacre of his brethren, the head of the Judenrat, Czerniakow, committed suicide.

Perhaps it was then, at the end of July 1942, that Kazik found an Aryan address for his wife.

They hadn't seen one another for weeks. Vera did not leave the ghetto, Kazik rarely crossed to the other side of the wall. She explains that he would come for a few hours, never longer, never stayed overnight. It turned out in time that he avoided the place that fate was going to designate for him as well.

In documents for the German Office on Indemnization, she wrote years later that she was pregnant at the time and she had a miscarriage after having been beaten by a German in the street. Should she be believed? She wrote that the father of the child had died in the ghetto.

For security reasons, who knows, perhaps he was spied on, she told everyone Kazik had left her, the bastard. Because he didn't want anything to do with a Jewess. Sometimes they spoke to each other on the telephone. The telephone in the ghetto, that was miraculous, it allowed them to be in contact, to hear one another, to nearly touch. But at the same time it could not be trusted, because the authorities listened in, spied. Indispensable tool for the black market, therefore for life, the most repeated phrase was "How's it going?"

She didn't know the taste of a Warsaw street on the other side of the wall. I wonder if she ever tried to experience it. Was it her decision, due to a set of circumstances, a lack of time, or desire? She had no desire, nor any reason, no one was worth the risk, to place herself in danger for a meeting, a conversation, an intimacy? Was she afraid? Perhaps she was tied to someone OVER THERE, in the ghetto, then why move, put herself in danger, justify herself?

Perhaps she would have lived this period differently if she had known the direction her future would take? What burden she would place on her future destiny?

She would have perhaps counted the months differently, and the days, the hours, and the moments. She could not, she was incapable of predicting what would be the finale? . . . If she had wanted to count . . . fifteen months, from . . . to . . . until . . .

She had to abandon this familiar room. And everything that was a link to Vera Gran. Erase all traces, and erase the proof. Cleanse herself of herself.

A light raincoat on her arm, a beret, a small handbag in her hand, neat and clean—Aryan. She notified her landlady that she would not return that evening, because they were holding a family council at her sister's on Nowolipki Street. She doesn't remember how much time she spent with them, if she had arrived in the afternoon or only in the evening. Nor can she remember the words, even if she tried many times to make them come back. "We have to separate, it's necessary," "She must leave," "Only she is capable of it," "She has contacts." The words remained stuck in her throat, they dried up, and remained petrified into silence. Just as she did, in the face of her duty—responsibility.

She remembers the fear. The helplessness and her inability to walk from one wall to the other, from the window to the door. With the reassuring thought that she was carrying a capsule of cyanide that would enable her to escape in case . . .

August 2, 1942, at dawn, they were awakened by a dry rhythmic sound resonating from far away. It was coming nearer. Dozens of pairs of boots. She immediately understood that it was a new raid by the Jewish police to round up people for the convoy. For several days they had been blocking off buildings; they dragged the people into the courtyard, to carry out the selection. "It's our turn," her mother lamented. They stopped in front of the building entrance.

But nobody pounded on the door. Vera went to the window. They were dragging the neighbors across the way outside. She saw everything in the clear air of the morning. They were kicking old people and those who resisted or who didn't have the strength to walk. They pushed, shoved, and bludgeoned them. They dragged the women by their hair. They were Jews. Both sides. Their own people.

This frame of Vera's memory has to be repeated.

In 1980 she wrote it down.

Amid bloodcurdling screams, the militia men dragged by force everything that had a head on its shoulder. At the sight of this woman brutally bludgeoned I wanted to scream. This loathsome deed was the work of the hands . . . of the pianist! I saw him with my own eyes. He survived the war. I want him to know that I saw him.

In 1995 she told it at the Shoah Foundation in California.

"He was across the way, directly in front of me, I could see him clearly. Szpilman, with his policeman's cap.

"Szpilman in person, the pianist. I cannot forget this. He dragged women by their hair. He protected his hands. His pianist hands needed special care. I have never spoken of this, I didn't want to wrong him. Now, I want him to know that I know. Far be it for me to want to judge whoever it may be. But it has to be known, it's history and it has to remain associated with a name. He knows that I know. And he remains silent."

She was haunted by this scene. The memory of it would often come back to her at different times. I have not found any confirmation of its veracity in the archives to which I had access, nor in the narrative of witnesses.

The time to pass to the other side had come. Her sisters forced her to leave. They were counting on her. They needed her help. When she left, she didn't say goodbye, so certain was she that this plan would not work.

She entered the courthouse at 11:00. The bailiff, bribed beforehand, did not pay any attention to her. She walked slowly to gain the time to rip off her armband. She looked around, searching for the man Kazik had told her was supposed to wait for her and escort her. She had to cross the immense hall, disappear in the crowd, never show any hesitation, and come out on Bialta Street. The sun was shining.

They walked for a long time. A new exercise. Don't look into people's eyes. Eyes speak, eyes betray. Keep eyes lowered. She had flat black shoes with low heels. She studied them intently.

5

She left the Jewish quarter
on August 2, 1942

She left the Jewish quarter on August 2, 1942, before noon. She changed her fate, her face, her hairstyle, her eyes. Curls brought forward on her forehead, glasses. Forget the stage, the lights, sing no more, don't even hum anymore. Can't be that person any longer. Erase her features. Keep her desires for better times. Ignore her accomplishments. Wait for others to help.

"I got out of the ghetto," she told me, "and I could not allow myself to refuse anything that might come along."

She thought of her mother, that perhaps by a miracle she would succeed in seeing her again, protect her, hide her, save her on the other side of the wall. Of her sisters, so important to her, who shared her childhood, cleaning ears, taking the first piano lessons. They saw her sing, imitate the guests, heard the applause, saw the little failures, the pride.

A woman in a doorway greeted her. She made her sit down on a stool and immediately applied herself to turning her into an inconspicuous blond. Vera said she couldn't remember much.

I doubt it. Rather, I don't know how that could be possible.

"All along I worked with my face, my voice, my figure. I valued, perhaps overestimated, my own image. Now suddenly someone came to transform me, to manufacture a new me, to disguise me. To destroy the person I was. In good faith, to save my life. But it was very difficult. I was pretty, famous, and celebrated. For my voice, certainly, for my voice, but also for the rest of me. My person. Vera Gran. And what next? Nothing? Forget everything? Her hands moving around my head, these cotton wads soaked in the nauseating liquid, I checked, 30 percent solution of hydrogen peroxide, not a word about my panic, the burning, the shock of the transformation?"

Her thick dark hair took on a reddish tint. Red locks fell on the ground. For a fashionable coiffeur, all that was lacking were bangs. It was done. Now, curl papers. Later, in the mirror, an unknown face she had to learn to live with.

Years later, she said that it was the sister of Professor Stanisław Lorentz who took care of her then; he was an art historian and had saved the priceless collection of the National Museum in Warsaw. He also came to the aid of Jews.

She didn't remain a long time in this apartment. She was shunted from place to place. People known and unknown, from room to room, doors that closed behind them, in front of her. She couldn't remember the addresses.

First she landed in Saint Roch Hospital, where Kazik had worked since 1940; she had not seen him, for the security of both. She spent several days in the office apartment of his colleague Dr. Tylicki, on Krakowskie Przedmieście Avenue; the following days with an intern at the hospital, Mieczysław Hilbe. He locked her in before leaving for work. She preferred staying in Mokotów in the villa of the Bednarski family, but her young host was in contact with the Resistance, and he organized clandestine seminars and meetings at his home. She couldn't stay there much longer.

"For two months I wandered throughout Warsaw. I hid with different people. They hid me. I was hidden.

"I had to hide—" she says it, still perplexed a half-century later—"me, hiding in my own city, among those who had applauded me. Before that I wasn't conscious of the danger. I had no inkling that behind the wall I could be recognized, and I had to be afraid of that. I was so naïve."

I have the impression that everything was about this: her subjugation. In the ghetto she was a star; on the outside, a Jew whom anyone could denounce. Anybody could become the master of her life. Point his finger at her. She was in other people's hands. Dependent. Her fate left to others.

She was forbidden to go out into the city. Immobilized and solitary after months spent in the crowd running everywhere, she was wasting away.

In her room on Na Skarpie Street (a good address in the German quarter), she leafed through the same worn book— *The Factory at Home.* A book of practical advice for living during the Occupation—a best seller: *180 ways of making your own soap, cosmetics, creams, ink, glue, lacquer, and how to dye and dry clean.* She had trouble memorizing anything at all. She didn't make the effort. She had nothing to dye or to make over. She had only one dress to change into, besides a skirt and a pullover. Everything was in somber tones of gray, earth colors.

Perhaps she placed the contents of her closet in storage before leaving the ghetto, like her furniture and paintings. Did she get them back one day, recover them? What happened to her jewels, necklaces, cigarette case, rings, brooches . . . a source of pleasure, an investment? Lost forever?

Not far from there at the Apollo Cinema—for Germans only—they were showing with great success, as everywhere else, *Jew Süss. The first really anti-Semitic film,* Goebbels joyfully jotted down in his diaries of 1939.

Wooden soles that clattered, the new invention of the Occupation. It got on her nerves. In a newspaper, an advertisement for Diana sandals—flat-heeled shoes, practical and solid. The Stero Department Store at 27 Hoża Street. People were still walking down that street?

Years later, she claimed to have seen Dr. Korczak with the children walking toward the death train. However, she could not have seen him. On August 5, 1942, she had already been on the Aryan side for three days.

She had no papers. Another good reason for not going outside to see the world. Nor a *Kennkarte* either, the identification card required since 1942 with the fingerprints of the index finger of both hands. Nor the *Ausweis* confirming employment. A residence card was required to obtain ration tickets.

The papers . . . She knew how to sing. She knew the way to the Sztuka, the crooked stage, the sound of the piano accompanying the emotions. The wall had two sides; she had belonged to one, now she belonged to the other. But still, not to those people for whom trees in bloom are only trees in bloom, and not a revelation, for whom raspberries on the bush are not a miracle.

From the window of a strange apartment, she looked at the street that was forbidden to her.

The sequence of hiding places in Warsaw succeeded one another, different, and today, after all these years, their chronology is no longer clear or of any importance. Was she first welcomed by Janusz Konecki on Na Skarpie Street, then by Bednarski on Naruszewicz Street, or the reverse? First by Dr. Tylicki on Krakowskie Przedmieście Avenue, and then by Mieczysław Hilbe? And yet these people took risks for her, they were responsible for her fate, and put the safety of their own families in peril.

Who organized all this? Who was paying? She doesn't know. Probably Kazik. Probably? He sought help from their closest acquaintances. He made the effort, he didn't let her down. He never disappointed her.

In her narratives she would never present Kazik as a hero. I cannot recall ever having heard her express gratitude toward him. For her, his help and solicitude were taken for granted. At that time as later. Always.

More than two years of memories compressed to the miserable size of an obituary. During this time, three autumns passed, three New Year's celebrations, as many changings of the calendar. Acting the role of the doctor's wife, briefly of the mother. Then mourning. She was a young woman. She wasn't even thirty years old.

In her memory of life on the Aryan side, there is more shadow than light. It seems that it could have been otherwise. All the same, she had left the wall behind her, and her life was opening before her.

She doesn't know who brought her to Babice, near Warsaw, where Kazik opened a medical practice. She saw him for the first time a month after fleeing the ghetto. She didn't know what he had done for her. She wasn't thinking. Everything was happening outside of herself. The effort he made, his tenacity. The first of September 1942, on the third anniversary of the outbreak of war, after being separated for long months, they were again alone together.

They sat next to each other on the bed. Perhaps because there was no other furniture.

I don't see any happiness in this scene; rather, a resignation.

Babice was five kilometers west of Warsaw. Paved with cobblestones, with neither electricity nor running water. They had at their disposal the old schoolhouse. The mayor of the village felt deeply honored that a doctor wanted to open his practice in such a place. Housing consisted of three rooms without handles on the doors. At the time, she was using the documents of a friend of Kazik's, Wanda Czajkowska.

They were assigned an apartment on the upper story of a house. They had to cross a hallway, then climb stairs. Some empty rooms, windows without panes. People downstairs, a couple with a child and a grandmother.

She tried to hide herself, disguise who she was, but reality turned out to be more clever than she. She wasn't cut out to be a nurse. She didn't look like a housekeeper. From the first day, she was considered the wife of the doctor, and she was treated with the respect due to her. The doctor of the clinic, that wasn't just anybody.

The house faced the church and the central marketplace, where all roads crossed. Had I been in her shoes, the place would have filled me with anguish; it was like being exposed on the stage.

She looked out the window; from the upper story, she had a better view than from the ground floor. Instead of handbags, the women carried pails of water, or logs of firewood, or else sacks of coal. They dressed in a bizarre fashion; evidently they did the best they could, mixing colors and textiles, as if everything hanging in the closet had come back into fashion. It was there on their backs and not buried with them.

The ones she saw from her window, all bundled up in their scarves and their Russian stockings, dragged themselves through the autumnal streets as if this was their lot in life, as if dressing according to the seasons only influenced their disguises but not the very essence of their existence. They had the right to live, to walk openly in the streets, to believe that one day their fate would do an about-face.

Then the snow came, making tracks more visible.

She saw people who she thought lived better lives. However, she did not see this as a reason to feel sorry for herself. She had enough with her own cares: how to make room for her two sisters, behind the armoire, and in the shed by the kitchen, how should they steal away in case of unexpected visitors, and where to? Patients dropped by to see the doctor at any hour; how was she going to feed her sisters, give them some peace, and in what corner could she place the pail?

The money they had was enough to meet their hunger but not enough to save anybody.

They were considered privileged, perhaps because her "wartime" husband had taken the Hippocratic oath. In reality, they had trouble making ends meet. From Kazik's family inheritance there remained two gold chains, a ring with little diamonds, and several gold five-ruble coins. This was enough to last for some time.

At one time, she doesn't remember when, she presented the Mainkes' little girl for baptism at the church. They were their neighbors on the ground floor. Alojz worked in a concrete factory; he left in the morning and returned at nightfall. Janka, his wife, took care of the children.

The infant, a little girl with translucent skin, was dressed in lace. They had given her a majestic first name: Jolanta. Vera, concentrated, serious, stood still, stiff as a board. It was as if someone were pulling her strings. A puppet? Usually it was she who controlled her own fate. But not there, "under the Germans." She put everything into playing this comedy, which was still, and always will be, synonymous with life itself.

Did the Mainkes know who she was? Were they pretending not to know? Years later she said that Jolanta had made herself at all cost erase the memory of this religious celebration in which Vera had participated. To be the goddaughter of a Jew was not acceptable at that time. Even if the godmother was a famous singer and the little girl dreamed of following in her footsteps.

Kazik, her husband, rose at dawn every morning and rode his bicycle to the hospital in Warsaw by back roads. That is what she remembered, that is what she repeated. It was the reality she created.

He earned 50 zlotys a month working in the surgery department of the Saint Roch Hospital on Krakowskie Przedmieście Avenue, and they paid his living expenses. At the beginning he lived at the hospital, then (according to his memories after the war) *in Babice, from where I went to work by bicycle.* The hospital remained intact until the Warsaw uprising broke out. In total: surgery and internal medicine—120 beds.

He received the authorization to practice general medicine in August 1942. A few days later he was certified as registered with the medical board, and that he had his practice in Babice. This document was necessary for his proceeding to register his bicycle.

In the Medical School Library, there is a note dated April 10, 1943, addressed to the medical board, stipulating that Dr. Kazimierz Jezierski had installed himself three weeks earlier in Babice, where "he holds the position of general practitioner of visiting doctor for the Social Security, and he has a private practice."

It is difficult to say whether this document describes an already established fact, or whether it was then that Jezierski opened his practice in this location near Warsaw. If that is the case, he and Vera would have spent one year without documentation. The archives contradict one another. I think that the last document is simply erroneous. Everywhere else their settling in Babice is dated the summer of 1942.

Praised be God!—it was the first visit by the parish priest, Machnikowski, a jovial little fat man—*I want to bless these premises, in the name of the Father and the Son . . .* Yes, she had no idea what these gestures meant. She knew neither how to cross herself nor how to pray. She fluttered her hands nervously, and he sprinkled holy water as much as he could. Respectfully he addressed her as "Mrs. Doctor." She thought it was the end and she had betrayed herself.

But no. He returned. He liked her breasts. "Show me your tits, Mrs. Doctor." She let herself be pawed if it gave him pleasure.

They talked, and it could have been thanks to him that she started going to church. She didn't know what to do— genuflect, make the sign of the cross—but she tried to imitate the others. She repeated behind all the people standing in front of her the whole ritual of prayers. No, she did not pray. What for?

She invented for herself the role of eccentric woman, crafty, mean, and inaccessible. The women confided in the doctor, by definition. They liked to talk to the doctor. "I have a pain in my chest," "I feel pressure on my stomach," "My sacrum is going to explode." She was cantankerous and unpleasant, disagreeable and aggressive, her blond hair all tousled, out of character for her, neglected. "I played at the slattern, crazy, insane perhaps?" They complained, never stopped talking, confided—they are drawn, they are impetuous—but not toward her. "The doctor is not in. I will make an appointment for you, yes, of course. The doctor will listen to you. Make an appointment, the doctor will know how to advise you. But as for me, don't ask me anything, leave me alone!"

Patients came from afar in carts. Vera moved like a shadow among the sick. The Mainkes remember her that way, taciturn, sinister, dressed in dark clothes. "She had nothing happy about her, not in her bearing, nor in her smile. A dress with flowers, stripes? She? Never."

"He forbade my singing. 'Not under any pretext can you open your mouth to sing. Even if you are alone in the house.' So, in other words, never." She paced the spacious rooms lengthwise and across. What privilege for the condemned. She wrote song lyrics in a notebook.

We live in confusion and the absence of feelings . . .
Treachery and lies, that is what we play at in life . . .

The words tear at one another. Memory is lacking. And yet she had hardly stopped singing.

Only a mother's heart can feel emotions . . .
Only she knows what it's about . . .

She moved the furniture that had accumulated over time. She looked for a shelter in the armoires. She fell sick, stomach ailments, a serious jaundice. She carried water, cut wood, and worked in the garden.

She remembered the advice of Stefania Grodzieńska for Jewish women on the Aryan side. She advised them to take the offensive. Not to be afraid, not to hide, have some initiative. "For example, in the streetcar, or in the park, sit next to a woman with some presence (that is to say, Aryan) and engage her in conversation. Loud and clear: 'It's raining cats and dogs and I didn't take my umbrella.' And so on. When people see you with someone, it never occurs to anyone to sniff out your doubtful origins. It's always you who initiates the conversation, and make sure they listen to you. You cut them short before they ask you any concrete questions."

She never had the opportunity to put this advice into practice. She rarely went into the city.

A Christmas tree up to the ceiling, with the Star of Bethlehem. On the table herrings, a platter of fish, a little vodka. She doesn't know, she can't remember how, she started singing. No one had asked her, because they couldn't have known that she sang. Traditional Polish carols—"Sleep, Little Jesus" . . . "They Came to Bethlehem" . . . "Glory to Heaven on High" . . . She couldn't say how she knew these words. The mayor, the priest, the neighbors. Alojz later said that she had "an unusual voice."

Cut off from the world, in the countryside, she lived on illusions. She did not know what was happening in Warsaw, in the ghetto. What they were going to do to them. If they lived, were still alive. That is what she believed. If she dreamed, it was only about them.

Only the heart of a mother . . . knows how to give a little warmth, and understand each pain . . . and when it stops beating for us, how hard it is, how hard it is to live . . .

She tired Kazik out with talking about her mother. She asked him to save her. She didn't know what had to be done, but there had to be a way of managing it. He reassured her, everything was on its way. Money was needed, they didn't have any, but they would manage.

For a long time she believed it. She spoke of it again, complained, begged. The leaves turned their autumnal hues. One rainy day she threatened to return to the ghetto. That's when he told her the truth. They had taken away her mother in the last raid—September 8, 1942. She had no chance without the "ticket to life." For her sisters it was a different situation, they were still waiting for help, and a solution for their survival.

She held in her hands a coded note from Maryla, written on cigarette paper. She showed it to me years later. For a long time she remembered the imploring voice of her sister.

The "tickets to life" were little yellow cards you had to wear on your chest. Someone wrote by hand a number on each, and added a seal and signature. Thirty-five thousand Jews could still be alive. For the others it was the Umschlagplatz, the place in front of the triage train station. Before serving death, this used to be a place of delivery; carts pulled by two horses came here to deliver cabbages and cauliflowers.

The Umschlagplatz, cabbages, and the final sentence. She began to knit again. She skipped stitches, she believed she saw musical scores. Then the wagons. Wagons she never saw, never even came near. She had heard it said that in a hospital not far from there, there was a room where women who were selected could for a moment redeem themselves and save themselves from the clutches of death. No, not her sisters, they never took that path.

From the clutches of death—she didn't give a damn for metaphors. The policemen, the Jewish police, pocketed thousands for these "heads" saved from the convoys. They took cash, gold, diamonds. At the beginning, a thousand was enough, and then ten thousand was not enough.

She was no longer there by then. She only repeated what Kazik brought back from the city. "How is it possible?" she asked. "Our own people, it's our own who round us up." In the ghetto, they were more detested than the Germans.

Before moving behind the wall, Maryla had entrusted her fortune to a Polish family. This friend, who she believed was a trustworthy man, was a policeman. She believed this was a guarantee of honesty. He promised to help her. To do something. Magic words that galvanized her hopes. "I'll turn these goods into cash, and we will give you the money. That's certain, that, right away." Did they even try, or had they only said they would try?

"What could a Jewish woman do against a Polish policeman?" Vera asked me years later. Kazik had tried to do something, with pitiful results. But he tried.

One day early in the morning, Vera was awakened by a pounding on the door. It was springtime and the birds were deliriously twittering; such insistence was easier for her to bear, she who never rose early.

"Mrs. Doctor!"

"He's not here, the doctor is not here, you know very well that he's not here! He will be back this afternoon, as usual."

"Mrs. Doctor, it's Mrs. Dobrzańska—" Mrs. "Good," well named—"open up for me. It's important, really important!"

And so on.

"Come to the window, please, you will see."

She thought the woman had perhaps brought her a present,

some buttermilk, or a chicken? She went to the window and looked out. Smoke. The ghetto was on fire.

"You see, Mrs. Doctor, the Yids are being roasted, they are burning." Her cheeks flushed, her eyes shining, with a broad smile.

They are being roasted. It's inscribed on her skin.

She could no longer keep straight the sequence of events.

Maryla had sent them a message that she would leave with a group of Jews working on the Aryan side, on April 19. Kazik was supposed to wait for her by the courthouse gates. Vera had prepared a hiding place in the apartment in Babice. She moved the furniture. Was it on that morning when Mrs. Dobrzańska woke her with this news that was supposed to send her into seventh heaven?

She waited. Kazik also, in front of the wall of the ghetto in flames.

He returned alone.

She remembered it was Easter, it must have been in 1943, because pieces of burnt papers kept flying, reaching even them, fragments from books, you could still distinguish some letters.

They invited her friend the musicologist Gerard Gadejski (with whom she had deposited photographs and paintings) so that he could play the role of kin. As if she still had family in the city. He remarked teasingly that she was uncommunicative and seemed embarrassed. Sometimes she said that it was at that moment she went to church for the first time. "A regrettable incident." Years later, she learned that her zealous devotion had aroused suspicion about her behavior.

I spent whole days at home and I was in contact only with my few neighbors, out of fear of being identified, she wrote in 1946. She took seriously her role as "the village crank." She had no other.

The summer of 1943; she remembered the long days of the heat wave. Kazik brought two turtles for her from Warsaw—

the markets in the capital were filled with them. They were certainly destined to be canned for the army, and a couple of wagonloads had been bought for the black market. Hers did not end up as soup. She called them Mr. and Mrs., even though she was not sure of their gender. They led a happier life than hers.

She already knew that she was alone, without a family, when someone visited them announcing that it was possible to buy passports for Brazil and even further. It was perhaps Gerard Gadejski; who else could it be? Who else would come to see them if not him? Just to be on the list, up to one hundred thousand zlotys was the down payment. It was said that in the Polski Hotel on Długa Street, where the last escapees waiting for liberty were staying, they were serving salmon and champagne.

She didn't believe in fairy tales. They did not have this sum. Nor such expensive hopes. The liberty turned out to be the gas

The Warsaw Ghetto uprising began on April 19, 1943. On May 16, Germans blew up the great synagogue on Tłomackie Street. Jergen Stroop, commander of German forces in the Warsaw Ghetto, wrote in a report: "The Jewish residential district in Warsaw no longer exists."

chamber. It was as if for Jews there was no other place where you were safe.

Life was less difficult in Babice, because in exchange for a consultation, people always brought something for the doctor. Eggs, lard, blood sausage, apples from the orchard, chickens. In the city people paid unheard-of sums then for the products that were bare essentials. Onions that were 1 zloty a kilogram at the beginning of the war had reached 25 zlotys after four years. Sugar rose from 7 to 95 zlotys, potatoes from less than 1 zloty to 4 zlotys.

She thought back to the holes in the walls of the ghetto where they caught little boys who were trafficking in contraband. On the armbands for these children they inscribed, for a laugh, *Service for Maintaining Order.* She thought that they had all disappeared now.

She became pregnant in the autumn.

She went to Warsaw several times, four or five times, not more. These numbers would become important later. Always for medical reasons. Consultations with known specialists. Alone or with Kazik. They had to walk three kilometers to reach Boernerowo, where they could catch the streetcar. It was hard on her. Under a fierce downpour. With the priest's cart, which was more comfortable. But it wasn't always available. They returned home in the evening.

The childbirth was a nightmare.

"What man could abandon a woman giving birth for the first time? Me, I didn't even know on which side this baby was going to come out. I knew nothing. He at least knew everything. And he left me alone. He went to care for his patients, as if there were no other doctors on earth! He abandoned me!"

She held it against him to the very end.

"The placenta was not coming out. I was fainting all the time. The midwife was afraid. My husband was at work in the hospital. Someone went by bicycle to fetch him in Warsaw. He came back, and he tried to help me. Without success. I was hemorrhaging."

They called an ambulance that transported her to the hospital in Warsaw. Her condition required an immediate transfusion.

"I remember that Kazik was standing near the window, and he was crying like a child. I have never had any luck with men. I attracted the weak ones."

They were desperately looking for type A blood. A colleague of Jezierski's, Dr. Wojciech Wiechno, stopped by chance in the room where she was lying. He gave his blood. The following days it was Professor Leon Manteufel who took over her care. They had little hope that she would survive.

Everyone, without exception, knew that she was Jewish. They kept the secret. She insists on that.

She returned to Babice in July. Rumors ran everywhere about the imminent Warsaw uprising.

She didn't have any milk. She gave her baby boiled milk, or rice water. The doctor hired a wet nurse. But the peasant woman saved her milk for her own child. Vera's little boy fell sick. He was always crying. He lost weight, he either slept or cried. Then he started to choke on all that phlegm. Until he passed away.

She became pregnant several times. She never said that she wanted to become a mother. I doubt she really wanted to be one. She spoke a lot about her giving birth and the complications afterward. About the only child she brought into the world, she said only one sentence: "He died of hunger." She never called him by his first name. She never said anything about him that I can remember. His hands, his coloring, his eyes. She had difficulty recalling his features. Without tenderness.

But in her Paris apartment she had a photo of the grave of little Jerzy Zbigniew, son of the Jezierski couple. In the Roman

Catholic parish, the mother of the little boy was registered under the name Weronika Jezierska, née Tomaszewska.

They listened to the radio. For that they could have been sent to the camps, tortured to death. Their son was conceived—according to the war calendar—a little after the battle of Lenino. He was born on June 10, 1944, a few days after the Allies had landed in Normandy. He could have brought hope.

They had him baptized. The baptismal certificate, filled out by the hand of Father Machnikowski, has been preserved.

The tombstone of the little boy who died after barely three months existed in the parish cemetery of Babice until the late 1990s. I tried to find it by comparing it with the ornaments of the neighboring graves, without any success. There are no traces of it.

Vera remembered the late months of 1944 as a time of perpetual movement. The insurgents crossed Babice, then the Germans, and the soldiers of the Vlassov army. There were mobs of deserters and bandits. Drinking bouts, rapes, barbarism. She saw numerous Germans shot down. The Russians enjoyed hunting down Germans. The sign *Doctor* on the house protected them against attacks from all quarters. Only those in need of help came knocking at the door.

One day the priest came to warn them that the German army was going to make a sweep through the area. She decided to flee. She went by cart to the neighboring parish house of Grodzisk. A large room, people lying on the floor, one on top of each other. She made her way through the sleeping people. There was no room. She found a place under a table; two women had to make room. She was numb, she couldn't manage to stretch out. She tried to sleep. She turned around; her eyes met the glance of the beautiful Nina Andrycz.

She was afraid. She was afraid that Nina would tell the truth about her, that the presence of a Jew in this place would endanger all the others who were fleeing. She knew that she had been

recognized by the way Nina turned her head, an eloquent gesture, in the blink of an eye, unequivocally. She didn't want to
frighten her; she dismissed it.

The night was long. She always wanted to thank Nina
Andrycz.

The danger passed, she returned to Babice. On January 17,
1945, a Russian soldier arrived in the marketplace on a poor,
winded horse that once was white; he was on his way who
knew where. But he was wearing a Russian uniform, which
was synonymous with liberation.

Several weeks later, Kazik came with news: in the neighborhood of Praga, the radio station was broadcasting again. The
next-door neighbor heard the first communication: *Hello, hello,
Radio Warsaw, Polish Radio.* I verified the date: February 11.
The most influential person there was Władysław Szpilman,
that's what people said. "Szpilman called the tunes at the radio
station."

And further, "I thought that he owed me a debt of gratitude."

She got on her bicycle to reach the destroyed city. She reached
the right bank of the Vistula by a pontoon bridge. It was in a
small apartment that she came face to face with Szpilman.

"You are not dead?!"

She would never forget this question.

"You are not dead?!"

She opened her arms.

"I am alive."

"What are you doing here?"

"I came looking for work."

"I heard that you collaborated with the Gestapo!"

6

You were working with the Gestapo!

You were working with the Gestapo!
    You are not dead?!
    You survived?!

The accusation seemed so blatantly absurd that her instinctive reaction to leave was followed by an imperative need to refute the lie, to absolve herself, to explain.

Following Szpilman's advice, she went to the police station in Praga.

"I went there because I had nothing to reproach myself for," she repeated many times.

The officer promised to transmit her statement to his superiors and "the authorities would notify her." Nothing happened. Two weeks later she returned to the police station.

She was received by someone else, who asked her to wait patiently.

She returned to the radio station; Szpilman remained intractable. "I don't hire people who collaborated with the Gestapo," he said. That's what she remembered.

She filed a complaint (in green ink, and preserved in the records of the court dated March 5, 1945):

The extremely vicious intent of this defamation repeated constantly, considering the nature of my profession, leads me to suppose that behind all this hides a deliberate cruelty, or a need for personal vengeance.

These accusations are groundless slander.

On April 30, at dawn, she heard pounding on the door. "Police, open up!"

Two men in black leather coats and wearing hats.

"Vera Gran-Jezierska? Get dressed, you are under arrest!"

She tried to defend herself, to explain herself. They started a rapid search. She had no idea what they could be looking for. They put seals on the door of the apartment. Kazik was not there.

They drove for a long time. She thought about death.

They arrived at the headquarters of the Ministry of Public Security in Praga. They took all her belongings and sent her down to the basement.

Her description of the time she spent in detention is filled with painful language: "the squealing of rats," "the bare concrete floor," "the huge locks," "the spotlights with all their power that threw a blinding light into your eyes."

"I was arrested, arrested," she repeated. And immediately after, equally loudly: "I am not guilty of anything!"

The interrogation. Several times a day. Name, first name, date of birth? What was she doing in the ghetto and outside the ghetto? Explain yourself, talk, don't hide your face. Be more clear, how, with whom, when. Why? With Germans? Furs, in dives? In exchange for what? The questions and answers were repeated, mistakes were made, errors, slips of the tongue. Holes in her memory. How did she survive? In what way? What for?

"What for?"—she was beginning to ask herself.

They made her undergo long and repeated interrogations,

with blinding lights, threats, insults to make her confess. Confess. If you confess, everything will be taken care of.

Confess? Confess what, she wondered. She was incapable of thinking. Glimmers of instinct between the blinding lamps. She felt as if the skin on her cheeks had exploded. I am not guilty. Repeat. Name, first name, date of birth, what was she doing in the ghetto? . . . She learned the alphabet of the routine.

Little sleep. The threat of blows. The pressure of what informers said, collaboration. Her husband also, they suggested.

She doesn't remember if she was more bewildered and cast down by a fever or by the dramatic absurdity of her situation. Or perhaps she was paralyzed by fear. They will beat her, send her to the ends of Russia, kill her perhaps. Sometimes she felt that they were playing with her. Once again? A blow, the rats, the light.

They asked for the names of witnesses; she gave them those of Szpilman, Ignacy Waksmacher, owner of the Paradis before the war, and of Jonas Turkow, who produced acts of entertainment in the ghetto. She did not think that anyone could still harm her.

She was alone in the basement, but sometimes they brought in someone else. She remembered a bleached blonde, arrested for looting. She came into the cell with a springing step, with a big fox wrap around her shoulders. She came back from her interrogation a caricature of herself—her makeup had run, her hair was a mess, her face was bruised and bleeding. "They were zealous," Vera remembered thinking, "just to show what they are capable of. Executioners—" she thought. "Before this, they had been of another nationality."

She liked this judgmental expression, full of the power of its meaning: "executioners." Who were they to make a judgment about her life, the path she took to reach her goal, her sacrifices?

The one who arrested her in Babice was called Jerzy. A certain Władysław Heller (much gentler) had been her interrogator as well. A Ukrainian, Jan Klusek (cold gray eyes, the face of a brute, pockmarked), took turns with Heller questioning her in the subsequent sessions. She remembered that one night he had turned up unexpectedly, drunk. He banged on the table with his fist and shouted: *Smack her face around, this whore, she'll sing you another tune!* She remembered the word "whore." She had the temerity to demand an apology. Later still, and on numerous occasions, she heard this word. As a label, about her, against her. WHORE . . . who sold herself for money, who satisfied the sexual whims of men—a whore, perverse, untrustworthy, bad.

No, she did not sell herself.

Had she ever had to do it?

She remembered that date, May 8, and the sirens screaming to announce the end of the war. She welcomed the "victory." The quote marks are correct, because who had won a victory? Not the Jews, not her family, neither her mother nor her sisters. She welcomed a world without Germans, but not without fear or a feeling of injustice—alone in her cell. Again locked up as during the preceding years, but this time—these are her words—"accused of collaborating with the Occupation forces who had killed my family!

"I screamed my head off!" she repeated. And added: "They would not listen to me."

She survived, that was her victory. She was beaten down, humiliated. That was her defeat. To whom did she owe something? And what?

She received a package of food. She did not know who sent it.

During the questioning, they repeated the story of her dance-school friend, Franciszka Mannówna, now known as Franciska Mann, who had a relationship with a Gestapo collaborator. Then they started combining their names, Gran/Mann, Mann/Gran, and vice versa. Like reflections in a mirror. THAT'S HER . . . the performer, she had collaborated, she wore furs and flaunted them, she, me, Franciszka, Vera, that's her! They knew the voice of Vera Gran from the radio but had not necessarily seen her in person. They had mixed her up with Mann, and they became one. According to hearsay, the affirmations, the promises, the so-called testimonies by others, both not only were arrogant but also had privileges. You saw them, they were seen, flashy in the everyday setting of the Occupation. In the ghetto, on the outside. They were alleged informers.

She said that she was at that time "a victim of the paranoia orchestrated by the German killers responsible for the genocide." She would not allow them to stick her with the "label of shame."

On the fifth or sixth day they transferred her to a narrower space and a dark cell, stifling, without a cot. They locked the door. She remained in this hole for a certain time. Hard to estimate. She remained there, crouching, because she could neither stand up nor lie down. She stayed there crouching because in prison that's what you do. She rocked back and forth the way orphans do. She fell asleep, perhaps to have oppressive nightmares devoid of any chronology and sense. It seemed to her that they had arrested Kazik, that he was not far away. She could almost feel him. She tried to contact him by whistling her hit song "The Letter." She thought that he would respond. *All soaked in tears, today your letter is only a souvenir.* Wasted effort. The hours seemed to stretch in her fever, her weakness and shortness of breath.

"We've got to settle her!" she finally heard. Settle!—the sound of it solemn, unequivocal. But this moment was put off, apparently, because she learned that they were going to put her in the hands of specialists. That was even worse, as the name of this "popular singer" meant nothing to them. "There, they know how to break even the strongest."

They threatened her, they offered her a cigarette, they scared her again. They blinded her, showed their rifles, showed their strength. It was a warning. They offered her only one possible solution, unavoidable, and very simple: to avoid deportation . . . she had to confess!

Minutes, then hours passed. In the constant dimness and monotonous rhythm of time passing. Confess? Moments of complete paralysis as if electrocuted and, again, the waiting. She had nothing to confess. The collaboration . . . never before had she analyzed this word. She had never examined it. It sounded like the name of a musical instrument. With a keyboard, something like an accordion. Five syllables, which she measured with the tapping of her fingers. After the third syllable, you knew what it meant.

She understood the seriousness of the accusations, the weight of destiny, her fate. At the same time she had the impression of participating in a game, with rules set by someone who placed her in front of a wall of established facts. She had to stand up to it. Oppose these calumnies.

There were times when she felt she was a rock. She would scream: "No! I'm not guilty!" and faint away.

In the records there is the following deposition:

I refute [the accusation of] having walked hand in hand with the German occupiers acting to the detriment of the civilian population in the capacity of an informer for the Thirteen—representatives of the Gestapo in the ghetto—I categorically deny having denounced Jews in hiding or members of the Polish Resistance.

She was under arrest from the first to the fifteenth of May. By then she hadn't sung for three years.

When she was released—I don't know under what pretext or who intervened—she fell into depression. She drew the curtains across the windows, she avoided people, and she remained in bed for days on end. She reproached Kazik for not understanding and not supporting her; he thought only of his hospital. And yet everything that happened subsequently she owed to him. Following the advice of a friend, Dr. Wojciech Wiechno, who had saved her earlier, they decided to intervene with his friend, the minister of justice, Henryk Świątkowski. He promised to help them.

He forbade their answering the summons of the Security Commission, and he advised them that he would transmit her dossier to the state prosecutor of the Supreme Court of the Ministry of Justice.

The next day, she went to the office of the prosecutor, Adolf Dąb, who recommended that she depose a "self-accusation" that would permit the start of the investigation. He assured her that this would gain her immunity and free time to gather the necessary proof. Prove her guilt or her innocence? She was not so certain. Her dossier was going to be under the jurisdiction of the specialists in cases of collaboration—the prosecutor Jerzy Sawicki, who prosecuted the executioners of the Majdanek camp, Rudolf Hess, the commander of Auschwitz, and his underlings. A man without pity. He promised that if she proved to be guilty, he would do everything to see her hanged. And everything began again: Name, first name, date of birth, how did she survive, what did she do in the ghetto, and on the Aryan side . . . with whom? How? Why?

Then on the street she ran into Jerzy Jurandot.

"You are not dead? You survived?"

"And Stefa?"

"My parents were left behind."

They threw themselves into each other's arms, sincerely, like old friends.

"In the suburbs of Warsaw . . . where?"

"In Mory."

"Oh, we were not far away . . . And you, where are you staying?"

"In Łódź for the moment, it's temporary."

He told her that after the case of Franciszka Mann, rumor had it that Stefa had also "made it with the Germans." "Gestapo agents," as Szpilman was said to call them. It was not clear; he insinuated more than he accused. But these rumors were beginning to carry weight.

At first Jurandot wanted to take Szpilman to court, but after thinking it over, he came to the conclusion that it wouldn't serve any purpose. It could have more liabilities than advantages. It risked causing trouble and creating a commotion.

The rest I learned from Stefania Grodzieńska.

"Jurandot went to Warsaw, to the radio station, where Szpilman worked. Many friends came to support him. They asked for Szpilman to come down into the lobby. The important thing was to have as many witnesses as possible.

" 'Mr. Jurandot, what a pleasure . . .'

" 'Is it true that you are saying that I collaborated with the Gestapo?'

" 'Not at all!'

" 'Oh, yes? Then you will get one slap only, for my wife.'

"The rumors stopped immediately."

From that time on, Vera wrote, *he was known as "the face you always want to slap."*

"If it was up to me, if after all this I could have gone home, I would have stopped struggling." But she noticed that several personal belongings were missing that had been confiscated during her arrest. A fountain pen, some photos, and her compact, a priceless souvenir from the ghetto, a testimonial to her involvement with and her responsibility toward the street children.

A few days later she went again to Praga. She was in a rage. She said she told the guard that she wanted to speak to the minister, Stanisław Radkiewicz. She admitted bitterly that she had to settle for Różański (another bald one!). She demanded that they return to her the objects taken and wanted an apology for the word "whore." She was shown the door. And they advised her never to cross their path again.

Minutes from the record of the tribunal of the district court of Warsaw, in the dossier Vera Gran-Jezierska—"Collaboration"—according to article 4, decree of August 31, 1944. These documents had not been taken out for more than half a century. Nobody had consulted them. I learned of their existence in 2009, having consulted numerous documents at the Institute of National Remembrance (IPN).*

I read the depositions made after the war, sixty years later. Are they less powerful now? Has their value diminished? Do they carry different weight on the scale of truth? The accusations made at the time, enclosed in cardboard folders of the court, have they fallen under the statute of limitations?

There were several witnesses. Three accused her.

The first deposition was from Jonas Turkow, actor before the war. He appeared before the court as a clerk of the Central Committee of Jews in Poland:

One day in 1942, in the ghetto, a certain Szymonowicz organized a party well supplied with liquor, lasting the whole night. The guests were Gestapo sympathizers, German and Jewish; Gestapo agents Lolek Skosowski and Adam Żurawin were present as well. Among them was Vera Gran. She partied the whole night.

I had heard the narrative of these events from the mouth of Vera herself. It's hard to know where Turkow got this story. Was he there himself? And in what capacity?

A certain Szymonowicz, a party well supplied with liquor . . . Gestapo sympathizers . . . She partied.

Even if he is only reporting what he heard, he remains convincing. And he would repeat this information several times, supplemented with additional details.

Turkow left Poland in 1946. In his memoirs, published two

*Instytut Pamięci Narodowej, the Polish institution created in 1998 to investigate Nazi and Communist crimes.

years later, he does not mention this event. By contrast he describes a party given to honor Chana Lewin, an actress from the Jewish stage, organized by wealthy people in the ghetto, Abraham Gancwajch at the head. Turkow was officially invited with his wife to this party.

Turkow greeted Chana Lewin and evoked *the essential role that Jewish theater played* "during these dark days we are living through." Then Gancwajch spoke. A supper was served. The party must have been a success, since the Turkows went home after the curfew, escorted by Jewish policemen.

I don't quite understand why he described this event, since it was an incident of the same nature that in his eyes was so compromising for his colleague.

According to the account given in the *Jewish Gazette* of December 5, 1941, this celebration in honor of Chana Lewin took place at the Nowy Azazel Theater, at 72 Nowolipie Street. The festivities were celebrating the twenty-five years on stage and in vaudeville of this great actress, known for her verve and temperament. A three-act play, *Love and Betrayal,* was staged. 15 zlotys per ticket. Other entertainment followed the performance, and a wonderful buffet.

After the liquidation of the ghetto, he said further on in his testimony, *Gran, Vera, supposedly fled to hide in the countryside.*

As proof that this was not true, he related a visit to a mutual friend (Gerard Gadejski, musicologist and member of the Resistance), where he saw photographs and paintings belonging to Vera Gran. He preferred to forget that she left them with Gadejski before moving to the ghetto. And that none of this constituted any proof of her presence in the city or her eventual relations with informers.

Apolonia Bugajska, daughter of Markus Bugajski, unmarried, sentenced to two years in prison before the war for Communist activism, confirmed all these accusations. She had perhaps not seen anything herself, but she knew that Vera Gran was strolling without armband, elegantly dressed; toward the end, between January and March 1943, she hung around the ghetto with Gestapo sympathizers.

Her conclusion: *It was public knowledge that Vera had turned over Jews and clandestine organizations after the liquidation of the ghetto.*

It's hard to fight what is known with such certitude, against a conviction that is so widespread. I am powerless against this all-powerful "I KNOW." I would stumble across it more than once.

I often thought of asking Marek Edelman, the legendary fighter of the ghetto, what were really the facts. I knew from many earlier talks that he had other things on his mind, and other preoccupations. He despised those at the time who needed entertainment.

It was he who gave me my first lessons in Jewish history and in human virtue. In the years after the facts, he was another witness for the prosecution in the first trial of Vera Gran.

On May 5, 1945, Marek Edelman, born in 1919, student, testified:

At the time of the Warsaw Ghetto, Vera Gran was close to the upper echelons of the Office to Combat Profiteering and Speculation, commonly known as "the Thirteen." Jurek Błoner, Janek Bilak, and Fela Godsztein, presently deceased, formally told me that during the period from January to April 1943, Vera Gran appeared in the ghetto without armband, in the company of Józef Lipski, notorious Gestapo sympathizer; she wore a black suit or dark coat with a big silver fox stole.

In Warsaw it was said everywhere that Vera Gran was an agent of the Gestapo and that her work consisted of flushing out Jews and Polish underground organizations. In general people feared her. I know that the members of the Home Army had followed the verdict of the Resistance tribunal in condemning her to death, but that the sentence was not executed because they did not know where she was living.

I know from Zofia Kopik, a friend of mine currently [May

1945] *at forced labor in Germany, that during the summer of 1943, Vera Gran went in a convertible with civilians, probably members of the Gestapo, to a restaurant on the corner of Jerozolimskie Avenue and Krucza Street. There the civilians took away a man and a woman of Jewish origin, friends of Zofia Kopik, to be exact.*

What to make of this testimony? How to understand it? How and whom to defend?

It was a difficult conversation with Edelman, on August 18, 2009, in Warsaw.

"What do you want to prove? Leave it alone, unless you want to write about her singing. The rest is all nonsense!"

What responsibility can you take for these fragments of memory that rise to the surface? What can you be certain about, which of them? None, who knows? Perhaps memory is only an element of the process, and memory modifies itself when being evoked. Perhaps memory does not weave a tapestry but runs along a particular strand, uniquely under the influence of the moment.

At first I thought that he was going to ask me to leave after fifteen minutes. What was I still looking for?

"What I said at that time was just anything. I was pushed into doing it, it was Turkow who asked me, and at that time it was good to name someone as an agent."

But he had never seen Vera, never heard her sing. Perhaps once, on Smocza Street, there was a line of fans following her. And among them some Germans.

His attention was elsewhere. What he is certain about is that she opened orphanages and she had taken care of hundreds of children at the same time. She did everything she could for them, she appeared on stage, collected money. She organized fund-raising concerts. He states positively that Vera was someone good, and an honorable person.

"She telephoned to the ghetto before the liquidation, April

18, 1943, to warn us that a raid was planned. She was really respected in the ghetto. In consequence we all believed her."*

He spoke of the beautiful sunny afternoon and the meeting of the commanders of the Jewish Resistance in Mordechaj Anielewicz's apartment on Nalewki Street. Preparations were going on for the Passover holidays.

Vera never confirmed this information. It's not the first time that the memories of the survivors cross and contradict one another. Vera, as I knew her, and from her stories, would have been incapable of transmitting to the ghetto this sort of warning. And what she told me, personally, was that once she had passed over to the Aryan side, she maintained no contact with the ghetto.

I then questioned Edelman on the subject of Szpilman.

"Someone perhaps got Szpilman out of Umschlagplatz, an acquaintance, or even a policeman. He could have been himself a policeman, this is not out of the question. So what? You could be a policeman and be someone good. I have known some who were placed there by the Resistance."

Edelman was perhaps right, just as Jerzy Giedroyc, a prominent emigration intellectual, before him, who advised me to put aside these inextricable and inconceivable stories.

How to establish the link between this narrative from the leader of the ghetto uprising and the reality at that time? Take notes, without commentary. These memories diverge from one another by more than sixty years.

I had two interviews with Stefania Grodzieńska, in 2000 and in 2008. The transcripts of what she remembered did not change.

"Vera immediately became the idol of the ghetto. She

---

*This concerns the preparations for the uprising in the Warsaw Ghetto, which was triggered by the rumors of the planned liquidation of the ghetto by the Germans.

appeared briefly in Jurandot's theater, the Femina. But Jerzy finally convinced her to go to the Sztuka. It was a prestigious café, not frequented by just anybody. Besides, it was also a chance for her to be a soloist.

"It was a limited space, a small platform, an extraordinary literary cabaret (uncensored!), excellent satirical writers. A duo of concert pianists. And Vera. Lolek Fokszański recited his poems, which had been admired before the war by Julian Tuwim, a prolific writer. Władysław Szlengel performed at the Sztuka a sort of spoken journal, using laughter to recast the daily tragedy of the sealed quarter. When the program touched on recent events in the ghetto, it gave rise to salvos of laughter from the audience.

"I know that it can appear awkward in the context of the ghetto, but the Sztuka was a club for the elite. It was like going to the Café Ziemiańska, where the Polish intelligentsia passed time before the war. At the Sztuka, you could find friends you didn't see every day in the ghetto. And even though it now seems unbelievable, there was a wonderful atmosphere there.

"Taking a pedicab was not within our means, nor ordering anything at the Sztuka, but we could talk about everything and nothing and for a while feel like it was before. They served coffee, tea, cakes, ice cream, and even alcohol. The customers at the Sztuka could still treat themselves.

"You only had to stop in the street to ask a question of the Jewish Gestapo—sympathizers, as we used to call them—to fall under suspicion. Of what? Collaboration, too-close contact, intimacy . . .

"As for Vera, I am sure that she had nothing for which to reproach herself. Perhaps the resentment against her came as a result of her status at the Sztuka? It was clear that she lived on the money spent by the clientele of the Sztuka. And many of them were morally questionable. But you cannot reproach Vera for that. She was not responsible for those people. There were traffickers, Jewish policemen, and sometimes Germans, they sat down, they invited her to the table. How could she have refused, made excuses, run away?"

Stefania Grodzieńska was aware of the ambiguous situation of performers in the reality of the Occupation. She knew that the Association of Polish Stage Artists had forbidden anyone from appearing in the official theaters on the Aryan side. However, for the ghetto the rules were more flexible. Jurandot had naturally contacted the officers of the association before opening the Femina.

For more than half a century Stefania had not spoken about her past during the Occupation. She had crossed it out of her memory. She never officially defended Vera Gran, which Vera had for a long time held against her.

Marcel Reich Ranicki, literary critic, was a translator for the Judenrat in the Warsaw Ghetto. It was he who translated the text proclaiming the deportation of the Jews on July 22, 1942. I had a long conversation with him about Vera Gran in his apartment in Frankfurt am Main in 2008. His wife, Teofila Langnas, who also survived the ghetto, sat next to him.

He considered his work in the ghetto like any other obligatory activity imposed by the context of the war. He did what was demanded of him—without harming anyone else, as far as possible. He earned money for himself and his family. He jumps when the word "collaboration" is used concerning him—he who was the editor and translator at the *Jewish Gazette*. (Ringelblum wrote that no honest journalist worked for the *Jewish Gazette*.)

"You mustn't treat the musicians who played in the ghetto as collaborators. None of them. I wrote criticism of concerts and performances. Collaborate—it was enough just to be in contact with the Germans."

"Like yourself?"

"Like me. I don't know what Vera Gran told them. The

important thing is that it was discussed. She was pretty, extremely attractive, that feeds rumors."

His wife repeats twice:

"In the ghetto, it was 'people said' . . . nothing concrete, but it was better not to be close to her. They talked about her. Nothing clear, nor specific. People were afraid. That is a fact."

"People said—" she used the expression, significant in the ghetto—"they said she lived with men from the Gestapo . . ."

Reich Ranicki: "I can swear to nothing, I cannot guarantee that she was the friend of a German. No, I am not certain, I know nothing specific.

"No, today, sixty years later, I am not sure that she tried to seduce the Germans. Don't ask what she wanted. That, she knows, not I. As for me, I survived without collaborating!

"No one was treated as a collaborator for having played Beethoven or Schubert. Not one of the musicians in the orchestra—and there were several dozen—was ever stuck with that label.

"If you want me to tell you that every Jew that survived has sinned, then you have come to the wrong place.

"You cannot exclude the fact that someone could have fallen in love with a Jew as attractive as Vera Gran. It's unlikely, although conceivable. Everything I know comes from gossip. The Germans were not too inclined to frequent Jewish women; they had their own *Blitzmädel,* with the lightning symbol of the Gestapo on their sleeves. Besides, all these things were regulated by the Nuremberg Laws of 1935."

Reich Ranicki categorically denied the idea that Szpilman was a member of the Jewish police.

"That is idiotic, like everything that Marianowicz, the satirist, said about me. It seems that he saw me wearing a policeman's cap. Me, who never wore a cap in my life, much less a uniform.

"For Vera Gran, I can't vouch for anything. I think that it is very probable that she never collaborated. Even though rumor at that time said the contrary. But what mattered in the ghetto was music. Words could not express what was happening. Despite this it was words—not music—that carried judgments and manufactured legends."

Israel Gutman, historian of the Holocaust, who participated in the ghetto uprising, judged Vera Gran severely. "Her whole life was an enormous lie," he told me. "It's the ghetto that made her, and it is there that she came into her own. There are people who want to live at any cost, and she was one of them. For me, she represents no particular moral value."

Symcha Rotem (born Ratajzer), who used the code name Kazik when he was the liaison agent for the Jewish Combat Organization (ŻOB) on the Aryan side and had gotten dozens of insurgents out of the ghetto, had nothing to say about Vera Gran. This world of cafés and clubs did not interest him.

In Paris I had a conversation with Ala, the wife of Marek Edelman. She also preferred to keep a distance from this reality. "We were elsewhere—as much in thought as in body and soul. In our projects, our actions, our struggle."

Jerzy Szapiro, professor of neurosurgery, who had lived in the building where the Sztuka was located and worked in the hospital across the street, does not remember having heard anything bad said about Vera Gran.

I have before me the final decision of the commission for verification of the Association of Polish Stage Artists, dated October 15, 1945, and signed by its president, Aleksander Zelwerowicz. The commission was without pity toward those members suspected of collaboration. They condemned more willingly than they exonerated, and rare were the extenuating circumstances. No mercy.

In this specific case, an unequivocal declaration was handed down. The judgment stresses that Vera Gran's comportment during the German Occupation was irreproachable.

The commission for verification of the Musicians' Union handed down a declaration shortly afterward affirming that the citizen Vera Gran Jezierska had not sullied her honor as a Polish woman during the German Occupation and in consequence she had every right to practice her profession.

"Szpilman no longer had any reason to prevent my working on Polish Radio."

On November 19, 1945, during a conference of the directors of European radio stations, Vera Gran performed "Her First Ball" with an orchestra of thirty musicians under the direction of Stefan Rachoń. Along with the orchestra, she was accompanied by two pianists, the composer of the piece, Władysław Szpilman, and Czesław Aniołkiewicz.

Vera affirmed that the only reason she was able to perform the piece was because Szpilman saw personal benefit in it. She was the only person who possessed the text by Szlengel, and in a way it made her the "owner" of the piece written for her. "Szpilman wanted very much to present the piece to the foreign guests. Naturally he was silent about the 'Gestapo sympathizer past' of the singer."

A week later, she received a registered letter. On a small sheet with the stamp of *the delegation of the Prosecutor of the Criminal Court of Warsaw, 95 Marszałkowska Street. Citizen Vera Gran Jezierska. The Secretariat of the office of the Prosecutor informs you that on the date of November 26, 1945, the prosecutor of the Court dropped all charges against you; the accusations have been found groundless.*

She didn't remember her sense of relief then.

She and her husband, Kazik, lived for several weeks in Warsaw, in the Mokotów neighborhood, in one of the houses spared by the war. On the second floor. The neighbors from Babice had moved to the first floor. She felt safe, protected, as if on the Aryan side. The snow was falling. As in Babice, there were no panes on the windows, and there was no electricity, but it was of little importance.

At night in a canvas-covered truck she and a whole group were going to Łódź, the provisional capital at the time, to give some concerts. After a few hours, she began to lose her voice. The next morning it was worse. She looked at the enormous posters:

The Polish Red Cross, at the Polonia Movie Theater, Łódź, December 31, 1945, at midnight—Celebrate the New Year with the chorus of Revellers ("Give Me Your Heart," "Tell Me Good Night," "Pappy and His Trombone"). Vera Gran with her repertory and the others: Andrzej Bogucki, Natalia Lerska, Hanka Bielicka, and many others.

Then she saw the public gathered in a crowd. She felt herself stumble. Her voice was hoarse. "Please excuse us, we will refund your tickets . . ."

The ovations were not for her. She tried not to give it any importance. Bad luck. But certain ill-intentioned people interpreted the illness: it was Security that prevented her from going on stage; a collaborator did not have the right to sing!

The next day, her colleague Ludwik Sempoliński brought her half his fee. She refused it.

She remained silent. She looked at the newspaper articles about her supposed diplomatic illness. Mieczysław Fogg, a singer she befriended, tried to reassure her. Once they were back in Warsaw he took her to an artists' café that was jam-packed.

All the texts of the songs she interpreted on stage and on Polish Radio during the 1940s have been preserved. I have in front of me an imposing pile of papers: manuscript format, yellowed, with carbon copies taped to them. They are stamped with the rectangular seal of the censors, "Reproduction Authorized," every time with the date and a signature. There is also the seal of the literary department of Polish Radio, sometimes crossed out in red pencil, with the annotation "No" and a signature. Vera annotated that it was Szpilman. It's not certain.

Vera always performed with piano accompaniment, rarely joined by other instruments or an orchestra. This continued for five years after the war in Poland and later all over the world—Paris, London, Caracas, Toronto, New York.

This is what Kazik said to her one day, but she didn't pay any attention then: "If you continue to worry about what people say about you, you will go crazy." She could not believe that the rumor would persist.

Again the following year, in the month of December 1946,

she was in her dressing room at the small Kukułka Theater on Nowy Świat Street. As was her habit, she arrived early to collect herself before the performance. In front of the mirror she found an ugly blue envelope with the seal "Confidential." The Central Committee of Jews in Poland asked her to be present for a case concerning her. No signature.

7

"I can tell you a few things"

I can tell you a few things, but you have to promise on the wounds of Christ that you will not say a thing to anyone."

She rushes me along, she pushes me in the hallway. Quick, quick in the nook by the table.

"And what are you, Catholic? . . . No? You are not Jewish, I don't believe it."

"I can swear to you on the life of my mother."

"No, not mothers, that's sacred."

"Then on what?"

"Then I don't feel like having you swear to me on anything at all. You just have to promise me that you will not vomit when I tell you this story. Unless you promise me to hold it in, or to run to the toilet. Promise? . . . Good!"

I would have promised her anything to be able to stay near her, swept into this world unconnected to time. I could touch it.

Sixty years after the ghetto, spring was here. In her Parisian bunker, Vera was enumerating the residue of all the personal wrongs done to her.

"Today, I am going to tell you. I woke up. I had the feeling that I was suffocating. My mouth was dry. I got up and passed between the fridge and all the cardboard boxes to reach the kitchen. I wanted to make myself something to drink, and I saw that some things were preventing the sink from draining. I wanted to throw all those things into the toilet bowl. I ran to the bathroom. I tried to make everything go away. Suddenly there was a gurgling sound, and I looked into the toilet bowl, and that's when I got everything in my face—excrement, piles of shit, from the whole building, a stink, tons of pestilential waste. I flushed and received a second barrage."

"Would you like some water? A compress for your head?"

"And that wasn't the end of it, it was going to get worse. What could I do? It started flooding the whole bathroom, liquid excrement, and solids, brown, black, yellow, tobacco colored. And I was standing in the middle of it, it never stopped, it continued pouring out, it splattered on me, and I was bathed in it. And I couldn't ask anyone for help. I couldn't flee, because all my things were there. I had to manage. It was my home.

"It happened on a Saturday or a Sunday. It wasn't even worthwhile to go see that bitch of a concierge, she would have rubbed her hands in glee, for sure.

"I ran out into the hall, and I sat down on the ground in front of my door, and I howled. My neighbors from across the way came out. I tried to tell them what had just happened. They thought that I had lost my mind! 'You have to go see the concierge.' 'No,' I cried, 'I mustn't go near her.' But she was already standing there in the stairwell, waiting. The concierge muttered, 'She should just call an ambulance.' She turned on her heels and left. I went back inside. I felt sick. The summer, the heat. It stank, it was horrible. I took a dustpan, but where to throw all that? What could I do with it? The concierge would gladly have had me swallow it."

She must have imagined it perfectly, or else she was playing to the audience—an exercise in the horror genre, *Disgust* its title.

"But that's probably not the worst thing that happened to you in life."

"And what do you think happened to me that was worse? I didn't have rubber gloves, she stole everything from me. I had to clean it all up with a towel, with my bare hands. It's indescribable what I had to go through. And then I had to bathe myself, wash myself, and clean myself up. 'Out, out, damned spot!' Do you know the classics? I am marked to the end of my days.

"Fortunately, I don't have much longer."

In little cloth bags, rolls of cotton. She takes them out and wraps them around her hands. It looks like a game, or the preparation for a fight.

"To place microphones, they take down the walls, saw through, screw, make holes. They spend their time drugging me. They are obliged to, if they want to do to me what they plan. I don't leave this hole, not even for five minutes, they have to knock me out if they want to prevent my protesting. Today I received a big dose, I don't know why. It must have driven them crazy when I stopped up a couple of holes the other day. I do it on purpose to annoy them. With cotton, it's like clay. Apparently, what I have done causes disturbances. They had to come and make repairs.

"They are destroying my brain. I know that it will leave traces. It's inhuman how tired I am. I know that the Brute is preparing new ambushes for me.

"The Brute—that's the name I gave him."

The doctors' diagnosis: persecution complex, maniacal syndrome of persecution. They don't know precisely when it set in. She was afraid of him for years.

Drowned in excrement. It's the expression of a defiling, of a humiliation, of an outrage.

Vera usually performed onstage in black, without jewelry.
But this bright portrait from a Parisian photo studio was one
of her favorites.

And then THEY came and didn't give her a moment of
peace, till the very end.

For a long time, I thought her illness was a manifestation
of what she had suffered. I tried to unravel the meanderings of
her narratives, I repeated my questions, I took notes, I returned
to them. I always interpreted in her favor the times she lost
her psychic equilibrium. But it was becoming more and more
difficult.

The feeling of being observed, followed, recorded, spied upon is a typical manifestation of a persecution complex. Cameras are installed everywhere, even in one's teeth. They are less likely to film you from the back, or on the toilet bowl. Everything is a menace. There is no help anywhere. The theory of a global conspiracy.

She writes on everything. In the margins of books and bank statements. On pieces of paper pasted on the refrigerator, or the mirrors in the bathroom, on every possible surface, the moment she finds a space between the recipes for desserts and lists of side effects of her medications, an ad for a new television station.

Written on a cardboard box of tights on sale from the Samaritaine department store:

Stolen:
1—large package of panties = 10.
2—in the hallway: removed, the cover of the doorbell by the door.
3—pulled from the wall, electric cable, almost new, it came from the outside and ended with a sort of "circuit breaker." I noticed it after the business with the extra television channel they tried to force me to pay for.
4—three pairs of sunglasses stolen.
5—expensive and very fine pencils from NY HB.
6—a plastic box filled with stamps—collected over the years—valuable—from all over the world.

When speaking of herself she writes "old toad," whose life is like a seesaw.

I look at her, her face; I can almost discern a gentleness, for an instant the shadow of a smile. It's an illusion. In reality, she is mean and authoritarian. She never gives in. She is the one who knows, who commands, who sets the rules of the game.

"What is the most important feeling that you experience the most?"

"Hatred," she says without thinking. She laughs. "I said that automatically, but it's true. Hatred and the need for vengeance. Huge. An enormous need to avenge myself against those who have hurt me. And the desire to do good for those who have been good to me. And there have been many of them. But these saints, the good, are those who are the least heard, you don't notice them. Good deeds don't make people think.

"I repeat to myself endlessly: never say anything to people—give the least information. The best answer is, I DON'T KNOW. Or, THE LAWYER DECIDES—DON'T LET ANYONE ENTER WITHOUT A WITNESS. Say nothing. That can also serve the enemy.

"It's best that I keep quiet, because if I open my mouth too many people will lose face."

The most important thing that happened to her, the most traumatic in her life, occurred when she was very young. When she was twenty-five years old, she spent sixteen months in the ghetto. It marked her forever, and she was haunted by it for the rest of her life. FOR THIS. For . . .

Not having gotten into the wagons with her dear ones, like others.

Not to have remained in the ghetto, because leaving it seemed to her the only salvation.

She left without a word, with the presentiment of tragedy.

Not to have been able to organize help right away.

Not to have saved her mother or her sisters.

She never got over that.

Like others, like so many others.

She was haunted by what she did or did not do, by the echoes of slander and gossip, by what she can justify one hundred percent: "I tried to save my family, but I could not do it." I wouldn't dare set rules for such a struggle.

The more time I spend with her, the more I dig into the subject, the more I consult old documents, the less I let myself understand. The more powerless I feel confronting this past. Not qualified to pass a moral judgment. What do I know, what can I know?

Did she have a choice? Choice always exists, but what does that mean?

I choose white bread or black bread, white wine or red wine, cake with poppy seeds or cheese. Or else: the sea or the mountains. A flowered dress or the little black one. Happy choices. But when it is: save my mother or my sister? My father or my husband? Suffer hunger or appease it? To be afraid or to be less afraid? Or to feel safe for a moment, thinking that what is happening is the work of a madman. And to feel better, thanks to these thoughts. Then, perhaps it was worth the trouble. It doesn't matter what brings you comfort. To be protected by a man, to temporarily free oneself from one's responsibilities, to have the piece of paper stamped with the seal of survival.

In every reality you find heroes, those who sacrificed their lives for others. They fire or are fired upon, they attack or turn their bodies into a shield. There are also normal people, ordinary. We are normal people. Courage is a virtue that cannot be required; what can be demanded is decency. I will not be underhanded, I will not willingly harm anyone, I will not betray you for a kilo of sugar. No, I am not obliged to help you, since it is dangerous. It's not my duty if it puts my life in danger, and that of my family. Do not judge me if I don't do it. I am only human. I don't want to deprive my children of a future.

Vera made no effort to leave the ghetto to go over to the Aryan side. Did she not feel like it? Was there no reason? Was no one worth the risk of a meeting, a conversation, an intimacy? Was there no one, or did fear paralyze her? Or perhaps she did not have the time? Busy singing, taking care of her mother, of the daily tasks. Perhaps there was also a man? What was her fear? No one knows.

I am using the lexicon of a world not at war. I am adapting it to a reality in which words had often lost their meaning. The period of the Holocaust had shattered the old models of behavior, loosened the rigors of moral norms. In the face of constant threat, people pushed back the limits of ethics. It's not up to us to judge.

But in the end it is also they, those who survive, who try to adjust to this past. Is it just them in particular?

What would you have done to save your skin? And to save your mother? To which of those condemned would you have opened the door to your home knowing what dangers awaited you? Who would you have helped while endangering the life of your daughter or your grandson? Do you know? You only think that you know. And in those cabarets in the ghetto, you would have looked down on those who were eating blinis with caviar while people were dying in the streets; that seems morally reprehensible to you, the subject of condemnation. Like Vera, who sang in the ghetto her songs from before the war. Like Vera, who used the songs to regain equilibrium, to recall the years before the persecution. Because the persecution weighed on the world, for a longer or a shorter time, on those who were conscious of it and on those who did everything to ignore the danger.

Life is expensive. Survival is expensive.

First, the price, the appraisals, the evaluation of the merchandise. If life is merchandise for some, for most people it is priceless.

Some had it written in gold letters: the idea of "dignity" or—equally out of fashion—of "honor." It seems that they are superior to the animal (i.e., primitive) instinct for survival. However, it's about survival, at any price.

The history of currency can also be the subject of controversy.

Some had dollars, letters of credit, and valuable objects; others had factories and apartments, paintings and musical instruments. Still others sold their furs and articles of clothing, their porcelains. Some had few things, others nothing at all. These people were the first to go.

However, the others saw everything they owned disappear, little by little. The war lasted not a month, not a year, nor two. People still had to eat and drink. Exhausting their resources. The sideboards, the dressers, the drawers, the shelves, and the storage units were emptied. Large families were reduced; only the strongest in good health remained, who also needed money for bread and to pay for a roof over their heads. Expelled, exiled, deported from one place to another, they tried to carry on. There were months when surviving proved possible and others when what occurred was impossible to believe. Ice cream and liquor were served less and less in the cafés, the orchestras had fewer and fewer musicians, the Jewish undertakers were making a fortune.

The price, the price, that constant need to pay. There were several lists of prices. One's eventual fate could be marked by inferior yellow Jewish tickets or the better Polish ones, which would come due a little later.

Grynbergs, Rozensteins, or Fiszmans had to pay thousands to stay alive, especially if they spoke Polish badly and they were circumcised. It was the same thing with little boys. For the women and little girls it was easier, but the problem of language, the eyes, the skin, the aura, the coloring . . .

Who set the prices? Who sealed the bargaining? Not always the smugglers or the scum. The sums, the expense, the liquidity put into play often depended on the neighbors, the concierges, friends sometimes. Because it had to be done, there was no other solution, obtain food or medication. Buy potatoes and bread.

Some had nothing left and still wanted to live.

It seems that everything has a price. Or to put it another way—demand determines the market. When the ghetto was reduced in size, when more and more trains left from Umschlagplatz, people looked for places on the Aryan side, safe addresses, viable papers. The prices started climbing.

In the autumn of 2009, after years of working on this book about Vera Gran, I had a dream. I was tortured systematically for a long time, without any chance of escape. They beat me, twisted my arms and legs, and mutilated my face. It was a powerful lesson in fear. I was in pain on waking up. I remained lying in my bed for a long time, until dawn, trying to understand who had struck me and why I was in such pain.

Without a scientific interpretation, someone (SOMEBODY) wanted to make me aware that pain can be absolutely unbearable. As a consequence, everything would be sacrificed to escape it. That morning, I understood that I was ready to do anything in order never to be in such pain.

Extract from Vera's diary:

October 14, 1986. Po tikhońku s uma skhozhu (in Russian: That's it, I am losing my mind). *My God, I cannot stand myself, and it's like that more and more often. I am no longer in control of all my thoughts—that is to say, stop myself from being submerged by my hatred toward the world—worse yet, I cannot control my language either, and my words come back to hit me full force, like a boomerang with two points, hurting only me. Without relief.*

I sleep in the morning—déformation profesionnelle. I don't like poetry very much.

The 6th of November, Sunday. I don't want to live any longer.

"You are not dead!?!"

That's how they were greeted by their neighbors, their friends, by those who now lived in their abandoned houses. The new owners of property that used to belong to Jews. It was not a cry of joy, nor of welcome. There was no relief. In the question mark there resonated a note of regret. Like a bad surprise.

You are not dead, therefore you succeeded, how did you

Vera Gran's senior transit pass (for free travel on the Paris bus and Métro), with an "official" birth date of April 20, 1918 (she deducted two years from her age)

manage it? How could this be? You are not dead when others are dead. You are not dead, so you must have bought your life from someone. Present among the absent.

At what price? Finally, how did you manage it? Just like that, by chance, with a bit of luck? Things didn't happen as easily as that. They knew the war. To escape, you had to pay. Pay the price of fate. By what means? Pay how much, and in what currency?

"And what is it to you? I hear it said once, twice, a hundred times—why do I have to justify myself? I would have loved to have seen what you would have done in my place.

"Did you hear? Shhhh . . . Do you hear? They are everywhere. Implacable. For them, nothing is impossible. Yesterday, they came in through a window in the bathroom, when I was there with a girlfriend, a few yards away, in the next room. We were speaking of Aznavour and his cunning, to distract their attention, to muddle the trail. And then, at a given moment, I got it full in the face. I like to turn things to my advantage, I like conflict, I like arguments and judging others. We argued about dressing rooms. Aznavour had placed me upstairs, where no one ever came. I burst into tears. On stage as in life, the wolves dictate the law."

After the war she fought very often, as best she could, for her money. For an increase in her pension or the reparations due her from the Germans for war damages, for the rent of her studio, where the tenants came one after the other, the interest from the bank, her investments, her savings . . . she was constantly making a scene at the bank. "Shit, I don't feel like giving you publicity. Go to hell!" "And at what percentage? I insist on seeing the accounts and in sequence." She carefully analyzed the banking transactions. All this to write in the end that she has nobody to bequeath all this hard-won money. Nobody except for animals.

She has lived alone for years. As far as she can remember, since she left Poland. Men came and went. Dogs, more faithful. And in time, neither one nor the other. Nobody to speak to. Yet she had to speak. Taking notes doesn't make any sound. It involves other senses. Hence the hours spent on the telephone. Speaking all alone or to the walls.

"Yesterday, for example, I dropped a flower behind the dresser. Deep, very far down, impossible to reach. I wept, I swore, I called out to it. I told it that I was there, right there, nearby, that I wouldn't leave it alone. It heard nothing, or didn't want to hear. It was dying, visibly fading away, I could feel it in every nerve. Help us to save ourselves, please."

On the wall she had hung a crown of thorns. She had made it herself. Out of fish spines. "Spines can also be beautiful." She collected leaves, roots, flowers. In the corners were pieces of her own sculptures. Dried branches. A network of things that hold memories and the unreal.

"All of my people were gone so quickly. How come I am still alive?"

"Perhaps you still have something to do?"

"In a religious sense? Maybe . . . The only thing that functioned relatively well before was sleep. I went to bed late, it's true, but I slept six, seven hours straight, without dreaming. Now I wake up after two hours. *Hoc rachmunes . . .* have pity. A beggar's lament. I wake up several times at night repeating these words. I enunciate them well, articulate them for a long moment, no longer remembering what they mean, nor where they come from. From the ghetto or from heaven? Have pity, have pity . . . And then the children didn't even have the strength to drag themselves over to reach the bread that had fallen into the street."

She's beside me, wedged in the past. She doesn't sleep anymore. She rhythmically rocks back and forth.

"The bed draws me, I can hide there, but at the same time, it terrifies me, as a place of torture, where the ghosts, the nightmares, and the anguish descend upon me too easily. I am going to lose the archives of my brain. I am rambling, I am going to end up doing nothing but rambling. How to escape it? How do I protect myself? More and more often I am submerged by a wave of fire, the flames of TERROR. My heart is beating rapidly, beads of sweat on my skin, and I have to suppress a scream of despair that wants to come from the depth of my stomach, my soul, my brain."

The Orwell year: 1984. She gave me permission to look in

her calendar. A firm order: Very little time. On the flyleaf she had written: *Five Jews have given to the world: Moses—the law, Christ—mercy, Marx—conscience, Freud—the subconscious, Einstein—that everything is relative.*

She had drawn a striped dressing gown of terry cloth over her flowered nightgown. It is held together on top by a safety pin, and she wears several of them on the lapel like you wear medals. "The accessories of a retired star." She chuckles.

An aluminum crutch with a white handle, pieces of toilet paper in the guise of handkerchiefs.

"I have to make time for her," she repeats. "I must take care of this old woman called Vera.

"My memory, my fate. Now everything is distorted. The goods are no longer fresh. They have completely broken me. And also, they believe I am working for Dr. Alzheimer. I can do nothing. I don't have the courage to do anything at all. I have been living in this state for a long time.

"I am becoming bizarre. The bridge linking me to others grows more distant at a terrifying speed. Several dozen years of solitary living (which means a whole lifetime!) distorts your point of view on communal life.

"Yesterday—a success. I made a telephone call to Warsaw. (You don't have to know who it was.) I heard a startled voice: 'Jesus, Mary, Joseph!' I took it for a nice expression of pleasure. The anguish was still palpable:

" 'Vera?'

" 'Yes, it's me. The one and only, the one you love.'

"And she insisted: 'Vera Gran?'

" 'Of course, it's me. Has my voice changed that much?'

"A long pause and . . . 'But, after all, you died last year.'

" 'That, I wasn't aware of it. But nowadays everything is possible.'

"And her sick husband came in. I heard her prepare him for the shock of a conversation with a corpse not all that fresh.

"And again: 'Vera?'

" 'Yes.'

"I have started pinching myself. It has to be me, after all . . . ?
We are no longer all that young these days! I have my little
share of ailments! And then tons of wrinkles—so, they must

Vera lived on rue Chardon-Lagache in Paris for more
than half a century. The narrow space was closely
packed with her stage dresses and shoes, sheet music,
and stills . . . alongside paintings and books (also her
autobiography, of which I found dozens of copies under
her bed). She collected the evidence of her own artistic
life and triumphs.

be right. All the same I asked with some circumspection if they knew who had published my obituary.

" 'What do you mean, who? Marianowicz, first of all.' He still remembered when the actor Edward Dziewoński (despite the fact that he was embraced by Alzheimer's, it seems) shed a tear at the announcement of this news and . . . he quickly started telling spicy stories about US. What a shame we never made it together, because I was very attracted to him. Unfortunately I was (for a long time, much too long) chaste."

The restless recycling of memories. She repeats, replays the past in her head, on her tongue. Without a moment's rest, without catching her breath, thus, without letup.

The drawers. How many have to be opened to find the true Vera? And where is she? Does she exist? At what depth, and by what devious turns has she hidden beneath layers of invention, intentionally? Screens of shadows and illusions superimposed. Recorded night and day, months after weeks, they increase and add up. They form a three-dimensional network that lives and devours. I don't know toward what image they point the way.

"Kiss my ass," she suddenly says to the lamp hanging over the table, in which, according to her, they installed, years ago, an extrasensitive camera.

Her eyes, accustomed to the darkness, search out another place where they might attack. She hears voices, the monotonous squeaking of the magnetic tape recording all her gestures and murmurings. Even those that don't exist.

"I avoid people. I flee them, I even run from the idea of meeting them. I don't have the strength to perform, nor to defend myself. I am most afraid in the morning. Do you know this fear of the coming day? I know that something bad is going to happen. I only ask myself, what? One day I left the house at three o'clock in the afternoon—I call this story the New Year's story—it was going to be a stroll and some errands. I always bought coffee to send to Poland. I was walking on the sunny side of my street. I crossed Boulevard Exelmans, then by the dry cleaner's shop I saw a magnificent Doberman. I was afraid that he was lost. Suddenly I felt violently shoved from behind, and something heavy came down on my shoulders and the nape of my neck. A menacing barking in my ears. I protected my head, and at that moment I felt something biting my rear. Then the dog ran into the jewelry shop.

"I am certain that he was specially ordered to attack me. Isn't it strange that its owner was specifically a Polish Jew, Rakower? The result: a bruise with slight bleeding, twelve centimeters long, and a torn jacket. It was a premeditated and precise job."

I know that she believes it. I try to follow her.

She asks me to fetch from her medicine cabinet some tablets for her nerves.

"I have to take my medication. Three white tablets a day, that's not very much. I remain stretched out on my bed, I look at the ceiling, my photos come toward me. The paintings wink in the corners, but not in a friendly way, they are menacing. The books, the boxes are oppressive. As if they wanted to smother me. The dust weighs, the dirt sticks. I don't wake up. Therefore, I am not dreaming."

8

The codes of survival inside the ghetto and on the outside

The codes of survival inside the ghetto and on the outside were different. Once within the confined area, acts that would have been condemned without recourse outside the walls were treated with a certain indulgence. Even approval. But not everyone, and not completely.

People had the right to sing. Vera had that right in the ghetto. Her counterpart in a similar café on the Aryan side, equally. In the same Warsaw, occupied by the Germans.

Vera had the right to appear in the theater. Or in a revue. However, her Polish counterpart, in the same situation, would be going beyond the bounds of what was considered acceptable behavior during the Occupation.

The first is the fate of a star of the stage.

In March 1940, the governor, Hans Frank, signed a decree concerning the regulation of Polish cultural activities. Before being able to perform in the theater—"within the limits of the primitive need for entertainment, and with the specific recommendation of lowering the artistic standards"—the performers had gratefully accepted jobs as cloakroom attendants or waiters. Aleksander Zelwerowicz worked in a stable, and Jerzy Jurandot cultivated tomatoes, Stefania Grodzieńska assisted a hairdresser. Those who found work performing in a café were considered lucky.

In the spring of 1940, on Chłodna Street, they opened a first little theater, the Kometa, in an old movie house. Its manager, Stanisław Heinrich, founded an organization bringing together the Blue Butterfly, the Golden Beehive, and the Vaudeville theaters. Immediately afterward, the Theater der Stadt Warschau was inaugurated in the building that once housed the Polish Theater, with Igo Sym as the director. He was known as the biggest playboy of the cinema before the war. He performed in the very select cabaret of Morskie Oko and was as admired as other stars such as Hanka Ordonówna and Adolf Dymsza. All the major writers wrote scripts for him: Julian Tuwim, Marian Hemar, Andrzej Włast. He was a favorite of society— charming, witty, and a conversationalist, he even performed magic tricks and was a sportsman. He played billiards and spoke several languages. His detractors called him the "handsome walker."

By October 1939, people said, he paraded around the capital with a Nazi armband on his sleeve. Lidia Wysocka, his co-star in *The Golden Mask,* confirms that she saw him wear a German uniform. It was rumored that he was an agent even before the war.

Thanks to the origins of his mother, he became a full citizen of the Reich (*Reichsdeutsch*). In the spring of 1940, he assumed the post of advisor for artistic affairs to the German governor. He also directed the Komedia Theater on Kredytowa Street and the Palladium Cinema, which had been rebaptized Helgoland by the Occupiers and was "reserved for Germans" (*nur für Deutsche*).

On theater posters: *In Search of the Beauty Mark; Under the*

Fig Leaf; Amorous Little Games; The Nectar of Ecstasy; Kisses and Drinks.

The following could be read in the report of the underground Association of Polish Stage Artists: *Entertaining oneself with inept and licentious performances is a disgraceful proof of stupidity, of intellectual vulgarity, and lacking in modesty and dignity.* The association called unanimously for a boycott of all performances in official theaters. "Official"—that is, consciously or unwittingly in the service of German propaganda that depraved and lowered the morals of Polish society. Performers who participated were said to "lack a sense of morality," of having "lost their dignity as an artist and citizen," or of having made "miserable choices."

Only pigs go to the movies, and the rich go to the theater could be read on walls. People threw stink bombs during performances, started fires, and put corrosive substances in the spectators' pockets or shaved their heads.

However, crowds continued to rush to the theaters in Warsaw. At the Theater der Stadt Warschau, tickets for operettas were reserved two weeks in advance.

The underground press castigated this public: *The majority of them are traffickers, profiting from the war—traders in illicit gold or speculators in fuel.*

The Warsaw auditoriums held eight thousand spectators a day. In 1940, admission to the Blue Butterfly cost two to four zlotys (the price of two kilos of meat). Then, in 1943, in a similar small theater, the Figaro, five to fifty zlotys, the amount a family of six spent for food daily.

The citizens' boycott called by the Polish Underground State was largely ignored. Was theater only, as was the stated goal, for the scum—the smugglers, the traffickers, the profiteers?

Attendance reached 85 percent capacity.

Igo Sym hired . . . he had the power.

In 1941, by order of Goebbels, he was put in charge of the

production of a propaganda film, *Heimkehr: The Return to the Fatherland.* The roles of the persecutors of the German minority in Poland were to be played by Polish actors.

Ten accepted.

We are all collaborators. On a more or less grand scale, for a day or a lifetime. All that differentiates us are the experiences and the circumstances, which allow us to gauge the extent of our compromises. History often places us in the context of a tragic choice. We collaborate with fate, we come to terms with it. We are capable of justifying nearly all of our weaknesses.

In the *Dictionary of the Polish Language* by Samuel Linde (published in 1855), the word *kolaboracja* (collaboration) does not exist. If at the end of the nineteenth century they spoke in Polish of *współpraca* (collaboration—working together) with the Occupation forces, the word *kolaboracja* had another meaning. It appeared in European dictionaries only in the twentieth century to describe a new reality with which nobody had been confronted until then.

This term originally referred to the Second World War and described a political or economic cooperation with the Hitlerian Occupation forces, an act of cooperation by the citizen of a country occupied by the authorities of Germany, Italy, or Japan to the detriment of his nation. This word was used for the first time in October 1940 with regard to the meeting between Marshal Pétain and Hitler in France.

Collaboration: French, also used in English.

In Polish: *współpraca* (Slavic etymology) or *kolaboracja* (Latin etymology).

Several words are derived from it to describe the phenomenon: *collaborator, collabo, collaborationist.*

The agent. He differs from the collaborator in that he is paid regularly for his services. He is an employee of the police.

And then there is the traitor.

There were some who meekly carried out the orders of the

occupying forces, acting in this manner to have peace, earn profit, save their lives. But there were also the ones with a double motivation: those who forced themselves to work with the enemy in order to act for the good of society, to do something that would be beneficial even within a limited scope.

I have the feeling that all those who survived are implicated.

Apparently, work guaranteed survival. The Hitlerian Occupation had deprived the Polish people and the Jews of the greatest part of their usual activities. Polish institutions had ceased to exist. Everything was closed: schools, universities, offices, banks, orchestras, sports clubs. Life in its old forms was dead. Every day, month, year of war brought changes and demanded that people adapt.

The Poles in their cities, the Jews in their part of town behind the walls, tried to confront daily life in order not to succumb too quickly to its traps.

You had to have a roof over your head, for yourself and your family, and appease the pangs of hunger. The fundamental hunger—the hunger for bread—annihilated and neutralized all others, and only art could soothe.

In 1940, the Secret Theater Council published an ordinance:

Those who infringe on the rules of our organization, either because they could not find an honest source of revenue or because of irresponsibility, opportunism, or lack of ethics, will incur a SEVERE reprimand!

They were unwilling to accept extenuating circumstances— the need to support and protect your family, the inability to find another job, the need to act on stage, with the encouragement and support of the public.

They added things up with the furious need to inflict the deserved punishment. In the name of a sense of decency and sullied honor. *If they had had a guillotine at hand,* wrote renowned actor Stefan Jaracz, *they wouldn't have hesitated to use it.*

Igo Sym was shot down in his apartment on Mazowiecka Street, March 7, 1941.

The record of the verdicts of the Special Military Court at the headquarters of the Union for Armed Struggle have been saved, a rare occurrence. Date, name of the condemned, a few words. Specified secret information. Professor Andrzej Krzysztof Kunert is certain that the order for the execution came from General Grot Rowecki in person.

July 5, 1943, the carrying out of the verdict of the Underground against Jadwiga Kossuth-Galewska, the second wife of Kazimierz Junosza-Stępowski, a young actress and morphine addict, was attempted in her home.

Junosza-Stępowski was sixty years old, with a record of great triumphs on stage (from comedy to tragedy). He was a respected and popular screen actor who earned an extremely comfortable living (he played the famous Professor Wilczur). During the First World War he served in the light cavalry of the Polish Legion. The Second World War caught him by surprise while he was performing in Wilno. He returned to Warsaw, working at first in the cafés the Bonesetter, the Golden Duck, and the Frigate. He was offered a role in *Heimkehr: The Return to the Fatherland*. He refused. However, he did agree to perform at the official Komedia Theater. He couldn't refrain from working in the theater! He played eighteen roles, while also performing in several sketches at the Golden Beehive.

I am afraid of nothing, he explained in a letter, *as long as life gives off sparks.*

He tried to shield his wife with his body. He died several hours later as a result of bullet wounds.

Maria Malicka was condemned in 1947, for having been on stage certainly, but also for *having entertained intimate relations with an agent for the Propaganda Office, Józef Horwath, and having received in her apartment German officers and employees of the Propaganda Office.*

She was twenty-four when she gave a phenomenal performance in Shaw's *Saint Joan* in Arnold Szyfman's Polish Theater. Marshal Józef Piłsudski and President Ignacy Mościcki came to applaud her. She appeared in many advertisements, including the ones for the Jabłkowski Brothers department store, for Pluton coffee and Piasecki chocolates.

During the Occupation she co-founded and worked as a waitress at the Actresses' Café, 12 Piękna Street, at the corner of Ujazdowskie Avenue, then at 5 Mazowiecka Street. Opened in April 1940, this café was known as the most expensive in Warsaw. It was also the most popular. Talented actresses thus showed that one could survive in another way. They did not perform the repertory imposed by the Germans.

Malicka left her work at the café to take advantage of a contract with the Komedia Theater. She wasn't the only one, she explained. Igo Sym's offer interested other well-known actors: Junosza-Stępowski, Józef Węgrzyn, Antoni Fertner, Stanisława Perzanowska . . .

In 1944 Malicka earned 250 zlotys per day, thus approximately 7,000 per month. Some said it was two or three times that amount.

After the war, she was considered the most corrupt actress of the Occupation.

Adolf Dymsza was also accused of having performed in the official theaters and of having been too associated with the Germans.

He was forbidden to perform in Warsaw; sometimes his name on posters was replaced by three stars, and he was obliged to turn in 15 percent of his earnings to the actors' retirement home in Skolimów.

For Marian Wyrzykowski, the real accomplishment was to perform in private apartments, to recite poetry in the service of his country. Lessons in resistance.

He also worked as a waiter. He had to live. Of course, some people thought that it was an absurd regression. Infantile. In life it is far better to do what is inherent in our nature, what is beneficial and enriching for others, rather than waste your talent.

It was a matter for debate. Is it better to perform in the theater or to serve Gestapo agents in a café? It was being discussed constantly. The stage, all the same, enabled one to keep a footing in the profession; running a business meant being in contact with the Germans on several levels.

Jan Kreczmar upheld the decision taken to boycott by the Association of Polish Stage Artists. He said that he felt better not showing a broad grin on stage while the ghetto was in flames, they were shooting and rounding up people in the streets, and the convoys were rolling toward Auschwitz.

The need to stigmatize actors' guilt during the war reached absurd levels at times.

Jerzy Leszczyński was reprimanded for having walked the dog of a German theater manager. They tried a violinist from an orchestra in Cracow for having shaken the hand of General Frank, who came to congratulate him for his moving performance.

The fever for verification of these actions permeated all the most important theatrical centers in Poland starting in the year 1945.

Condemnations included being rebuked, charged with infamy, having heads shaven, or being beaten up. An actor could be suspended as a member of the association, forbidden temporarily from practicing his profession, banished from the stage of the capital.

In the autumn of 1944, the writer Janusz Minkiewicz was one of the first to give his opinion on the subject. He had collaborated with the official theaters during the Occupation. He explained how important an actor's work could be at this time. "Artistic hunger was as strong as physical hunger, and the need for laughter, satire, and amusement had taken the lead over the rest, including the Warsaw Ghetto, Theater—oh, how macabre!—of Death." He spoke ironically about the mixture of professions during the war: "Actors became waiters; the waiters, directors of businesses; painters became speculators; and confidence men, writers." He abstained from all judgments about those who did not want to leave the stage as well as toward the others who decided to devote themselves to the business of serving others.

After the war, the verification carried out by the Association of Polish Stage Artists had the purpose of objectively evaluating the "activities" practiced during the Occupation. With a fine-tooth comb they went through the dossiers of all those who worked during the war.

The Polish Underground State demanded the respect of all fundamental laws of the moral code of citizens. Passive resistance and the boycotting of the institutions managed by the Occupation, as well as orders issued, were among the most important principles set forth. It was stated that the need to work was not reprehensible in itself; rather, it was carrying out tasks with excessive zeal, more than was required by the need to earn a living and support a family. They called that the limit of vital necessity. It was an obligation to "stigmatize those elements that were harmful."

Some people are born for the stage. Applause gives them wings and carries them through life. They do not know how to function otherwise. How can they find their place in a reality that doesn't help them? What do you do to prevent losing your star status?

According to the professional organization to which they belonged, they broke the terms of civil disobedience by going on an official stage. And they defied the boycott. However, they saw other people doing it, they knew them, met them, and even performed on stage together. And why would it be worse to perform on stage than in the cafés? Open a bar? They wouldn't know how to go about it. They knew how to perform.

You cannot perform in a closet! It cannot be done alone. Do you understand, Mr. Writer? For others, it is always easier.

Furthermore, the public wanted to see them. Tickets were sold. Not only for *The Nectar of Ecstasy,* but also to see the works of Polish authors such as Aleksander Fredro, Włodzimierz Perzyński, and Gabriela Zapolska. And those who improvised as restaurant owners, in what way were they better? Because they embodied a heroic style of life? What about the others, those who went on stage? They perverted the meaning of the vocation for which they were responsible. Did they no longer have a sense of shame? They were the elite; as an example, they should have been wearing this unshakable honor on an armband. They were not uncompromising.

To not read any newspapers, avoid the theater and the movies, because they are all collabo—col-la-bo: pronounced with a stage diction, it is completely repulsive.

But to the point of depriving oneself of the pleasure of performing on stage?

The second fate is the one of an author of anti-Semitic propaganda stage plays.

The Propaganda Office launched in the spring of 1942 a contest for a play that would support the struggle against typhoid—this was understood as supporting the condemnation of primitive Jewish environments, primitive and backward, the breeding ground of all sorts of diseases. Forty works were submitted.

The first prize was awarded to Halina Rapacka for *In Quarantine.*

Daughter of the great actor Wincenty Rapacki, she had the theater in her blood. As a young actor, on tour, she appeared with family revues in Warsaw, Lwów, Łódź. At the beginning of the war, she sold soap in cafés, with little to show for her efforts. Then she tried to write for cabarets and for the *New*

Courier, a German newspaper in the Polish language that was part of what people called the reptilian press, a rag, a whore paper, a shit merchandiser.

The paper was boycotted, as was she, even hidden behind her pseudonym, "Misantrope." She provided scripts for German theaters managed by the Occupation authorities: *The Magic of Lies, My Celibate Wife, It's Not Me—It's Her . . .*

To the friends who still spoke to her, she explained that she had to work because her mother was hungry. She was ready to do anything for money. She said it herself, the witnesses of her fate also. I don't know what her limits were, nor what she was capable of doing. Writing works for the theater about Jewish vermin was not beyond the bounds. After all, they existed, those lice-ridden and dirty Jewish buildings that spread diseases in the streets and contaminated the world.

The message was clear: Jews constituted a moral and physical danger. Preventive measures had to be taken. She was proud of her reward.

In Quarantine was staged for the first time in Tarnów, on August 1, 1942. That is where the Touring Theater was inaugurated with the intention of spreading the propaganda of this piece and of its message. At first it made the rounds in the south of Poland. The fees of the performers who participated in this enterprise matched the maximum levels of German fees, up to 1,500 zlotys a month. The price of the tickets was reduced to 2 zlotys (as opposed to the usual 6 or 12). Before every performance a doctor made a little speech on the subject of typhoid, on dirt and the role of Jews in the transmission of infections.

The ghetto had already been sealed off for months. Helping Jews risked incurring the penalty of death.

The play was performed in Cracow in the autumn of 1942, and in Warsaw in January of the following year.

The Touring Theater gave performances on Hoża Street, in the old Urania movie theater. As in other large towns, the performances were met with protests and attendance was weak; the performers experienced acts of sabotage. However, Stanisław Lorentz, who was in charge of culture for the Government Delegation for Poland, testified that nevertheless this project produced the anticipated results because it reinforced significantly anti-Semitic tendencies.

Someone said that Halina Rapacka "was not made of patriotic material." Perhaps that is possible. Perhaps there is a sort of inability to see the context of one's own life in proper perspective, to respect the norms imposed by the code of morality.

She was sentenced in absentia, because she had already gone to England. She was condemned. She never served her sentence of ten years.

A third is the fate of the Jewish Everyman.

Szepsl Rotholc was a featherweight boxer. Before the war he had won a hundred matches. He was considered a hero. And that was to be lasting. But in the ghetto, there was no room for a ring, and he became a Jewish policeman. With professional smugglers he corrupted the policemen. He had to earn a living, he had a wife and a son, but he also wanted to help others. He managed until January 1943, until the end of the Warsaw Ghetto.

It was Jonas Turkow who advised Rotholc to start an investigation to establish his innocence.

On October 8, 1946, the office of the Central Committee of Jews in Poland convened the citizens' court. The announcement of the citizens' court was mentioned in the *New Life*—the official organ of the committee, published in Yiddish. On the agenda for the near future was a study of the cases of the boxer Szepsl Rotholc and the theater director Michał Weichert as well as the singer Vera Gran.

In November 1946 four public hearings of the boxer Rotholc took place in the temporary meeting hall of the Central Committee of Jews in Poland. Attended by crowds, the sessions caused a major stir among the survivors. The bill of indictment stipulated that the Jewish Police was a collaborationist organization that acted to the detriment of Jewish society. A particularly severe sentence was given to those who had remained among its ranks after the liquidation of the ghetto.

"I could not help everybody. If I remained, it was to help the Jews," Rotholc tried to say calmly. A moment later, he cried out, pounding on the table with his fist, "I wanted to save my wife and my child."

I watch this scene with growing despair. Here is the testimony of a woman acquaintance of Rotholc. She told how he did not help her during a raid. It was another policeman, a friend, who caught her, and a moment later threw the child of another Jewish woman out the window. "The Jewish police of the ghetto were worse than the Germans," she said.

It was not the first time I heard the statement.

"A gang of degenerates," as it was called by an old member of the Jewish underground. Especially those who remained there until the end, after the 22nd of July, during the deportation. He showed them no mercy. It was an "abscess growing in the Jewish organism" that had to be eliminated.

During the work of deportation, was it possible for someone in the police to accomplish his duty in an "innocent" manner?

They would have preferred to see in Rotholc a hero. An active member of the Jewish Combat Organization, for example. Where to find the courage? He had joined the police. He became part of the civilian patrol. His duty was to "protect the Jewish population inside the walls of the ghetto." Then everything happened too fast, new regulations, orders given, the threat of losing one's family. Who can demand heroic behavior of others?

November 29, 1946, the court found him guilty of *participating in acts of extermination against the Jewish people.* He was shown as a symbol of shame, symbol of the security service so loathed in the ghetto. The final decision fell—*request for rehabilitation denied.*

Apparently all the survivors had a score to settle—from Communists to Zionist Jews. The order of the day was to eliminate from Jewish society whoever had collaborated in any manner possible with the Hitlerian authorities. The decision of the court would prevent them from occupying important positions in the new society.

Scores were not settled straightaway. The reality of the postwar era proved dangerous for the survivors. The return to places occupied by other people was difficult. They hunted Jews in the trains. The pogrom in Kielce in July 1946 drove out of Poland many of those who had chosen to stay in their homeland after the war.

The wounds of war were too raw, the losses too painful. They did not want to, or could not, look one another in the eyes.

They decided to create their own court, because they disagreed with the verdicts of the state courts in cases of collaboration.

In January 1949 the Jewish community protested against the acquittal of theater director and critic Michał Weichert, who had been director of the autonomous Jewish Social Mutual Assistance Organization in the Cracow Ghetto and was absolved because he had acted "without criminal intentions."

It had been three years between the Rotholc trial and that of Weichert. The citizens' court had presided over twenty-five cases of presumed collaborators. Eighteen were given a guilty verdict, and seven were acquitted.

The idea of purifying the atmosphere was instilled in people's minds, wrote Marek Bitter, representative of the Communist Polish Workers' Party, within the Jewish Committee.

Before putting in place the Jewish court, the Polish judicial system had tried eleven cases: eight people were condemned, five of whom received a death sentence.

There were strong feelings of rejection for the Jewish administrators of the local governments of the ghettos, considering them as equally responsible for the Holocaust. I would have been worried about the fate of the president of the Warsaw Judenrat, Adam Czerniakow, or that of Łódź, Chaim Rumkowski, if they had survived. Using every means possible, Rumkowski had bargained with fate, and the Germans, much longer than people in Warsaw. He might have expected a more intense examination of his behavior in the ghetto and the most extreme relations he maintained during the Occupation. He survived with others an unbelievably long time, until the summer of 1944. He went beyond the limits of moral justification according to the chronology of events.

I am astonished by Jewish intransigence, then, in this struggle over principles. To demand rebellion from those for whom rebellion meant death. All that they could do was to soften the impact of the blows.

After the annihilation, after everything they lived through, they felt the need for moral purification, to make condemnations, to stigmatize. The price of survival fell under the blows of their severe judgments.

These postwar trials are painful to me.

To try on the costume of another doesn't hurt. To wear for a moment the clothing of others doesn't contaminate us with their experiences. To interpret a role for a moment doesn't cost very much.

Perhaps it is worthwhile to play this role for a longer time?

A reflection in the mirror. Of oneself. The same eyes, the same contour of the hair, the forehead, the same grin.

I would have wanted to live. Too much? But is there a gradation in this matter?

Among 2,500 Polish actors before the war, approximately two hundred appeared in the official theaters and revues during the Occupation. Less than 10 percent. Some of them were outstanding artists: Maria Malicka, Adolf Dymsza, Stanisława

Perzanowska. Among these two hundred collaborators, fifteen were pointed out publicly. The condemnations were published in the underground press; the sentences, the beatings or shaved heads, were public.

Commissions for verification of facts created a contempt for those tainted by their ignoble acts of servility. The disappointment of the misunderstood, powerless in the face of the severity of the judges. The polemics, the bitterness.

You may have read that it was not about vengeance, but my impression is that is exactly what it was about. An imperious desire to stigmatize the traitors went hand in hand with a silence about the unbroken ones, which provoked equally toxic reactions.

The catalog of terminology for the defense was voluminous: acting in favor of or receiving support from the underground organizations, hiding or helping Jews, blackmail by the Occupiers, the need to support a family. Or else, something as ordinary and as simple as just following a friend, we were playing along, or supporting a friend.

After the war, the director Leon Schiller gave an exposé focused on the verification process in which he stated once again in very clear terms, succinctly and categorically, that infringing on the interdiction to play on stage constituted a serious offense, not only in relation to the Association of Polish Stage Artists but also to the people and the state.

There were different degrees of offense, according to the person who had committed it. Famous actors, important, who were well off and could not justify their actions by the need to earn a living, were not subjected to the same treatment as less prominent actors, poor and needy artists. Whether they performed several times was also part of the evaluation. Also treated differently were the people who had signed a lasting contract of collaboration.

They stressed the fact that the guilty had acted of their

own free will; the Occupiers had neither exerted pressure nor required anything. It was thus even more humiliating to find oneself charged with having acted "in the service of German propaganda in the domain of the theater."

Was this in fact collaboration or only not following the organizational discipline set by the authorities of the Association of Polish Stage Artists?

I wondered if during the period of the Occupation in everyday life, the artistic milieu was as divided as it would be later, after Liberation. The people of the Comet or the Melody—did they shake hands with the waiters in the popular cafés of the artistic milieu, and with those who were organizing underground performances of Polish classics? Did they look away when their paths crossed by chance in the street? An abyss seems to separate the revues *Ah, the Little Women, Under a Fig Leaf,* and *Oh, What Legs!* from *The Forefathers* by Adam Mickiewicz, *The Wedding* by Stanisław Wyspiański, Sophocles, or Juliusz Słowacki.

With time, the censorship of German propaganda became less severe. Encouraged to perform a repertory on the verge of pornography, theaters staged such Polish comedies as *Fanfan's Happiness, Madame Dulska's Morality, A Young Girl's Wish . . .*

The trivial repertory of the Comet, the Scala, the Boheme, the revues with their sixteen puns, spoonerisms, and plays on words like "raw prunes, stewed prunes" drew crowds very different from those attending underground evenings, the secret poetry readings, intimate and modest. The young went from house to house to recite "Alarm" by Antoni Słonimski or "Polish Flowers" by Julian Tuwim. Twenty to fifty people in an apartment, with a feeling of danger, an atmosphere of secrecy, of national ritual. Decidedly far removed from emotions evoked by farces in the manner of *Pierogis with Cabbage* or *Gouzi Gouzi,* performed in the autumn of 1943 when the streets were theaters of bloody executions. On the poster columns, next to notices listing in red type the names of those executed, were posters for the play at the Miniature Theater, *Let's Dip Our Feet.*

The performers who had participated in the artistic life under Soviet Occupation in the Eastern territories underwent verification without any harm. The subject of activism in the Soviet theater was not newsworthy at the time. Those performances did not carry any culpability. Juliusz Osterwa, when he performed in Wilno and Grodno, was not met with criticism, whereas his performances in Warsaw were protested. In 1944 Stanisława Perzanowska was condemned for having worked in the official theaters of Warsaw, but nothing was said about her being the acting director of the Wilno theater under Soviet Occupation. In the same way, no verification procedures were applied to the theater life of Lwów, authorized by the Soviet authorities. And the actors who performed Fredro or Zapolska were never placed on the index.

Bohdan Korzeniewski, director and co-founder of the Theater Council in the underground, severe and intransigent toward the Polish performers, refrained from ever judging the choices of artists behind the ghetto wall. Stefania Grodzieńska remembers that Jurandot had asked his advice, in front of witnesses, about opening the Femina Theater in the ghetto. To avoid eventual reprisals.

An alibi. One can always be found. And it is not always synonymous with moral transgression. All this would be so much easier if seen through the eyes of the theater.

What card would Vera have played on the Aryan side?

9

"In the above deposition,
I have told only the truth"

n the above deposition, I have told only the truth and nothing but the truth."

They repeated their own memories like magic formulas.

The above-mentioned: "I am ready to testify under oath."

"I have spoken the truth."

"I have told you everything I know."

They repeated this as if to justify their own fate.

The citizens' court of the Central Committee of Jews in Poland had studied the case of Vera Gran, accused of collaboration with the Gestapo, from December 1946 to January 1949. More than two years, nearly twenty-six months, had passed in sorting out the problem of her alleged cooperation with the Occupiers. About fifty witnesses were heard—close friends and strangers, artists, doctors, lawyers, waiters, a priest, a gardener, and a glazier—dozens of hearings, public and in closed sessions, to finally arrive at a verdict.

In Vera Gran's apartment I found hundreds of copies of this verdict. She always had them at hand. It was her weapon.

She was thirty years old when this psychodrama took place. She had lost everything: family, support, and illusions. Everything, or almost everything, had failed her, aside from her voice and a few friends in whom she had less and less faith.

Remembering, recalling, looking back was a torture, but one to which she had to submit. She would have done anything to prove her innocence. She wanted it. She believed in self-purification—she herself had to return to the past and bear witness for herself.

She had not been allowed to forget. Neither before nor after. Never.

At the time, she still did not know this.

I "hear" them—the depositions of the witnesses. They speak of events dating from only a few years earlier. Difficult not to remember. However, they somehow become completely confused in this not-so-distant past.

This is what happened, these are the facts, the variations repeated and transmitted as if by a game of "gossip." They bounce back as echoes, at once more distant and stronger. A new picture transforms the preceding ones. Echoes are echoed. Here are the witnesses with their own faults, who are, at the same time, the victims of past evils.

The complete citizens' court was composed of its president, the lawyer Aleksander Ołomucki; judges Szymon Rosenberg, Bernard Borg, Genia Lewi, Anatol Truskier; the clerk of the court, Karolina Ney; the prosecutor, Piotr Kowalski; and the lawyer for the defense, Antoni Landau. For a long time the court weighed and measured justice. That is to say, memory and truth. They pronounced the result of their research. But everything remained as before.

Nobody convinced anyone else, no one changed what was remembered by anyone. I don't know for whom it would have mattered, except for the accused.

Even more than fifty years later, this case leaves a bad aftertaste. It gets lost in meandering innuendos and insinuations.

I have the feeling of being caught, just like Vera, in this web of contradictory testimony.

I don't know what really happened in the ghetto between Vera and her principal detractors. I know the accusations and their repercussions. I know the numerous testimonies, narratives, and variations of a rumor. A world of accusations that take on greater amplitude with passing time, that inscribe increasingly larger circles.

Who were her accusers, and what proofs of Vera's "crime" did they possess? Weren't they themselves caught in the traps of the process of "survival"? To survive, but at what cost? Who has the right to judge the survivors?

I have the impression that it was in somebody's interest to keep alive and maintain hostile feelings toward her. It's as if someone wanted to hide something from his own past and throw on her the responsibility for his own wrongdoings. Turn away attention from his own base actions in the past.

These thoughts come from my knowledge of memory, not truth. Because in these situations that reach the limit, there is not only one truth. It is the sum of individual pictures.

What was it about? Her beauty, her temperament, her success? Or was it her aloof and independent side? About opportunity, influence, money?

What provoked this resentment that evolved into aggressiveness and eventually into desire to confront her with accusations that were more or less certain or illusory? What was the most difficult to bear for these people? Not the poor, obviously—they did not accuse her—and not her colleagues, the regular customers, the strangers.

Dozens of questions were asked. Difficult to classify them by order of importance. An overview, and a detailed view.

Did they see the same woman? Did they actually see Vera Gran? Vera the loving person? Vera Grynberg?

When she went out into the street, she wore the obligatory armband that marked each inhabitant of the ghetto. But she was seen parading around without it, violating the obligatory rules. She was seen wearing a fur coat, fur in the ghetto, a symbol of luxury, a special privilege, particularly after the German ordinance was put into effect during the winter of 1941 that all furs—coats, articles of clothing, and collars—be turned over. She kept a moth-eaten gabardine, she had "nothing presentable to wear." But one thing is certain: no one ever saw her wearing astrakhan or chinchilla. Even those who said in their testimony that she "consorted with the Gestapo agents" and that she frequented the Arizona, a suspect club in the Britania Hotel run by "the trash of the Jewish Gestapo." They said she also appeared on the Aryan side, when she never left the ghetto even once—except when she escaped definitively.

Did she have a double?

What was Vera Gran's reputation in the ghetto?

Dawid Sznajer, age forty-two, president of the Central Committee of Jews in Poland, branch in Otwock, glazier: "In the ghetto, it was said that Vera Gran was among the people working for the Gestapo . . .

"Even in 1941, I myself read in the underground press to beware of certain individuals—informers for the Gestapo. The name of Vera Gran was listed. I know that in 1942 she was sentenced to death by the Resistance."

Adolf Hoffman Zieliński, age thirty-six, worked for the underground organization of the Security Corps: "In 1941 I was informed that certain Jews in the Jewish quarter were collaborating with the Gestapo. I heard among others the names Kohn, Heller, Anders, Milek, Gancwajch, Szternfeld, Mirski. It was also said that these individuals spent time with the performers Franciszka Mann, Vera Gran, Szpetówna. I have personally seen several times Vera Gran frequenting different clubs in the Jewish quarter in the company of this type of individual.

Her behavior was very casual, which leads one to suppose that she entertained intimate relationships with these men from the Gestapo. On the whole, Vera Gran had a bad reputation; people thought she was dangerous and avoided her. However, I have never been brought any concrete evidence showing any harmful activity."

Gerard Gadejski, age forty-seven, performer, musician, living in Warsaw: "I have never heard anyone say that she behaved in a manner unworthy of a performer. She was never involved in any scandal or indecent incident."

Elżbieta Gadejska (Irena Neumark) worked within the ghetto walls with Jonas Turkow as an employee in the office of the concert agency: "Vera Gran had an irreproachable reputation. She was involved in charity work. She gave the impression of being someone poised and very discreet."

Zygmunt Jankowski (appears in the records also under the name of Maciej Czarnecki), age fifty-six, co-proprietor of the Café Sztuka, worked in the ghetto in the capacity of director of fuel distribution, in Umschlagplatz: "Whoever would say that Vera Gran collaborated with the Gestapo is a liar and a slanderer. We knew very well what was going on. We had been warned to beware of Franciszka Mann, of Szternfeld, of Lipski. Lipski became a Gestapo agent at the beginning of the liquidation of the ghetto. We could not throw anyone suspicious out of the café. The Wentland sisters had a terrible reputation, and they also frequented the Sztuka.

"Vera Gran had no relationship with people who were suspect, neither with the Germans nor with the Thirteen. In the ghetto people did not have a bad opinion of her, and everyone found her socially acceptable. I never heard anyone say that you had to beware of her."

Leon Piotrowski (known under the pseudonym of Henryk Fuks), age fifty-five, Warsaw: "I have known Vera Gran for about ten years, only as a singer up until the war, but in the ghetto I also saw her socially. I have nothing to say against her behavior. All these suspicions are without basis in fact."

Wiktoria Cukierman and *Irena Rechtszaft,* waitresses at the Café Sztuka, living in Katowice: "We saw her every day. We can attest to the fact that she was never in contact with individuals suspected of collaboration; we knew those people by sight and by name.

"Vera Gran's behavior inspired respect and sympathy as much from the clientele of the Café Sztuka as from the staff. We know from her bosses, the co-owners of the Sztuka, that her behavior was irreproachable and that she lived modestly."

Krystyna Żywulska, age thirty-three, author of the book *I Survived Auschwitz:* "People talked about a group called the Thirteen and listed a whole series of names, which was repeated endlessly. However, the name of Vera Gran was never mentioned as suspect. I am particularly sensitive to the various degrees of collaboration. As a consequence, if I had heard anything ambiguous about Vera Gran's behavior, I would never keep it from the court."

Izabela Czajka Stachowicz (Gelbard, born Szwarc), writer, Katowice: "I knew Vera Gran before the war; I met her often in the ghetto. In my capacity as director of the Udziałowa Café (the Participant), 16 Sienna Street, I hired her sometimes for shows. I have always felt confidence in her, a great sympathy and gratitude for having made easier those terrible years in an inhumane period.

"She did not disappoint me. All this business and these so-called insinuations are, in my opinion, just hearsay, rumors made from whole cloth. I never saw her with a German. The people suspected of collaboration, we knew very well who they were, just like people who were under suspicion (even if there was no concrete information). She never belonged to any of these categories."

Jerzy Jurandot, age thirty-seven, author: "I often came across

Vera Gran because she was active in the artistic life of the ghetto, and I never heard a word said defaming her in this milieu.

"I state categorically that Vera Gran did not collaborate with the Gestapo."

Romana Wajnkranc, age thirty-five, co-proprietor of the Sztuka: "In the ghetto her friends were the most respectable people. I was constantly in the room, I was there every day, and I never saw Vera Gran in the company of suspect people. We closed the café at around eight or nine o'clock in the evening. Vera Gran was on good terms with everyone associated with the Sztuka; we used the familiar form of address among all of us. I know that she was friends with the baker Blajman, a well-loved person in the ghetto, and his wife. They wouldn't have come near her if they had the least suspicion."

Aleksander Jasielski, age fifty-seven, member of a cooperative, head waiter of the Café Sztuka until the summer of 1942, then a waiter in the clubs of the ghetto, lives in Warsaw: "I have known Vera Gran since 1930. For a short while she sang in the Capitol Cinema, which I owned. Then I saw her again at the Sztuka from the beginning. As a co-proprietor, I took on all the functions of the head waiter. I knew all the regulars at the club.

"I can formally affirm that during this period, Vera Gran was a regular in the place and participated in evenings in the company of Gestapo agents: Szymonowicz, Mann, Fürstenberg, Mirecki, the Czapliński brothers . . . I saw them drinking together. And then there was this celebration in the apartment of the Jewish Gestapo agent Szymonowicz.

"As a server, I brought him the dishes he ordered. After quitting my job at the Sztuka, I saw Vera Gran again twice in the company of these Jewish Gestapo agents, in the garden near Ogrodowa Street on the corner of Żelazna Street and at the Melody Palace. I have never heard it said that she was [otherwise] personally associated with the Gestapo."

Władysław Szpilman, age thirty-seven, pianist: "I have not heard anything bad said about her."

Who frequented the Sztuka?

Romana Wajnkranc: "Nearly every day at the Sztuka were people you could qualify as dangerous, people from the Thirteen and others suspected of collaboration with the Gestapo. I know the names: Gancwajch, Fürstenberg, Kanel, the three Wentland sisters, Hendel, Kohn, Heller. I was also told to be on guard against others whose names I did not know. The rest of the audience kept away from them. In the café there was a platform, a stage with a piano where the performers appeared. The suspect types I mentioned played at being the lords, they demanded faster service and all sorts of privileges. I have to admit that with the enormous tabs they ran up, they were the basis of our existence."

How do you explain that Vera Gran sang at Szymonowicz's home?

Kazimierz Jezierski: "It is impossible that during the Occupation my wife ever went to sing at the apartment of a Gestapo agent."

Elżbieta Gadejska (Irena Neumark): "Perhaps she was afraid of the consequences and she agreed to make only one appearance. Everyone trembled before Szymonowicz. She told me that this performance was a nightmare."

Romana Wajnkranc: "Knowing the relationship between people in the ghetto, I can state that not obeying an order, or refusing to appear in the home of a Jewish Gestapo agent when requested, could put the person in question in danger."

Zygmunt Jankowski: "Refusing was to expose oneself to potential reprisal."

What does the witness know about Vera Gran's collaboration with the Gestapo?

Piotr Piotrowski, age forty-seven: "I know about Vera Gran's case since she came to me in my capacity of president of the Musicians' Union. I was in the Resistance. I had detailed information on all the performers inside the ghetto and outside. On Vera Gran I had only favorable reports. After the war, I was no longer involved with these cases, I did not participate in the commission for verification."

Józef Jamiołkowski, proprietor of the Paradis Café, Warsaw, since 1946: "During the Occupation, especially toward the end, people said that Vera Gran was to be avoided. Her name was linked with that of Franciszka Mann, known to be working for the Gestapo.

"In the ghetto, I managed a card-playing club for a certain time. On the other side my material situation was very difficult. I received help from people who had been my colleagues— some Aryans. I changed apartments several times. Someone suggested that I find a safe hiding place through Vera Gran. I spoke to my people. Their reaction was immediate: I was forbidden to contact Vera Gran because she was working for the Gestapo."

Władysław Szpilman: "After Liberation, at the end of March, Vera Gran came to see me after a broadcast—she told me that there were rumors about her insinuating that she had worked for the Gestapo. She told me about her visit to the Ministry of Public Security and that she had been set free and declared innocent. Several days later I met Turkow and Colonel Alef. It was in 1945. Both told me that they were looking for Vera Gran. She was arrested two weeks later.

"After the Liberation, people said that Vera Gran was alive but she did not show herself, certainly because she had collaborated with the Gestapo. But she came to see me and I told her that she would do well to pass through the verification process. Miss Bochenek of the National Bank told me in no uncertain terms that if I hired Vera Gran for a broadcast, they would never want to shake hands with me again.

"My colleague Zeimer said that Colonel Alef told him that he would put a bullet through the head of Vera Gran because she worked for the Gestapo. In Poznań, speaking with Wejman about performers, he also told me that Vera Gran had worked for the Gestapo."

Mrs. Piękniewska told the story that when she was taken in for questioning in December 1942, in the Gestapo prison on Szuch Avenue,* she had seen in the next room Vera Gran accusing a Jew as a conspirator.

Colonel Alef (Gustaw Alef Bolkowiak), former chief of the People's Guard in the Warsaw Ghetto: "Personally, I would not have shaken the hand of Vera Gran."

Helena Zakrzewska, age thirty, Warsaw: "Within the framework of the Jewish Combat Organization, I was a liaison agent for Dr. Płockier on the Aryan side. In the spring of 1943, just before the uprising in the ghetto broke out, Dr. Płockier sent me on a mission; I do not remember now if it was to observe an act of execution or simply to keep watch in a café on Ujazdowskie Avenue. A certain Skosowski, 'Lolek,' a notorious informer for the Gestapo, was there in the company of Vera Gran and another individual. The observation or carrying out applied to all three. Now I cannot say for certain if it was about executing the sentence or just observing these three individuals. I remember that time was of the essence—'before it was too late.' Vera Gran was suspected of denouncing Jews on the Aryan side."

Irena Twardak: "Nothing of what I know about Vera Gran

---

*At 25 Jan Chrystian Szuch Avenue in Warsaw were located the offices of the information services of the SS during the German Occupation and the Gestapo prison.

during the German Occupation is based on solid facts. I heard the rumors circulating in Warsaw insinuating that she was working for the Gestapo. Some people said it loud and clear during the summer of 1943 when I was in the Polski Hotel on Długa Street. None of the people who gathered there are still alive, and it would contribute nothing to the case to reveal their names. If you believe that accusing someone of collaboration with the Occupiers cannot be based on rumors, I believe that I should not be heard as a witness. On the other hand, and I speak from experience, this sort of rumor is never completely unfounded."

Krystyna Żywulska: "I am the vice-president of the Superior Council of the Polish Association of Former Political Prisoners. On the Aryan side I worked with the Polish Workers' Party, and I had access to the list of names of people suspected of collaboration with the Gestapo or else condemned to death by underground organizations. There were among them actors and Aryans and Jews.

"I never came across the name of Vera Gran, but, by contrast, Franciszka Mann was on the list. Very often I saw distributed underground newspapers or mimeographed sheets with lists of suspected individuals, but the name of Vera Gran was not among them."

Gerard Gadejski: "Jonas Turkow reminded me during the liquidation of the ghetto of the rumors concerning Vera Gran's relationships. He underlined the fact that the rumors were not verified and that one had to be careful, knowing that in this atmosphere of terror, it was impossible to verify the information circulating. On the other hand, he had no reservations about Vera Gran's behavior in the ghetto.

"Our Commission for Verification at the Musicians' Union had studied the charges against Vera Gran, and no suspicion could be confirmed. I know that Vera Gran has many fine qualities; I think that these rumors came out of her personal relations because of her difficult temperament—vain and somewhat arrogant."

Jerzy Lewiński, public prosecutor, Łódź: "After the liquidation of the ghetto, I learned from people in the underground milieus with whom I remained in contact that apparently Vera Gran was an informer on the Aryan side. During this period a great deal of information of this sort circulated, in part verified beyond doubt by the underground information service. The collaborators were the actress Mann, Skosowski, Próżański, and others.

"After Liberation, Vera Gran came to me seeking my advice.

"I had difficulty understanding what would lead a person rather well off, who had no contact with the Germans, to propose her services to the Gestapo. I answered her that she had to ask for a complete and detailed investigation. The result of this investigation would serve as the reliable basis, and nobody would pay attention to rumors if the court declared her innocent."

Maria Piękniewska, née Grochowska, age thirty-four, married, worked since 1939 as a nurse with the Polish Red Cross in an underground organization, living in the ghetto until January 20, 1943: "In the summer of 1943, right after Corpus Christi, I was arrested during the night under the accusation that I was Jewish. That night they brought me to the Gestapo headquarters on Szuch Avenue. They told me to wait in a room until someone came to confirm my origins. I remained there for several hours. At the beginning the neighboring room was empty. I was about three and a half yards from the door, which had been left slightly ajar. In the morning two Germans and a woman entered that room. I remember that they asked her something in German, she answered in Polish. She gave the name of a Jew and his address.

"My interrogation lasted a long time; I denied everything. They let me leave because I was breast-feeding, they just kept my papers. Early in the morning I found myself in the courtyard. A man from the Gestapo pointed out a woman standing in the distance and told me that it was the woman who had made a deposition in the neighboring room: the famous singer Vera Gran. He said, 'She collaborates with us, she turns in Jews, and she remains free.'

"I did not doubt the words of a Gestapo agent. I immediately made a report, which was recorded and transferred to the unit in charge of surveillance of performers.

"I again had a conversation about Vera Gran on January 17, 1945, in Pruszków. The performer Turkow asked me how much truth there was in the allegation that Gran had collaborated with the Gestapo, because he suspected her of denouncing his wife, Diana Blumenfeld. I think that at the time Turkow still did not know the fate of his wife and daughter.

Note: In 1932 he married the singer and actress Diane Blumenfeld. In 1933 they had a daughter, Margarite. Both survived the war.

"In 1948 I received a visit from Szpilman, to whom I repeated what I had reported about Vera Gran. My advice was that she should not be broadcast over Polish Radio. He asked me if I believed that she had collaborated with the Gestapo. I answered him that in my opinion it was the truth, since I saw her with my own eyes in the building on Szuch Avenue."

Vera Gran did not own a striped dress, in which she was seen by a witness named Jabłońska. After her departure from the ghetto, Vera's appearance had changed so much, it was difficult to recognize her. She had blond hair and wore glasses. And according to another source, "hair that was almost red, curls on top of her head, and light eyebrows and lashes."

What was Vera Gran's behavior in Babice?

Gerard Gadejski: "When patients arrived, Vera hid in an armoire because she wasn't declared as a resident. I had warned her to come out only at dusk."

Jan Machnikowski, parish priest, Babice: "I've known the citizen Jezierska since she moved to Babice in September 1942. I understood that she had to hide, because she didn't often go out of Babice.

"Judging from my relationship with them, I concluded that they were very honest people. I have never seen anyone suspicious at their home."

Stefania Pruszyńska, age sixty-one, nurse, residing in Babice: "She took care of her home and made the appointments with the patients. The first year of her stay, she never left Babice."

Kazimierz Jezierski: "The political situation required a normal way of life. To make a good appearance. My wife was anguished. And (it was my idea) I followed her with a hammer, just in case, to 'neutralize' any eventual blackmailer. When I say that my wife was anguished, I am thinking of her inner state: she behaved like someone whose life was hanging in the balance. My wife went very rarely to Warsaw, until suddenly it became necessary."

Janina Mainke, age twenty-three, neighbor in Babice: "She very rarely came out of her home. She did not run errands, she made friends with no one, and showed a great piety. All this made me think that Vera Gran was hiding. For almost a year she did not go to Warsaw. When she did go it was because of her pregnancy."

Did Vera Gran associate with Franciszka Mann after leaving the ghetto?

Kazimierz Jezierski: "I have never heard it said that Vera Gran was associated with Mann."

Stefan Kisiel, Warsaw: "I came across Vera Gran during the Occupation in 1941. I heard it said that she was a friend of Franciszka Mann and that she had maintained this relationship until November 1942. Citizen Lidia Perec was with me at that time, and she told me that she had seen Mann seated at the same table as Vera Gran in a restaurant on Złota Street near the Palladium Cinema. Perec had heard about what Mann was up to and preferred avoiding any danger, so she left the place. The two women were relaxed, they did not seem worried or anxious, which was the usual attitude of all the Jews at this time."

Józef Jamiołkowski: "Her name is linked with that of Mann and also that of Mirecki, a friend of the latter. It seems that on Napoléon Square at Baudouin and Zgoda Streets there was a café where they all went. Gran knew Mirecki from the time they lived in Lwów."

Romana Lilian, singer, Warsaw: "I remember, it was toward the end of the year 1942, I met the violinist Henryk Rajngold in Warsaw on Marszałkowska Street. He warned me to beware of the dancer Franciszka Mann and the singer Vera Gran. He said they hung around most often in the main post office on Napoléon Square. As Gran had a bad reputation in the ghetto, the words of my friend Rajngold did not surprise me."

Tadeusz Płucer Sarna, age sixty-nine, former proprietor of a boarding house, Śródborowianka, retired: "One Sunday between February and September 1943, my daughter went to Warsaw with her husband. On her return she told me that she had seen Vera Gran with Mann in the street. Both or one of them wore a leather jacket and leather shoes. My daughter hid in a doorway so as not to be seen."

Has the witness seen Vera Gran in a carriage on the Aryan side?

Józef Jamiołkowski: "When he was asked if he had seen Vera Gran during the Occupation, one of my colleagues from the Paradis Café stated that his friend the actor Ścisławski had told him he had seen Vera Gran riding in a carriage with a man from the Gestapo."

Stefan Kisiel: "In the first months of 1943, a Jewish police-man, Józef Szapiro, came to my hiding place in Saska Kępa in Warsaw. His wife was also hiding there. He told me several times that he had seen Vera Gran riding in a carriage without any care in broad daylight on Nowy Świat Avenue. He was wondering how it was possible that a famous Jewish woman who looked Semitic could allow herself such a thing at times like these. My wife, Irena, heard the same statements."

Aleksander Jasielski: "I have never heard that she was riding in a carriage in broad daylight on the Aryan side."

Adolf Hoffman Zieliński: "In 1943 I saw Vera Gran once in a carriage on the Aryan side with Kohn in the direction of Jasna Street."

Emilia Mazur, Warsaw: "I saw Vera Gran in 1943 in the streetcar going from Babice to Warsaw, dressed with an inso-lent elegance—all eyes were on her."

During her trial, which lasted two years, Vera Gran was inter-rogated more than ten times.

She made categorical statements:

Within the walls of the ghetto, she had never seen Fran-ciszka Mann anywhere other than Hirszfeld's Café, 16 Rymar-ska Street, and at the Femina Theater, 35 Leszno Street.

She had never been to the Britania Hotel.

She had never sat down at a table with Kohn or Gancwajch at the Café Sztuka.

After leaving the ghetto, she had never ridden in a carriage in broad daylight in Warsaw, she never went to cafés on the Aryan side. She never went riding in a carriage with Kohn.

With her friend the pianist Goldfeder, she had received dona-tions for charities from Heller and Kohn. She and Goldfeder knew that they were Gestapo agents. They believed that they should get as much as possible from people like them. And now that the war had ended, she believed that it was appropriate to ask a Gestapo agent to buy a ticket for a fund-raising concert.

Never at the Sztuka, nor in any other club, was she in the company of Mandel, Czapliński, Gancwajch; Mirski, the friend of Mann; Rosenberg, the husband of Mann and officer of the Thirteen; Szymonowicz; or any other person who was a suspect, like the collaborators of the Thirteen, officers of the security office, or people known to be agents of the Gestapo.

Lipski was a colleague at work, but during the time when they performed at the Sztuka he was not a member of the Gestapo.

She had never performed in private apartments. Once she sang at Szymonowicz's place. She knew what was required of her. It was for a family celebration, perhaps a wedding; she sang for five hundred zlotys from five o'clock to seven in the evening.

She did not know Lolek Skosowski at all.

She had never heard anyone speak about a café that was located on Ujazdowskie Avenue, and she had never been there.

During the period when it was forbidden to wear furs, she never wore any. She had always worn the obligatory armband.

Antoni Landau, the lawyer for the accused, put in evidence a gift to Vera Gran by the wife of Czerniakow, president of the Judenrat, in gratitude for her social work. A silver compact on which was inscribed: *To Vera Gran—The Children of the Streets Shelter in Section III of the Service for Maintaining Order— January 1942.*

Heading: VERDICT [underlined]

The People's Court of the Central Committee of Jews in Poland, composed of. . .

After examining the dossier of Vera Gran, accused of having maintained relationships with notorious persons known for having been agents of the Gestapo during the German Occupation between 1941 and August 1942 inside the Warsaw Ghetto, and from August 1942 on the side called "Aryan":

Certify [underlined, in spaced type]

—*that proof for the allegations held against Vera Gran has not been provided and in consequence, we have come to the decision to reject the charges brought against her and pronounce her acquitted.*

Followed by the signatures.
Certified copy. Secretary of the Court.

10

She never called him "my pianist"

She never called him "my pianist"; yet she spoke often about him.

He never called her "my singer."

He never said anything about her in public.

Władysław Szpilman's statements in the trial of Vera Gran never left the courtroom. His memoir of the Occupation, titled *Death of a City,* was published in the fall of 1946. He does not mention her name once.

The idea for the book was born right after Liberation, in a cramped apartment on Targowa Street where the first station of Polish Radio was installed after the war. That's where writer and critic Jerzy Waldorff found Szpilman again for the first time since 1939. He didn't know how he had survived. They had even camped out for a certain time under a grand piano. Szpilman played and told his story. Waldorff saw in this fascinating narrative, as he used to say, "a slice of the German guilt that was so many-sided" and "all kinds of suffering inflicted by the Germans on the oppressed people."

Fragments of these memoirs were published in the cultural weekly *Przekrój* during the summer of 1946—Jerzy Waldorff's "Memoirs of Szpilman." The book came out a few months later. It was one of the first personal accounts of the sort relating the difficulties of survival for a Jewish family in occupied Warsaw. The book was both a trump card and a responsibility.

Władysław Szpilman was the only surviving member of his family. More than half a century later, Roman Polański made his life story into a cinematic symbol. But even Polański, who had lived through a similar experience, was not capable of explaining where the instinct for survival came from, and how it manifested itself. What saves a condemned man in an impossible situation? What is this mysterious gene of survival that helped a person in these wartime circumstances not to perish? Not to be killed when others are killed? To go to Umschlagplatz with the others and not be taken away in the wagons, to play the piano to survive?

What does one do? How do you find yourself in the right place, neither too far nor too near, but just within reach of the rescuer? And how to react when a brother, a sister, a mother, and a father leave on the path to death? How then do you give yourself permission to live? And then what? Wander among strangers, die of hunger, reach your limits, and again fall upon someone who will feed you and give you his coat. How do you do that? And is it only a matter of chance?

How to manage the feeling of guilt? Or the feeling of defeat? The ties that bind at those moments are perhaps impossible to loosen.

The film adaptation by Czesław Miłosz and Jerzy Andrzejewski of Szpilman's memoirs, *A Robinson Crusoe of Warsaw,* mutilated by the censors, was never finished. When the authorized version, *The Untamed City,* was released, Miłosz withdrew his name from the project in protest.

The Pianist, a version of the memoirs listing Władysław Szpilman as the sole author, was published in Germany in 1998. It quickly became a worldwide best seller. It was translated into a dozen languages. In Poland it was published in 2000.

Jerzy Waldorff, whose name was removed from the title page and whose role in the drafting of these memoirs was ignored, published in 2000 an article in the daily *Warsaw Life* accusing Szpilman of being an impostor, a plagiarist, and a thief. Szpilman's son, Andrzej, author of the "new version" of the memoirs, offered a certain amount of money to Waldorff and convinced him to renounce all claims concerning this work. Władysław Szpilman died in July 2000. Three years later, Polański's film *The Pianist* won three Academy Awards in Hollywood—for best adapted screenplay, Ronald Harwood; for best director, Roman Polański; and for best actor, Adrien Brody.

The Warsaw Ghetto is the central setting of the story of this pianist during the Occupation. The author describes the paralyzing feeling of being closed in, all the more cruel as it has the taste and semblance of freedom. Even in his dreams, his Polish friends appear to him wearing armbands, as if it were a clothing accessory as elementary as a necktie. The omnipresent lice invade everything, including bread and money. Sometimes he would stumble over corpses lying in the streets. He remembered the sound of twenty-dollar gold pieces that traffickers were counting and which drowned out the sound of the piano when he was playing at the Café Modern on Nowolipki Street.

He devotes many pages to the Café Sztuka, which he calls *the largest club in the ghetto, with big ambitions*. He praises the talent of the singer Marysia Ajzensztadt, saying that she could have been famous had she survived. He mentions his colleague, the pianist Goldfeder, and all those who participated in the "Spoken News"—the satiric chronicle of the goings-on in the ghetto, a feature of the stage on Leszno Street. He even mentions that he *achieved a real success with his song based on the*

The pianist Władysław Szpilman at the Polish Radio recording studio in Warsaw, August 1946

waltz from the opera Casanova *by Ludomir Różycki, with lyrics by Władysław Szlengel.*

Not a word about Vera Gran, nor the fact that he had arranged this song, "Her First Ball," especially for her in the ghetto.

Natan Gross wrote in 2002 after the international success of the book and the film *The Pianist:*

In this documentary narrative the name of the major star of the Sztuka is missing—Vera Gran. I was indignant. Not only because Szpilman was the regular accompanist of this popular singer, but also because he gave himself sole credit for the enormous success of this piece written by Szlengel for Vera Gran. Without Vera Gran's interpretation on stage of "Her First Ball," Vera's showpiece, neither the text by Szlengel nor the musical arrangement by Szpilman would even have been noticed.

Szpilman eliminated Vera from his book. He had banished her, expunged her from his life. He had excised her from his story as if their paths had never crossed.

I cannot pretend that this did not occur. Especially in the situations where his words could have saved her reputation.

In the public arena he simply ignored her. He was silent to the point of killing her.

Was this a way of protesting? Keeping his distance with regard to the accusations weighing against her? Was he denying the existence of their performance together to avoid falling into the dirty quagmire of accusations? What dictates such a decision—prudence, foresight, fear? What makes one turn away from friends with whom one shared the experience of a time of tribulation?

The mud slung at her—could it have splattered on him? By chance or for specific reasons? Perhaps his survival also came at a price? Perhaps she knew? Was he afraid of her faults or his own? What did he fear? What accusations? What consequences?

The interrogations were carried out between 1946 and 1948, and the case was causing a sensation. I am trying to understand: perhaps he did not want to be identified with her. In his book he does not mention the name of Józef Lipski, who also performed at the Sztuka and who was accused of collaborating with the Gestapo. Apparently he did not want even the slightest possibility of a connection being made, that the slightest link, even tenuous, might be considered.

Why? Because Vera was accused? Because he was jealous of her success, of her talent, of the interest she aroused? Did he want to discredit her? Deprive her of something—but of what?

The ghetto was the past; now he had things in hand, and in any case, he had influence.

For several months, over a year, they saw one another every day in the ghetto. They worked together. They rehearsed, they gave performances. They performed and received applause. They ate, they were afraid, they sweated together. In any case, that's what you'd think. They had to agree on the movements, the measures, the refrains; they certainly had to talk about the latest regulations, the movements of troops at the front, their repercussions in the ghetto, signs of what would, must, or could happen. Did they mutually ask each other for advice? What to do, escape or remain?; if yes, then how? In the face of danger in such a situation, you must have conversations, ask yourself questions, hold each other's hands, cross your fingers . . . Exile, deportation, hunger for bread (not so extreme for them), the desire to stay with the family but also to escape, to go some-where, toward the unknown, to work. Would they need per-formers over there? What is it like to be afraid together, side by side, when one is so young—a man and a woman? No one has ever suggested that they ever entertained a relationship that was other than professional. Sometimes I wonder if this mutual hatred in its final guise doesn't exactly prove it.

They were so close in the most difficult of times. What hap-pened? And when? Who hurt whom? Who knew too much, or knew something he or she shouldn't have known?

And after the war? Would it have been easy for me to learn, like that, of the accusations brought against someone I was close to for a long time, and I knew what that person was capa-ble of? He knew her in the ghetto, backstage at the Sztuka, during rehearsals or during time spent together after perfor-mances, when the audience was gone and they were resting after performing and slowly recovering, preparing themselves to go out again in the sinister darkness . . . Szpilman, did he make use of what he knew about her?

Why did he believe the rumors rather than his friend from the stage with whom he had shared such difficult times? As for me, whom would I have believed? Is an accusation enough to refuse to help a survivor? And why had he preferred to refuse? Perhaps his conscience dictated his actions? And I, would I have given work to Vera after the war?

What happened between Vera and Szpilman in the ghetto during the months they worked together and lived side by side? How did the Café Sztuka change as the bad news kept coming? How did the jests become tiresome, and the usual acts just routine, and the bravos die out?

Is it possible that Szpilman took on the cap of Jewish policeman in the summer of 1942? If yes, then why? Out of apprehension, foresight, fear? Was he a member of the police, or a volunteer? And if that is the case, I have no proof whatsoever. Did this occur before the deportation of his family, or after? Did he believe that life could be bought, or only the feeling of security? And for how long? How did people envisage this at that time? How does one think when living the inconceivable? The experience not yet lived of an approaching annihilation?

Integrated into the ranks of the police, gaining access to places that could offer a chance of survival, for a little longer. It wasn't impossible, historians say. Therefore, possible. Possible that the one who joined the police is the same person who saved someone from transport to death.

In his memoirs, Szpilman calls the Jewish policemen "thugs," contaminated by the spirit of the Gestapo. He shared the opinion of his brother, Henryk, who, even before the great raid, refused to join the police. *As soon as the uniform was put on, the police cap was on the head, and the truncheon was in hand, they became vile.*

In the historical landscape after the Occupation, special principles were in force. Accusing others was like an instinct to survive. Settling accounts was the daily occurrence of a tally that was anything but heroic. People counted the betrayals more than the real acts of the struggle. They accused more easily than they exonerated.

The idea of justice was understood in a particular way, difficult to explain.

I have trouble understanding, yet I should understand, this ease in making accusations in the postwar period. Settle scores, verify facts, let them explain themselves. The retribution of justice. The accounting of faults included those presumed. The detailed account of sins. The numerous trials of traitors, of collaborators of all sorts, not all opportune or won.

At the end of his life Szpilman told how after the war Vera Gran had come to him to Targowa Street, to the canteen of the Polish Radio station, to ask him to give her work. He refused, because Turkow had told him earlier that she had collaborated with the Gestapo. "He knew and I didn't? How did he know?"

"It appears that" . . . "it was said"—those who know, thus those who survived, are the ones who use those expressions. It was easier to say in 1945 that someone had collaborated than to do so later.

Szpilman's book reveals new aspects not only of the past but also about memory and responsibility for words spoken. For truths enunciated. For what makes life at the time it happens. It is not possible to unsay with a simple gesture years later. It is not possible? It turns out that it is simpler than I had believed.

Did Szpilman feel himself demeaned? He had to accompany her, play for her, or only next to her. She was the star, and he only accompanied her. In his mind he had the impression of playing a secondary role—the accompanist of a star. Was he forced to do it? Who originally made this arrangement between them? Who was more important? Who felt more important?

Professional rivalry is an essential point of view to decipher these two fates. Professional jealousy? But, after all, he arranged melodies for her. It means that he felt esteem for her as an interpreter of his own musical ideas. Or did he have no choice? There was no other singer at the Sztuka.

Competition. The need to be the better one, more important on stage.

Szpilman considered himself a great artist before the war. That is what witnesses say. Vera was also a star. Some say that Leon Boruński was a better accompanist than Szpilman. Vera had an influential position; she could find work for Szpilman in the ghetto. After the war, it was Szpilman who ruled as master at the radio station. As the musical director, he could dictate his own terms. That is what he did.

It's important to understand the milieu in which they lived, this specific microcosm, full of fireworks and artistic illuminations, imbroglios, jealousies, rivalries . . . Perhaps there wasn't room for two stars? All the same, it seems they had to work together, complement one another; one couldn't go on without the other. And yet, even when he speaks of his successes in the ghetto, like "Her First Ball," the composer doesn't mention the name of its first interpreter.

Or perhaps it is about feeling disappointed? Someone said that they heard said, it seemed . . . But can this resentment be inherited, passed on from one generation to another? Andrzej Szpilman behaves as if his father had a secret that can't be revealed. Dark, fearsome. Do not touch it, or else it will be disclosed. Every person potentially able to discover it, Andrzej Szpilman considers a threat.

I can imagine another scenario. Each person knew something about the other, considered incriminating in the postwar context. He had attacked first out of fear of being attacked himself. He found the means of neutralizing a potentially embarrassing informer more quickly, someone who knew something and could make use of it. And Vera, as she herself claimed, knew too much.

Vera Gran ended up telling a few scenes from Szpilman's life in the ghetto. She never showed any signs of good will toward him.

Not when she told how he had come to her, poor and humble, asking to be hired ("brazen and pretentious—all the same, I recognized his talent as an accompanist"); nor when she told how she had the crazy notion of creating a piano duo at the Sztuka, an idea that he had opposed ("egoistic, rapacious, envious, he wanted to play the first violin"—sic!); nor when she made fun of his mania for Yardley brilliantine, which seemed to her a decadent whim, considering the conditions of life in the ghetto ("only this grease could put some order in his hair").

She tried to minimize what he said about the magnificent assortment of alcoholic drinks in the Sztuka, the sums raked in thanks to the number of customers who came to see the shows. She cooled the fiery outbursts of the virtuoso pianist. She made fun of him because he could not get used to the idea that he was not playing in the most elegant club in the ghetto ("a megalomaniac, he could never have played elsewhere!"). She minimized the size of the café but not its importance. He preferred to see it as immense.

She did value his arrangements and other songs.

She described several times her meeting with the two Szpilman brothers at the café's bar. She did not spare the details. She mocked what the pianist remembered in order to construct his legend—the abundance of spirits in the bar, the succulent côtelettes de volaille or boeuf à la Stroganoff.

Corrections of memory:

"I was seated facing him. Henryk came to see his brother at the bar where Szpilman took his meals—like the rich. You could have anything with money. Szpilman profited from everything. The most tasty coffees with the richest whipped cream. And here he was eating his ice cream with an enormous quantity of whipped cream. His brother said to him: 'I'm hungry.' He didn't move, did not look in his direction. He didn't turn his head. Not the least embarrassment."

A subsequent variant:

"He was getting ready to devour a cake topped with a thick layer of whipped cream when a yellow skeleton, famished, came up to the table. Szpilman did not stop eating, pretending not to hear anything when his brother let out in a breath: 'I'm hungry.' The poor man stood for interminable minutes while the maestro finished eating . . . He left without a word. He never came back."

How much credit can be given this narrative? Is it possible to treat a hungry person this way? A member of one's own family? Even a stranger?

Words create events, they give them a more lasting consistency and are more telling than what really happened at the time. There is no ghetto now; there is no spring or autumn day when the famished brother of the pianist comes asking for help; none of the participants exist anymore, no witnesses; only the words remain. And the images they help to create.

Painful words. Destructive, like a blow to the face, like an insult. Can you believe them or not?

And what meaning do they have years later?

Władysław Szpilman always refused to speak about Vera Gran. He said that they had been part of two worlds that had nothing in common. He downplayed her career before the war: "She sang hiding behind a pillar for a Jewish audience. And her background didn't help."

He scoffed at the idea that it was she who had hired him at the Sztuka in the ghetto. *Stupidity! She was a manicurist. And I, I was writing melodies that were popular!*

He stressed the fact that he did not consider her his equal, neither in music nor socially.

It did not sit well with him that she *had played the star* in the ghetto. *The waitresses spoke to me about it. She wanted to repaint her dressing room in red. In those days, in such times.*

He kept his distance from her, but he continued repeating that he had nothing against her. *I did not accuse her.* At over eighty years old, he swore that he told the truth.

Szpilman "triumphed." I wonder why I put this verb in quotes. He won neither a contest nor a race, but it seems at times that the survivors played among themselves a perfidious game. The game of memories—cast as memoirs, put up for auction, pieced together, dreamed or transformed. No lies in these games. But an omnipresent fiction. Without proof from any side.

His version of events has won the world for him. I am not capable of confirming that it is true. It was his own. Vera was cut out of this picture, taken out of the frame, like an enemy of the people from Soviet photographs. Excluded from the reality of which she was a part.

Note: Transcriptions of general information taken from interviews with Władysław Szpilman can be found in the archives of the Polish Information Services. Taking into account his numerous travels abroad, he had aroused the interest of the Secret Service, especially in the second half of the 1950s, when he was giving concerts with the Warsaw Quintet and had renewed contact with the prewar violinist Bronisław Gimpel.

Gimpel had a pivotal role in a large investigation into the musical milieu of Polish Radio.

Excerpts from the "operational interview" of November 20, 1969 (summation by the inspector of the Second Division of the Ministry of the Interior):

Evoking with indignation the collaborators with the Gestapo and the Jewish policemen, [Szpilman] mentioned the Thirteen and added that he was informed about those implicated in the Jewish police: Nowogródzki, Jerzy Lewiński of Warsaw, Gombiński, residing in France, Zajdenbojtel, also known as Kruszewski, Vera Gran, living in France, and others.

This information is repeated several times in the records of this case.

The lawyers from before the war, Henryk Nowogródzki, Jerzy Lewiński, and Stanisław Gombiński, had in fact worked for the Jewish police in the Warsaw Ghetto.

After Liberation, Szpilman drew up a report on the subject of the police officer Lewiński. According to his statement, he had contributed to the expulsion of this person from the office of the prosecutor. He recognized the policeman Zajdenbojtel (Kruszewski) in 1945 in the street and was responsible for his arrest (which lasted a short time).

Why was he saying all this? It's as if he wanted to deflect attention and place the responsibility on others.

The following excerpt:

When Szpilman was working at the Polish Radio, Vera Gran had come looking for support and work, which he was not able to offer her because he knew that she had collaborated with the Gestapo in the Warsaw Ghetto.

What was his motive with this statement made to an officer of the Secret Service? Did Szpilman know something that he had not revealed in the trial at the end of the 1940s? He was threatened with being forbidden to travel abroad if he did not agree to cooperate with the Secret Service. What was the use of offering up of his own free will this information about an old friend from the Sztuka?

11

"The Jews dreamed of having their own Mata Hari"

The Jews dreamed of having their own Mata Hari. Young and pretty, artist and whore. And if she wasn't a whore, they would turn her into one. With one gesture, they made me into a Mata Hari. It was the Jews, they did the work all by themselves. No Catholic had anything to do with it.

"And besides, I am not sure that Mata Hari was one of 'those girls.' I saw on television that she was proud in front of the firing squad at her execution. Standing very straight, with a hat on her head, insolent, she refused to let them blindfold her. She wanted to look. To see how they were going to take her out. And the Jews, they dreamed about it! A Mata Hari of their own, 'pure blood.' Little Vera? Perfect, let them have her. I am obviously guilty of the death of Christ and of Mohammed. I am also guilty of the war in Israel. Of everything. I am Jewish. They are Jewish. They and I, we were in the ghetto. This does not set us free from the feelings of injustice we experienced. Nor of the guilt. This does not make us all into certified saints.

The Ducretet-Thomson record company printed
postcards of their performers. Vera Gran's photo
was taken in the Vallois photo studio in Paris.

Death is not a certain acquittal. We have the status of survivors, for many, still suspect. The tragedy always begins again,
constantly reborn. It grows, it grows again in me. Look at this
inscription on the wall":

*Help!! The Szpilman and Polański clique wants to kill me!
HELP ME!!!*

She had written these words with bold strokes in red ink on
the walls of the hallway, in big block letters. She had to have
climbed on a chair or raised her arms very high. She made corrections several times. Added: *The pianist, my accompanist, they
paid one another off. They have each other by the short hairs . . .*

"It's there, that's the truth! A pack of mangy dogs, dirty liars. I know this man's book. Unspeakable lies. It is driving me crazy, this whole tissue of lies! Everything was mixed up, manipulated. They were biding their time, and making money, and still they come after me. They track me down from every side. At night they come into my home, they enter by the windows or break the locks. They grab everything. They've stolen my photographs, my papers; they take and destroy anything they want. They drug me so that I won't wake up before noon. They want to destroy me. Who? It's forbidden to ask the question.

"I was not prepared to be a whore like in Amsterdam and remain displayed in a window. I closed myself off, I walled myself in. It is he who has turned me into a whore. He films me nonstop. Even in the toilet—I cannot go without being watched, I always have to cover myself. It's unbearable. I am completely shattered. One day I'm going to throw all that in his face. I wish that his life would end in the same suffering that he unjustly inflicted on me.

"They come every night. To rob me. Sometimes they trip over the shopping cart that I place in front of the door as a barricade. Yesterday he must have slipped; he sent everything crashing to the ground, ruining my clean sheets. I'm in the hands of a madman who wants to reduce me to crumbs. He has stolen an important document, and turned my old flannel nightgowns inside out. He also ripped my underpants.

"I am always on the alert, all the time, everywhere. They film me twenty-four hours a day. No doubt about it. They spend crazy amounts for this. Unimaginable amounts. I won't say who is paying; it's a certain man who worked with me at the Sztuka. Surely you knew him. Don't say his name.

"He takes everything from me. He stole piles of books, inscribed to me and dear to my heart. He put cheap paperbacks in their place. It's unbearable. He has blood on his hands. And furthermore, he has destroyed all my recordings at the radio station."

There are no mirrors in her apartment. From every place, photographs look at us. In poster format, or smaller. The picture of an attractive woman with dark hair, expressive lips, and an irresistible seductive glance, conquering all before her.

After her death, in shoeboxes and forgotten plastic bags, I found dozens of negatives, mostly of photos taken on vacations. They show her in action, as in a kaleidoscope, Paris, Rome, Caracas, Venice, the sea, the mountains, the beach, the slopes of the Alps. Often with a little dog, Punia. Never with a man.

"I don't like people," she repeats. "Not men, either. I used them from time to time, but I don't like them.

"In this photo, this large photo on the poster kiosk, that was me, me after all that, after the ghetto and the unleashing of calumnies across continents, after the horror and the filth of the accusations. Me? Me, the great me. Believe in me!"

She was very pretty, not tall, nimble, with a feline grace, but she didn't like her body. She could charm, she was coquettish, she took pleasure in seducing. She cast her net and pulled in her catch, but she was not interested in sex. She spoke with revulsion about the body and corporeal things, and with contempt for masculine lust. Was this also the result of what she had lived through during the war? For her, what was really the greatest tragedy at the time? What was happening on the sidelines of the performances given in the apartments of German officers and of their collaborators? In the thousands of testimonies recorded in Yad Vashem, it is rare to find, even among the most upsetting, narratives of sexual abuse or testimonies of submission to masculine violence. These painful stories are still being kept in silence. I do not know how many women paid this price for the right to survive during those years.

Vera the star could not bear "carnal gymnastics," as she called it. That the fate of the world depended on it surprised her. That's how it begins and it ends. She considered the sexual act as rape. She did not give in to the passion of the other. Perhaps she did not understand it. She never spoke of love, either.

She played with men according to her own rules. She did not want, or did not know how, to give herself totally, nor lose herself in loving. She controlled herself at all times, never drank alcohol. Always on guard. Nature made her that way, or was it circumstances?

On the back of a bank slip from September 21, 1999, she wrote:

I have never spoken to anyone about my sexual life. I have never spoken about God—these two emotions, the two "acts of love," are too intimate, too powerful for me to be able to find the adequate words. Those who need to express themselves about this subject are exhibitionists. And besides, they only know how to use metaphors. The people who discuss this subject are part of the caste of "asexual" abstainers who do not really know what strong feelings are. I doubt that this sort of discussion can awaken in them something that they do not possess. That's why I am skeptical about "believers" who need a church, a synagogue, a Mecca, or any other place of this sort to practice an act so important in life.

"Everyone wanted to hear me talk about my lovers, no one about my hemorrhoids. I have sung hymns to love my whole life. To what end?"

Photos on the wall, on the shelves, on the ceiling, visible from every position and all angles. She is looking at her, she is looking at herself. The young looks at the old; the good, the bad; the triumphant, the vanquished? Where does it come from, this need to confront her own face, or her beauty, or the portrait of a star?

She was very clearly doing the promotion for herself; she kept under her sofa small, worn wooden cubes, ready to stamp out her image. She paid for the printing of hundreds of photos.

"That was forty years ago. It's the past. It's lost. I was still relatively pretty. In any case, that's what they said about me.

All that was flattery. Actually, I had admirers for the different parts of my face."

This memory gives her pleasure.

"I had an admirer who loved my nose. It's changed, this nose, everything changes. My dimples were popular. And my lips. I had pretty lips. At the time I still wore makeup. I made up my eyes and lips. People also admired my complexion. It was like alabaster, smooth, firm, solid, covered with a fine down. They called me 'the peach.'"

Boo-hoo! She was pretending to cry, she squirmed like a little girl . . . *Vsë propalo. Vsë.* All is lost. All.

"Another anecdote. I was standing in front of a store window on a major thoroughfare in Tel Aviv, Dizengoff Street, perhaps. Two men were next to me, not badly dressed, well groomed, not bad looking. I heard one say to the other: 'Do you recognize her? You know who it is?' A glance in my direction. 'I see. How did you recognize her?' 'By her chignon. And you, how did you recognize her?' 'By her nose.' I started laughing. I will never forget it. I couldn't control myself. Generally I don't allow myself to be approached. But there, I turned around and I smiled. 'Ah, you see, it *is* Vera Gran.'

"I remember a similar incident in Paris. I had just arrived then, and I was in the north of the city, near the legendary neighborhood of Montmartre. Evening was falling. I just couldn't believe that I was in Paris. One moment I heard behind me: 'You saw who it was?' A man's voice. And a second: 'Who?' in Polish. It was completely unexpected. I burst out laughing. It's a little pleasure of mine. It was touching and surprising to be recognized on Place Clichy, far from my usual setting, from my country, my language. You know who it is . . . 'Verochka, it was Verochka.'"

She admitted she had been a coquette. And she always needed to be one.

"Men? No, I didn't have any problems with men, I had a lot

A portrait from the stylish Natkin studio in Paris, 15 avenue Victor Hugo

of those little poodles running around me. They all wanted to sleep with me, obviously. They didn't know that I was moral, because of my mother, my education, my ignorance. Nobody wanted to believe it. They always asked me, 'How much?' I was so young. I didn't understand what it was about. They all wanted to sleep with me. They certainly must have thought that as I was a singer, I must have a 'licentious nature.' Big mistake. It was only on stage that I was so courageous, a woman of action who goes on the offensive. I took the time to learn the alphabet of survival in that little world."

She remembered an actress from before the war, Wacława Szczuka (known as Wawa), her massive figure and her special, particularly lascivious monologue. "And he kissed my hand . . . Oh la la, and what if I became pregnant after that?" She often repeated these two verses, and found it hilarious. "Oh la la, and what if . . . ?"

For a long time that summed up her concept of sex.

She recalled an admirer with a bucket filled with roses who had pushed open the door of her hotel room. "It delighted me until the moment when the man started getting ideas. On the spot he left empty-handed. Or else, Lord preserve me, they threw themselves on me. 'You will be mine, you will be mine!' That also happened, like in dreadful novels. He threw off his clothes, and I gave him a slap in the face. I didn't scream for help, I was ashamed. I am a little provincial that way. Sexual matters were not my strong point. They never were. I like to excite them, *c'est tout.* That's all."

"Therefore love, without the organs?"

"Yes—*charmer,* to charm, give compliments, flirt. Lightly, with intelligence and humor. Nothing more. And since I had my virginity taken in an unspeakable way, it has marked me forever. *Voilà! Charmer,* be charming. Even with women, that's why they often thought that I was a lesbian. I had a few of those lesbian encounters.

"Yesterday I was watching a program, not bad at all, channel surfing. I went from the Casino de Paris, to the Moulin Rouge, to land at the Lido. On all three channels . . . only bare asses, and bare asses, and more bare asses!!! Bare asses and bare titties. Piles of them. Certainly pretty, young, firm, but there were so many, they lost their interest and their attraction. Women don't know how much they have lost by giving up that small indispensable part of mystery."

Is she still recording all the time?

"No."

The first lie of the day?

"I am going to tell you something. I have never seen a man's member. Never! I have always closed my eyes. Since the beginning. I hated the whole business. I remained lying there like a dead tree trunk and waiting for it to be over. I am awfully glad that I don't risk its happening to me anymore.

"I love monkeys, but what I hold against them is that they parade around bare-assed. And with the little business that comes out. I think that they should be more discreet. The only visual contact I have ever had with the male organ is with monkeys. I am an aesthete.

"Men only interest me from the waist up, to the head.

"I have been asked what I would do when no one remained whom I could target with my charm. Because I love being charming, even today. That was my great passion. What would I do if I had no one I could charm? I would charm the wall. Even a wall.

"Try bread with margarine, some honey and a little bit of yogurt. You'll see how good it is. Margarine has taste, butter none at all. They say margarine is fake, but I prefer it. I have a whole technique. Be careful, because if the honey starts dripping and it gets over everything, then I will kill you. It's already dripped somewhere, that's it? It drives me crazy when things become sticky. The honey is good? *Poproboi, raz w zhyzni, ne khochesh, ne nado, khodi griaznaia.* Taste it, once in your life, but if you don't want to, then you don't have to, stay dirty."

"You look very pretty."

"I was pretty on stage . . . In Łódź, for example, after the war when I sang with the chorus of revelers, 'Give Me Your Heart' or 'Instead of good night, tell me . . .' Or the following year at the Roma. That evening was advertised as the gayest in Warsaw; it was in 1946, the ruins were hardly cleared. And afterward, a whole series of concerts for the New Year, I was wearing a décolleté dress, gold with sequins, and the encores, the bravos wouldn't stop. A real Polish winter, cold outside and warm enthusiasm inside. The jokes, and the Christmas tree— those were the good times."

On a scrap of the *Evening Express,* I read: *Vera Gran: The great art of a magician, a warm and fascinating voice, a singer in a class by herself . . .*

"They took my photographs in color at the time for the covers of magazines, in an aviator's cap, my favorite, à la Tamara Łempicka, or on a motorcycle, in the summer, with a fan. This accessory I always had in my hand, perhaps because it had belonged to my grandmother and we had managed to save it from the ghetto.

"From my earliest years I had heard people go into ecstasy over my beauty. I was not aware of it. There were days of course when I said to myself with a certain pleasure while combing my hair in front of the mirror: 'I am pretty today.' What a shame that they didn't stress the fact that I was (and I am always!) funny. I knew how to move people to tears in my way of interpreting songs—but I also provoked bursts of laughter when I was clowning. And the sense of humor is based on intelligence—but that they don't accept and they don't forgive.

"And now I am making a little ball with my fingers, and that means I am putting on a red nose. And I am a clown, a funny clown. I can do what I feel like and say what I want. I am a clown, a funny person, a bitter entertainer. Clowns are the most serious. Everything that's bad disappears completely."

At one time she collected herbs. She made bouquets. She gathered leaves of maples, ferns, and lime trees. In her books there are dried rose petals everywhere, jasmine and hydrangeas. But she accepted with distaste the bouquet of lilies I brought her.

"I can't bear cut flowers in an apartment. God, how one can

change! When I was young, and I was collapsing under flowers, I loved this type of homage. It was for me the most extraordinary gift, coming straight from the heart. Today, an obsessive thought takes away the pleasure of admiring them. I know that I am witnessing their slow agony, the inevitable disintegration that precedes their death. I don't throw away flowers given to me that are still pretty, but I know what is going to happen to them and it paralyzes me. I see myself.

"If you were to ask me if I wanted to be born again, to relive in the same way this life that has not been dull at all, I would refuse. Too much suffering, disappointment, and bitterness. It's not worth the effort. What a cruel struggle!

"No one turns around to look at an old man, and even fewer at an old woman. I've asked myself why I continue to dye my hair, put on makeup. The answer: to make people turn around . . . for me! Question: Make whom? Answer: At least me!

"I feel like disappearing from people's sight, as if old age were shameful.

"I had a revelation when I understood that the harbinger of social death is the telephone that has fallen silent. I was almost proud to accept this knell—the alarm of old age—with dignity. Now, I've had another revelation in listening again to the tolling [of the bells]—the alarm of advancing old age, of solitude that settles in—the mail! The mailbox also became silent. Empty, a somber silence in the mailbox. And it is only going to get worse. If I could, I would telephone myself, but as for the letters . . . Who knows, maybe I will write myself a letter from time to time, which I would answer. Then, it would be the first time in my life that I would be completely sure of the discretion of my addressee, therefore free with my confessions. It's a brilliant idea. Finally, a charitable soul with whom I could be in total symbiosis.

"I have invented pretexts to force myself to leave my apartment. I try to take the longest route. From the habit of observing the people I came across I learned to recognize the lonely women. They have a lost look, they are not part of the spectacle of the street. The indifference and the awareness that nobody looks at us anymore. I think that for years I have been caught in the mesh of a serious depression."

It was April 20, her birthday. With a pink marker she drew a large heart. She wrote: *I wish you, my darling, you know what.*

Further on: *I am completely alone. The telephone remains silent—it is dead. Death and the hyenas are waiting. It's been years since my poor mother brought me into this world.*

One shouldn't live a long time. There remain only the Lilliputian pleasures of time running out. One can only expect gathering disappointments that swell and are painful.

You do not know, God be praised, you cannot know, what it means to be totally solitary. The people I knew from my DEgeneration are old; they are also sick, they don't know absolute solitude. They live far away—and, to complete the picture, in a foreign, ENEMY *country.*

In twilight she wakes up, in twilight she eats, in twilight she falls asleep. She spends a lot of time seated at a table crowded with objects, where she always has to make room for a plate, a cup, and the jar of honey. Today she had to push aside one of those shoeboxes filled with strings and colored thread, ribbons and braids for dresses, and lace for cuffs. She plunged in her hands in a graceful gesture, almost choreographic. She untied the knots, unwound threads, and arranged them by size and color. She rewound them. Arranged everything.

Vera, who is rather small, has relatively large hands. But fine-boned hands. She willingly showed them on stage. Demonstrative and agile. Swaying gently, bare. "Medusa," this is what they called this exercise in the dance school. Centuries ago.

People had paid homage to them with gold, amethyst, pearls. But with time they lost their usefulness. They faded when no one looked at them. There they are, spotted with the passing time.

"I hate Jews."

"You are Jewish!"

"By blood. But fortunately I had a transfusion! I am an atheist. And besides, I don't belong to any mafia. Neither Catholic, nor Jewish, nor Arab. I am not a good candidate for the mafia. The Jews have been killing me for fifty years, because I am Jewish! I detest them—because they are Jewish. Connect the dots."

Then, a moment later:

"I am a real Jew, and since I still have my pride, I don't renounce myself to play another role. But that doesn't oblige me to remain silent. To be silent about what I know about my fellow Jews. And as a Polish woman and proud to be one, I would not have kept silent, either.

"In the night, I had another telephone call: 'You're just a whore, we're going to get rid of you.' Stabbing with a knife in the back. And so on. When I hear the telephone, my brain turns to water. The night is gone to hell."

"Later, you tried to find a new goal? A new meaning to life, perhaps?"

"I don't know if anyone has ever tried to find that. I survived. I had to play hopscotch with fate every day. The farther away the war, the more it hurts, the more I feel alone."

"Why did you enroll in a dress-designing class in the fall of 1950 in Warsaw?"

"Because you never know. Because I had a premonition. Because it happened that I couldn't squeeze a note out, my throat was so closed."

"Five years after the war in Poland, after the ghetto, what could still happen?"

"Everything."

"And what happened afterward?"

"I wanted to escape. Flee. Nothing else. Blindly."

"To Israel? Why?"

"What do you know? What do you think you know? Poland was a cemetery. The odor of burnt corpses. I was an enemy to myself. I had no other place to go."

12

To the Ministry of Public Security

To the Ministry of Public Security:
 Could you please send me the necessary documents to facili-
tate my departure for Israel, where I have the intention of
settling permanently, to take the nationality of that State and in
so doing renounce my Polish citizenship? 12.10.1950. Vera Gran.

Why Israel? It seems that in 1947 she had been baptized. With what goal? Had she thought that by doing so she could remove herself from the jurisdiction of the Jewish tribunal? There's no doubt that she made the decision to leave for the Jewish state subsequently, following logically the court verdict and everything resulting from it.

I searched for her baptismal certificate. It is not either in the parish of Saint Michael the Archangel in Warsaw's Mokotów, not far from the place where she lived after the war, nor in Babice, where she eventually could have had herself baptized by Father Machnikowski, an old acquaintance.

Just before her departure she invited "a whole bunch of women" to the Marzec, a well-known café in the Square of

Three Crosses. She ordered coffee and cakes. "They sat down and devoured everything." I don't know why, but there was anger in her tone when she said that. There always was. I noticed it several times.

She had told no one that she was leaving, that she had signed papers, that it was for always. They didn't know that they were invited to a farewell party. Vera was afraid that someone would sabotage her plans. It could have happened anytime, she repeated. She put on her most joyful mask.

The document with which she left the country, hardly larger than an ordinary envelope, a wretched little piece of paper, bore a complex name: Official Identity Card (Israel). It allowed Vera Gran (born 20.04.1918; she had already begun to make herself younger) to leave the country within a month starting October 26, 1950, by the border crossing at Zebrzydowice. It expired on the 12th of December. The photograph on the card was an unflattering close-up: she had a wide face, a smile showing white teeth. "I am laughing because you want me to be crying." In the expression in her eyes you can see the cavalry charging. She was always proud of her talent as an actress.

In her request to the Ministry of Public Security she had also written: *Profession: Performer. Level of education: Secondary. Civil status: Celibate.*

Why had she written "celibate"? In documents or in daily exchanges, she departed from the truth. Since the outbreak of war, with Kazik Jezierski, they had taken advantage of the official privileges granted to married couples. Before her departure she returned the discount card given to wives of officers by the national transportation system. She had also made sure that the Jezierskis, husband and wife, were living together, in conformity with the administrative documents: Weronika and Kazimierz, lieutenant doctor.

She couldn't manage to leave her home on her own strength. The morphine prescribed by Kazik did not succeed in reliev-

With Kazimierz Jezierski, her husband during the war years, taken in
Warsaw, where they lived together following the liberation

ing the severe pains that came to her at night and which lasted
until the next afternoon. In her suitcases she had a few dresses,
some musical scores. Drafts of the lyrics of songs and copies of
court documents. In her handbag, two bills, of ten- and five-
dollar denominations, the amount allowed to be taken abroad.
Her neighbors the invaluable Mainkes took her to the train
station. They placed her in the train like a package—yes, that
is the word, an object, a piece of wood. Her feelings were paralyzed. She tried to struggle against this state.

Her destination in the next few hours: Vienna.

Why had she left her husband?

In a letter that she never mailed to Kazik—anyway, she was
sure that he would read it only when she was no longer there—
she tried to find the answers to this question. She tried to
analyze the condition of her illness—"this darkness that com-

pletely weighed down her soul"—acknowledging that nothing could make her glad, that she had to force herself to live, that she was violating the laws of daily life. Misery had left "a mark too deep and too visible."

You were a friend to me in my distress, but I was a stranger to you in sorrow.

Agreements in effect in time of war cannot always be taken for granted in time of peace.

It seemed as if she begrudged his succeeding in living, and what's more, his obvious happiness, despite everything that had occurred. She declared her love for him, all the while saying that this love was the enemy of their living together in the future. Because he would not be able to help her. Twice she mentioned suicide as a redemption. She understood that her bitterness and her sorrow were pushing him into the arms of another woman.

I don't know what it means to leave for always.

Consciously, without being forced, she closed the door of her homeland behind her. Did she have it in mind to make a new beginning or to drown the past from which she was detaching herself?

Later—the magma. Difficult to differentiate thoughts. Fear distorted by pain, a slight fever—her sleep was like a swamp. The damp cushions with the insignia of the railroad line. She did not regret her decision, and yet she felt an orphan. She was changing her address, changing fate. Was she really? She was still performing.

At dawn the train stopped. Zebrzydowice. The border.

She saw through the window guards in uniform and several men in leather overcoats and hats. She no longer had the strength to struggle, she just wanted to be on the other side. "Uniformed security officers," she thought. She tried not to give in to the panic that was growing in the wagons. They were checking the papers in the manner of the Gestapo. The threat that weighed on all subsequent events. Comparable to that other, during the war—her dependence. Any means is acceptable. The goal is survival.

The word "confidential" printed at the top of the Ministry of Public Security papers immediately aroused the interest of the functionaries in the service. By what right did she have these documents? And the official permission? They separated her from the rest of the passengers to undergo a special inspection. A search? If necessary. They couldn't take more from her than had already been taken. Striptease was not her strong point, but these were common people. The interrogation proceeded.

The questions, just as before. Who, for whom, how, why? A singer? A trial? They said her name aloud. Gran? Grynszpan? Let her go on her way, it's better! Sweaty, unshaven, not exactly smelling fresh. But like the others, see, all powerful. She despised them, and yet she was in their hands.

They tried in vain to reach the prosecutor's office to clear up the situation. The train remained in the station.

One of the customs officers found among her papers the words of a text by the poet Julian Tuwim, the words of a famous Russian song. "The Night Is Dark Today." You can sing it? And in Russian? *Pa russki?* She asked for some hot coffee in a glass, and in exchange, she brought out the only bottle of vodka that she had with her. In her suitcase she also found some Polish sausage. She sang loudly and hurriedly, as if her life depended on it. She knew perfectly how to play the chord of nostalgia. She had reached the summit.

Night was falling. They had to take leave—"The Last Letter" (*Take care of yourself, I know everything, you will never see me again if you don't feel right with me*). They wanted more, and she didn't want to stop. She confided to Saint Anthony (in another song) that she had *lost her heart at the edge of the fields . . .*

The edge of earth; she felt the blood beating in her temples, the edge, the piece of uncultivated ground between two fields—over there, where she is going, are there fields? Why go there, since the apple trees and the lupines were no longer in bloom? They drank from the bottle, passing it from hand to hand during several songs. It was later than ten o'clock when she finished her performance. Her voice was hoarse. They let her leave.

During the hours that followed, the passengers lived only to speak about this concert given on the platform. She did not repeat the experience when there was a brief stop in Czechoslovakia. In Vienna they tried to convince her to stay. Perhaps she should have. Perhaps then her destiny would have taken another, completely different form, would have given her more peace?

She said that intuition had dictated that she continue her journey, go to Israel, where she would feel profoundly "at home." If not, she would have been judged as if she had something on her conscience—at least she thought so, which is what she tried to explain years later. Yet she had nothing to hide.

She didn't remember much about Italy. On November 26, a Sunday morning, on the bridge of the boat taking them, she watched the retreating shores of Europe. She evoked the words "belonging" and "roots," then Hitler and Stalin, and, still more, "claws" and "hell." Sharp pieces of her past invaded her thoughts. She tried to be rid of them as in a bad tale for children. To soften them. To be able to dream, if only for a moment, that to recover from the wounds of war was still possible.

A new beginning. A new day, a new page, a new song. Certainly new, but in what way, and to what extent, since they come from my body and out of my experience?

Does the beginning presuppose a change? What alteration for a skin marked by her previous existence?

In a notebook of lined pages, she wrote in green ink the Hebrew words that would henceforth serve her to name the world.

Kaha—so-so. *Ein davar*—never mind. *Yhije tov*—it will work out.

Further on, a more laborious apprenticeship:
I don't understand Hebrew,
I am not ashamed,
I don't want to,
I would like,
I am not saying . . .
SEIR—song.

Perhaps she was thinking of that evening, still in Warsaw, when on returning home after a concert, she had been attacked in the street and threatened with a revolver. She wasn't afraid; this didn't frighten her anymore. They had taken her handbag. Inside she had photographs saved from the ghetto. That's what they said in the local newspaper article under the heading of events of the day. Bizarre that she was carrying them on her.

Pictures, pictures.

Mother, small, heavy, she drank tea from the saucer while crunching on a sugar cube. She preferred it like that. She had big hands, worn. She had a worried glance. As if she knew more . . . Mothers have a lot in common everywhere in the world. As a joke she would say that on Mondays she would sprinkle her landing with pepper, so that she would sneeze; that brings good luck.

Kazik returned home from the security prison where he worked on Rakowiecka Street. His smell. Different. She saw him briefly, usually in the afternoon she went out to rehearse or to give a concert. Why did he take a position there? Not for her sake, anyway, although he sometimes suggested it. They needed money, and she didn't have any regular work. From performance to performance, Katowice, Łódź, Cracow. The hotels, trains, the cramped dressing rooms, the blinding spotlights. It didn't seem that bad, but she had to earn a living, therefore to travel in every direction and get all sweaty. Certainly in luxury, but all the same.

A prison doctor under contract. He sent in his application in

June 1947. After the Liberation, he worked as a surgeon in the hospital in the Wola neighborhood. He was mobilized in the spring. In the staff hierarchy of the Polish army he had the rank of lieutenant. She remembered, three stars on his epaulets. She had a slight weakness for uniforms. She had seen that he carried a pistol. He found this rank as burdensome as it was satisfying. He worked for a while in a boarding school for children of officers of the Soviet army. She did not know how he had arrived at Rakowiecka Street. Perhaps this might have been in relation to her case. She wasn't interested in knowing. She lacked any political knowledge and instinct. The prison, symbol of the Communist dictatorship, didn't mean much to her. What's more, Kazik did not have the habit of confiding in her. What use was a doctor for prisoners who were going to be killed? His name appears in the transcript of the execution of Cavalry Captain Witold Pilecki, the founder of the Polish Secret Army. And certainly on those of others who were condemned.

She remembered the strange people she used to see at home, on Odolańska Street. A German woman prisoner hired as household help, for whom Kazik acted as a guarantor, escaped and was never found again. Despite this, Kazik brought in still another prisoner. But this prisoner also, after having hoed the garden and transported all the coal from the basement to the attic, proceeded to make his escape. She was supposed to watch him, but she forgot. Not a trace of him. Despite the fines for this sort of negligence of duties, they didn't complain about the lack of money. Kazik was a little carefree. She liked his easygoing nature. And besides, when he took her on his motorcycle, on Krakowskie Przedmieście Avenue, pedestrians would turn around to look at them.

I don't know if she was aware that he had started working for the Ministry of Public Security. Nor if this had any bearing on her case. That seems impossible to establish. On December 27, 1950, he signed a document committing himself to the strictest professional secrecy. It can be assumed that he had been subject to this before as well.

Oval face; eyes golden brown; hair blond-black (sic!—elsewhere: chestnut brown). Distinguishing characteristics: none.

"We lived together eleven years, Kazik and I," she said to me one day, "and yet we didn't know each other. He didn't know me, and I didn't know him, either. We never had the time to get to know one another, to talk together. Our professional obligations did not help. He worked during the day and I at night. We crossed each other on the landing or in bed. That's all. He satisfied me very badly and very awkwardly."

A handsome man. High forehead, his hair combed back, a clear complexion with a slight olive tint. An expressive mouth, full lips.

Two photos, one of him wearing a coat and another in uniform. At the Institute of National Remembrance there are several dossiers labeled "personal" for Jezierski, Kazimierz, son of Zbigniew, born in 1914. Blue-gray cardboard folders, greenish with age, colors faded, with numerous stamps and various different certificates. There are many reference symbols, civilian, military, next to others crossed out by red felt pens. Inside are the files of a civil servant of the Ministry of Public Security. Doctor, no personal fortune. Languages spoken: French—fluently; German—elementary.

Married. The documents state: successive wives—Weronika Gacka (1947); Weronika Grynberg (1949); and Weronika Zofia Tomaszewska (1949). All the same Vera. Adequate changes were brought to the biographical notice of each one.

His wife's profession was always listed as "performer." First of Polish nationality, Catholic, from a family of artisans. Shortly afterward, of Jewish faith and bourgeois antecedents.

None of them has a judicial file registered with the Ministry of Justice.

The descriptions of the parents of the two spouses change in the series of documents and certificates. Who authorized the go-ahead for these changes, and what was the margin of the permissible? First of all, and very precisely, listed as Aryans, they become in time citizens of Jewish origin. In green ink on graph paper Kazimierz Jezierski has drawn their silhouettes.

Eljasz Grynberg, of Jewish faith, teacher. (Never, in anyone's memory, had he ever held that position. I don't know if he would have been capable of it. He was by nature rather destructive.)

Liba Kaplan, of Jewish faith, housewife, corset maker. (Seamstress for the torso. Vera never mentioned this trade. Did she sew custom orders? Corsets for lingerie and for evening wear. But also belts and medical corsets.)

Several years later he gave more information about his own parents. He used the administrative categories to tell a sort of story.

I want to specify that the actual first name of my mother was: Amelia. I mentioned the name Wanda because I referred to a birth certificate which had been changed during the Occupation. My father's first name was: Jerzy. I mentioned the name Zbigniew Jerzy for the same reasons that I stated above.

In the *Biographical Dictionary of the Medical Profession* published in 1999, I read:

Jerzy Jezierski born Rubinsztejn (1886–1940) in Suwałki, son of Lejb and Sima née Jezierska. Member of the Evangelical Church, confirmed in 1920. [It's certainly at this time that he changed his name to take the maiden name of his mother, Jezierski.] *Obtained his diploma in 1915, with a specialization in surgery. Practiced in Warsaw.*

Imprisoned in 1939 in the Soviet Union in unexplained circumstances. Deported to Starobielsk. His name appears in the list of war prisoners of the NKVD of this camp (registration number 1094). He died in Kharkov at the age of fifty-four.

In the statements that he made to the administration, Kazimierz never mentioned these facts. Nor in his private conversations.

I found these documents during the summer of 2009. I can't hide what a surprise their discovery was. Jezierski became someone brave and responsible. He deserves even greater admiration than before. Saving Vera, his Jewish wife, being Jewish himself; although rebaptized, it was not the same thing as for a Polish person. I know nothing of his fears, and yet he must have had them.

Is there such a thing as the vanity of survivors? Does it exist? Was it only their own vanity, innate and unchanged by the events of the war? She never praised to me the courage of her husband. She never acknowledged that he put himself in danger for her, that he tried his best, that he placed his existence second in importance for her survival. Not a word on the subject. As if it were taken for granted by her, as if it were easy and required no effort or particular attention. Did she not know how to be grateful? Was she the only one like that? Perhaps humiliation negates the reflex of gratitude. Blunts the instinct for mutual responsibility. Perhaps.

These same documents, at the very end of my work on the fate of the Jezierski family, revealed still one more secret. In the spring of 1952, Vera had been gone from Poland two years. Kazimierz, her husband for a long time, as they themselves said, as well as their friends and the administrations with which they were in contact, wrote:

According to the Civil Code, I am a bachelor, and I have never entered into any formal union.

The real name of my wife is: Grynberg, Vera. The other names were pseudonyms because of the Occupation. I lived eight years with her and have been separated from her for a year and a half.

Signature, in blue ink.

"Vera Gran is paged by the captain," she heard over the loudspeakers on the bridge, once they were well under the jurisdiction of maritime law. She did not feel safe among them, and therefore refused all the more firmly the glass of cognac that this Polish-speaking officer offered her. He insisted in the name of friendship and a safe crossing. He tried a subtle compliment: "I know you, madam . . . as an artist." He became even more pressing, threatening. "I also know . . . the case!"

Electric tension. Tight throat. Alarm. Increased vigilance. Weakness also.

The monotonous motion of the water only exacerbated her troubling thoughts. Her nerves, insomnia, sailing toward the unknown. She felt her head spinning. She had to get away, right now.

He was drinking, he quickly started calling her by her first name and wanted to put his hands where he wouldn't have dared if he considered her a lady. She remembered his laughter when she finally reached the door after blindly bumping her arms. She remembered these words: "My crew knows what to do when I entertain whores."

How old was she? More than thirty. She was alone, without family; the Germans had killed them. Alone, without a man; she had left him. In the name of what, she no longer knew. She was no longer capable of giving him the happiness that he needed. After what had happened, impossible to experience lightness of being. I. B. Singer said about these women that they will always stay on the side of death. Now she found herself in the cursed space "between the two," in the place that could have been a blessing, renewed her strength before the next confrontation. She wasn't given time to rest.

It was necessary to remain vigilant. She had to learn to defend herself. Claw, punch, and bite. For the first time? Not the last. The ripped dress, the hair a mess, and the captain's promise that he would destroy her in Israel because he had enough proof of her collaboration with the Gestapo. He wiped the back of his hand against her bruised cheek, undid the bolt, and opened the door. She fled. She was sick for the rest of the voyage.

In Haifa she was greeted with the same routine as in Zebrzydowice, only now as "acted out by members of my own people." She was the last to disembark from the boat. In a fur coat, fur toque, and boots. December. The sun was burning.

No one was waiting for her, and she was not expecting anyone. She had no money; during the trip she had bought some soap. She stopped short, blinded by the light. She rubbed her eyes. Dark stains on her cheeks, mascara, tears, some tenderness perhaps? Something fell next to her—an orange. Right afterward she found herself surrounded by strangers. Welcome to her new homeland.

I have always wondered why she left to go there particularly. Why didn't she stay with her husband? Didn't she feel safe with him? She didn't love him? A risky decision to leave everything behind: her man, her career, her country. And this only a few years after the war and its cruel and extenuating circumstances. Should this be seen as an act of courage or rather as an act of desolation and despair?

Of all places in the world, she chose the one she knew the least, and for which she had the least affinity. Had Poland become unbearable to such a degree for her, and why?

She felt wounded and under surveillance; however, she did not blame the Poles, but the Jews. It never occurred to her that to come to live among those who had survived the war would revive "the case" and result in adverse comments. Didn't she sense that choosing to live in the young Jewish state with the weight of what she had lived through during the war could provoke a storm? In principle, the young state of Israel did not want to look back. The memories of the Occupation carried with them death and humiliation. And the humiliation seemed to be the most painful. The new Jews in their own state would never experience it. They had to be strong and brave. They had to build and fight. Always hold your head high. Never become a victim condemned to be burned.

They treated the tragedy of the Jewish diaspora during the

war as a painful blow, which had soiled their honor and contradicted the legend of a country being built.

Barely two years after the creation of this state, they promul-
gated a law to pass judgment on the Nazis and the people who
had helped them. This law included war criminals as well as
collaborators. At the time in Israel, the members of the Council
of Elders (the Judenrat) as well as the capos of the camps were
treated with contempt. Most of the Jews spared from the Holocaust and judged over there were accused of collaboration with
the Nazis. Up until the beginning of the 1960s, almost forty
people were convicted.

It happened that the survivors would recognize, in the streets
of Haifa or Tel Aviv, their persecutors in wartime, their fellow citizens. They were often chased and heaped with insults.
People didn't mince their words; the heaviest stone hurled was
"Gestapo sympathizer." In the Israeli civil code, collaborators
were placed on the index in a special way. The need for purification was as important as the need to inflict a punishment.
The Jewish collaborators in the eyes of their accusers found
themselves covered with opprobrium for having participated in
the crimes of the Nazis. Motives were not studied in detail, nor
were the reasons for the collaboration. There were no mitigat-
ing circumstances. There was no attempt to understand. Those
who handed down the verdicts were convinced they were acting for the best.

She knew nothing about the Promised Land of the Jews.
Before this she had rarely tried to picture it—desert-like, wild,
unfamiliar. And here in front of her eyes were the alleys of Tel
Aviv, similar to those of Warsaw; the dusty shop windows, with
piece goods like in the neighborhood of Nalewki. The light
was more intense, but in the streets the language was familiar,
a hubbub neither completely that of hawkers nor that of people
praying. And when she saw on a newsstand *Our Review* next
to a title in Hebrew, she felt at home. She made a sign with her

hand that she wanted to buy it. She heard: "If you want a Polish newspaper, it is enough to say it in Polish." Vera couldn't believe her ears: the tone, this accent, everything was like home.

She had forsaken Poland for a cot in a miserable boarding house she shared with others. For some shady admirers who promised her the moon if she would give herself to them. For the vision of a heritage that turned out as illusory as the rebirth of the Promised Land of the Jews.

She did not mention her homesickness, her nostalgia for Warsaw. The first letter (a little gray envelope, a stamp with Comrade Bolesław Bierut) was from Jezierski and reached her four months after her departure. He told her that he spoke with her ("My little fish—Rybeczka!") every day, for long hours. He mentioned the health of the dogs, who although receiving little care were in good health. He referred to his tears but quickly turned it into a joke, speaking about a hunting party during which he had killed nothing.

He described his loneliness in this room that had not changed much and where hung the little yellow curtains she had made herself. "I feel you as a living presence, as a person with whom I speak and cultivate with great care." He compared the pain of reading her letters to some distant melody, extremely pure. He was moved thinking about her, her successes (she must have spoken about them to him); it boosted his morale.

"What is this story that happened to you in Poland?" they asked her with a nonchalant air, as if it were nothing, but to make her understand that it was known and that it could be used against her. Or if she agreed to fulfill certain conditions, the affair could be silenced, forgotten—well, at least not mentioned. Until the next time, when she would have to buy herself out again.

The defamers were everywhere. The blackmailers also.

What was the difference between them? What rapport with the blackmailers whose activities during the war cost the lives of thousands of people?

During the Occupation, these blackmailers turned the Jews over to the Gestapo. They denounced them for money or on their own initiative, thinking that it was the thing to do, or that things would be better that way. Or that they deserved it, just as Poland deserved to be a pure nation, Aryan, without the masses of Jews in long overcoats and skullcaps on their heads.

"She's one of them, and capable of anything . . ." was whispered, murmured with growing insistence. She had the impression that they held a grudge against her for everything. Her past, her beauty, and more recently—in Tel Aviv, openly—her relationship with a married man. Wherever she went she could feel the mean looks and words. Finally, in the spring of 1951, as in Warsaw right after Liberation, she went to the police. She produced all her documents and insisted that they start proceedings to give her a written work permit.

She obtained it after several weeks. With the Histadrut union card she felt slightly more safe. She was invited to participate at the performance for the fund-raising Police Ball. For her it was the symbolic beginning of her right to a new life.

A photograph of her, "lips sensually parted" in the Gypsy cabaret style, appeared on the cover of the Israeli weekly *HaOlam HaZeh*. She performed for a radio broadcast on Friday afternoon, prime time. She hired an agent to organize concerts for her. Everything seemed to fall into place. She waited for the first performance, paralyzed by stage fright.

On May 30, 1951, the Ohel Theater was completely sold out. She remembered the baskets of flowers that couldn't fit in her dressing room and that she finally put on stage. The room was packed, and policemen were along the walls. At first she had difficulty freeing her voice; nervousness made her lose her color, deafened and smothered her. She sang with full voice only during the second part of her performance.

She doesn't really remember having felt any joy. Right afterward she accepted work in a cabaret, while waiting for better proposals; it was always better than sewing. One of the first evenings a drunken colleague attacked her in her dressing room. She fought back violently. "You Gestapo whore, you'll see . . ." She was sick for a long time.

I believe that leaving Poland was a mistake. Leaving to go there. There, where the echoes of war were still resonating, and the ashes of the crematoriums were still warm.

She needed to purify herself. She continually washed her hands like Lady Macbeth. She didn't just want to be clean. She wanted to be recognized as such.

Survivor of the Holocaust. Victim of the persecutions of war and now destroyed by her own people, by the survivors.

On July 6, 1952, she embarked on the *Negbah* in Haifa, destination Marseille. She had cabin 56 in second class, just next to the space reserved for the synagogue. During the night of the 12th to the 13th—she remembered perfectly because she is afraid of the number thirteen—she was awakened by a violent noise, different from those familiar and characteristic of a seagoing voyage. When she got up, the water was up to her knees and still rising. She had trouble opening the door to call for help.

A pipe had ruptured in a neighboring cabin. The water flooded her suitcases arranged under her bunk. *As a consequence of being in water for a long time,* she wrote in her claim to the insurance company, *my clothing has been ruined and was destroyed, and as a result is beyond usage.* Further: *I am a performer by profession. What I possess and what I presently brought to Europe constitute my only property and my only goods. I traveled in the capacity of a tourist, but I had hoped to be able to present myself before a French audience as an Israeli singer.*

She demanded to be compensated as a consequence. She complained equally of the scandalous behavior of the employees responsible for serving the passengers, who neither tried to help her nor paid her any particular attention.

She proceeded with a minute description of the damaged goods:

A small cloth suitcase. A leather suitcase (value 35,000 Fr.). A silk summer suit (value 25,000 Fr.). Two black cocktail dresses (35,000 Fr. and 30,000 Fr.). A roll of white silk material (20,000 Fr.). An embroidered silk blouse (4,000 Fr.). A dress handbag. Sports bag. A pair of leather gloves. A sports jacket and skirt. Chiffon material for a caftan. Material (georgette) for a blouse.

13

The train from Marseille pulled into the Gare de Lyon

The train from Marseille pulled into the Gare de Lyon in Paris at the end of the afternoon. She could never explain to me why she had chosen Paris.

No one was waiting for her.

It was July 13, 1952.

The fatal thirteen. Unlucky thirteen. The thirteen of the pogrom. This superstition was the strongest in her. Her whole life she kept adding new adjectives to it.

She looked for the Métro to go to Montmartre. It was the only neighborhood that she recognized in Paris. I don't know if it was just by reputation or from personal experience. Sometimes she said that she came here with her mother when she was still wearing her school uniform with the sailor collar.

From her mouth, French sounded like a sinister growling when she tried to ask for directions.

Her wardrobe was stiff and sticky from sea water, and the colors had all run together. Just the thought of this made her burst into tears. She had nothing to wear. She had nothing in which to appear on stage.

However, it was summer; she wasn't going to freeze. Perhaps the insurance would come through and give her some small compensation.

She observed the city in full excitement on the eve of the national holiday. The hubbub of the cafés, the tables on the sidewalks, the appetizing smell of food, the echoes of music. On the surface, this foreign daily life appeared sympathetic to her, welcoming. But as well it was everything that she did not know. The language was separate from the words and the meaning. The names of streets and human exchanges belonged to an unknown order of things. Just like these people who appeared so happy.

She had before her eyes a fairy tale, and it seemed to her that she had only to reach out to enter this magic circle.

Her head was spinning. She questioned the mournful thoughts repeating in her mind. You are alone, too bad, you have to make do. It was your choice.

She moved into a small hotel that had been recommended by a passenger on the boat. Vera . . . Vera, very well, Vera, the *r* hardened to be better understood, Gran. No, not Grande, yes, grande, it amused her. Gran. In her room she could take three steps in length and two in width. She sat down by the window and drank water from the tap.

The next day she went to see the windows displaying lingerie in the neighborhood of the Moulin Rouge.

It reeked of luxury. It was in Paris that she first saw nylon stockings! Stretchy and easy to wash. They fit the calf so prettily. Unfortunately, they were subject to runs. Too expensive for her purse.

Staring at her from the covers of magazines, in full color, were Gina Lollobrigida in René Clair's *Belles de nuit* and Edith Piaf, the nightingale of Paris, recently married.

She never met the incomparable performer of "Hymn to Love." They were approximately the same age, approaching forty; Edith was younger by several months. Piaf was world famous at the time. Paris received Vera Gran with indifference.

Several years later, in America, they called her the Polish Piaf. They compared her voice, deep and smooth, to Piaf's singing "La Vie en rose." "When he takes me in his arms . . .": Gran interpreted, in Polish, the famous song. Listening to her sing, some people said that she seemed even more alone than Piaf.

She remained in contact with the Mainkes, her neighbors in Poland. In 1952, she sent them a case of oranges for Christmas. She did what she could to be in contact with their lives from a distance. In their letters the Mainkes worried about her, they said that if she had a child she would be happier in life. But maybe this was a speculation. Perhaps, living alone, she was reliving her youth? They were taking care of the grave of the little one.

In fall 1955 Vera appeared at the Hotel Commodore on Boulevard Haussmann. To packed audiences. She said that she could have continued this, but she had dared to rebuff the advances of the director. He called her a Gestapo sympathizer and fired her on the spot. She then proceeded to get a contract with the Dinarzade cabaret. A tangle of machinations and cover-ups by journalists resulted in the same consequences. According to Vera, everybody was after her for her charm. They wanted her. They stalked her. And once rejected, they promised to avenge themselves. With the "Gestapo Affair," of course.

I don't know if this was the reality, or if all this comes from her painful memories. Perhaps she reacted more extremely to insults that her colleagues at work would have reacted to with a condescending shrug of the shoulder.

She told me one day about a dream in which she sent postcards from this world to her mother and her sisters. She knew that this was the only news to reach the other side. In her dream, she hesitated whether to tell them the truth, or cheer them up by telling them about her daily life, or confide the sufferings that life had reserved for her.

She hadn't succeeded in shaking her doubts before waking up.

She held on to several postcards referred to in this dream.

In each one her face was crossed out.

I chose a few. She wanted it to be this way. They were the symbols of the greatest stages of her conflict: the struggle, the blows, the bad choices. The shadow of victories. Fate perhaps would take another form, but in the album of her life, these chapters were the most important. I read them among hundreds of pages written in the heat of the moment. Notebooks, pads, calendars.

There is no continuity in the narration of destiny. Nor in daily life, nor in memory. There are some traces, fragmentary pictures to reconstruct the past.

Caracas, 1954

A burning wind. A stormy sea. Fever for a whole year. Caracas is fixed in her memory in the dampness of afternoon siestas. For me it echoes what I. B. Singer said about those strange women for whom the war has not completely consumed itself. Even in this tropical fairy tale, they are still possessed by the dybbuk and a host of phantoms from the past. And the eroticism that is the proof of emptiness. Because "those who were on the threshold of death, remain dead."

She had given in to the promise of calm and a desire for heat. And to an illusory thought that the protection of others would liberate her from fear, that a friendly presence would calm the chaos.

Someone she knew, whom she sometimes called her friend but later, her enemy, had insisted, ever since she left Poland, that she should come visit her. This acquaintance named Stefa had become wealthy thanks to her husband's businesses. He bought vodka and traded it against wagons filled with furniture, watches, and valuables looted by the Russians. He sent gold and dollars to Venezuela by different means. The presence of her friend the singer, for whom she no doubt had admiration, would soothe Stefa's wounded ego.

She gave some performances in the Atelier Bar, which was located in the elegant Hotel Potomac, of which there is no trace today. Nor of the faithful and passionate public that was so gratifying to her, or of her songs, or of the applause and enthusiasm.

But there remained the memory of excursions across Venezuela, which Christopher Columbus called "the Blessed Land." Afternoons at the beach in good company, radiant faces, dancing. She on the main square, Bolívar Plaza with its pigeons, in this city of a million inhabitants. The strolls by the Caribbean Sea. There are photos, several of her on the balcony in an elegant summer dress. What gave the greatest pleasure was to have opened a bank account in her name for the first time in her life. She said that she used to caress her checkbook.

She enjoyed visiting cocoa plantations. She stuffed herself with chocolate. On the back of a photo she had written, not sparing of herself: "Well, I wasn't skinny . . ."

One day, the president of the Jewish Community of Caracas summoned her for an interview. If she had the intention of remaining much longer, she should explain her past with the Gestapo. Where did he get that? From Stefa and Staszek, the couple who had invited her. They had given him some documents. Not flattering about her.

She left the country shortly afterward.

In the airplane she realized it was Paris she missed, not Warsaw. And she told herself that attitudes changed quickly.

The blackmail exercised by this couple didn't stop on the other side of the ocean. Right after her departure they denounced her to the French authorities for collaboration with the Gestapo. That is the reason why she never obtained either French nationality or passport.

Shortly afterward she drafted a short note that I consider most significant. On graph paper, in ink as green as grass.

I am trying to explain her actions, not to accuse her.

This note explained to me the past and the present, why she struggled for herself in her profession, for the stage, for her image as a star.

My profession has more drawbacks than advantages. You have to love it as I do to be able to accept everything. It's like with a man you love, you can tolerate more easily his faults than those, however slight, of people you don't like.

My profession is a drug that I have consumed for so many, so many years that it's an integral part of my existence, not only material, but also moral and psychic. It's like a hunger; you want the bravos, the spotlight, the stimulant that is called "stage fright," the hunger to be in the ring, where you have to wipe out your adversary, with a song, but also seduce the masses, often hostile, critical, and changeable. The need for this stimulant is no less than for a drug. And unfortunately, even sensible words, dictated by reason, don't alter anything in the matter. Friendly warnings do not bring solutions. The drug is stronger.

Israel, Spring 1956

Marseille, like before, only in the opposite direction. A journey by boat without incident. Haifa. She calls this trip the pilgrimage to her spiritual homeland. Happy to have been invited to perform on stage.

And then came an image that took root in such a wounding manner in her fate. And in my way of picturing her.

"Let the truth shine through." These words resonated as a warning and the threat of a lynching.

Children were distributing flyers carrying this inscription in the streets, in the cafés, in the entrance of the club where she was performing. Songs in Polish, in Hebrew, in French, in Russian . . . a unique recital by the singer. They called for a boycott of "the Gestapo whore."

Neither her agent, Wallin, nor the management of the club could see who was behind all this. A certain K.—you could change last names on a whim—had spread the rumor of her vile collaboration. This time when she left Israel, she promised herself not to return there so soon.

Dinarzade, 1958

Starting two years ago, everything in my life was going to change, and rather for the better. I had made records for Ducretet-Thomson, where Charles Aznavour was recording. I had finally found a studio, and I was hired at the Dinarzade, something I had dreamed of for a long time.

I told myself that I would do anything to keep this work. I ingratiated myself with Madame Wagner, the director and partner— might as well have a woman on my side.

I had to win over the barman, the director of the room, and all the waiters. Each of them, including the bathroom attendant, could put a knife in my back. Each of the five members of the orchestra thought he was God and wanted the honors! They drowned out my voice even when I had a microphone. A bunch of boors, exercising their power.

Jealousies, garbage, dirty tricks, gossip. She barked this out.

London, August 1959

It was Feliks Konarski (Ref-Ren) who found her again and invited her to London. She was to sing in a newly opened theater with Marian Hemar as emcee. The authority and the support of Hemar seemed to her an invaluable help.

She left in her own car, a white Renault. Her colleagues were waiting for her in Dover to keep her company and help her learn to drive on the left. In the Polish clubs in London, she again saw people she had lost sight of for twenty years. It happened that she didn't even recognize them. She made enemies.

In the *News,* a Polish weekly for immigrants edited in London, they published a short article with her photo and listing her concerts. Someone said the paper received letters of protest.

During this trip, she recorded several programs for Radio Free Europe, songs by Hemar, who accompanied her and made commentaries.

It's a miracle that I have not poisoned half of humanity to avenge myself of the wrongs that they continue to inflict on me. It's a miracle that I have not tried to kill myself a hundred times over. It's a miracle that they consider me someone normal, that I continue to develop in my work as well as intellectually, in a word, that I can function with this parasite that hangs on and devours me, poisons me and paralyzes me.

And a little later, a long digression on Dreyfus, a French officer of Jewish origin, accused of betrayal and condemned. She thought that he was, after all, lucky, because he was defended by the great of the world, among them Émile Zola with his text "J'accuse!," who called for his acquittal.

I suspect that God reserves the greatest trials for the strongest. I feel myself to be a moral gladiator. Without this strength, I would have already swallowed this capsule that I had made for myself for the first crisis—that is to say, after my imprisonment.

London, 1960

She had left her country ten years earlier. Ten years since she had been cleared of all suspicion, recognized as innocent, and the accusations had been judged unfounded. Time enough to heal her wounds.

She was introduced to Ben Koller, who organized performances for which he hired émigrés. One of her friends was continually praising him. Vera noted: *Young, Jewish, sexy, insolent, great mug, and very, very arrogant, who should have from the start won my sympathy, if I had not through professional distortion acquired the habit of being on guard against this type of man. This new expatriate Polish Christ had deigned to show a little interest in me, he invited me to drink a little gin that I had to pay for out of my own pocket. I allowed him to kiss my hands, then on the cheek, to put his arms around my waist; to use the familiar form of address with me on the third day, while I continued to use the formal.*

Upon her arrival she had warned the master of ceremonies, Feliks Konarski, and his colleagues that she refused to have anyone invited to attend rehearsals. She didn't like to show herself when she wasn't ready. She worked through every note of her performance.

The day before the dress rehearsal, Koller arrived. He came to kiss "your little neck" and to assure himself that "you will be mine." She showed a certain displeasure. Koller exploded. *He vomited a flood of insults and curses. He left in a flash and quit the theater like a bomb, showering insults and threats.*

And the result followed the same well-known sequence. He started telling "stories about her abject collaboration," and to drag her through the mud. He claimed that if no one had yet succeeded in destroying her, he would take care of it.

The bored little world of Polish immigrants now exploded. She placed Koller on her list of executioners.

She systematically updated this list. She recopied it in her diary. She had difficulty erasing things from her memory.

1959, 1960, 1961 . . . and a little later (spiral notebook with lined pages)

For a long time she had no fixed residence in Paris. She lived in hotels, with friends, rented rooms.

They were full of moths, full of cockroaches. When I came home from the cabaret, I grabbed the broom and brush that I left by the door. When I turned on the lights, they were swarming on the ceiling. I beat them, I swept them, then I ran to crush them. Me, I am maniacal about cleanliness, it drives me crazy. My clothes were full of moths, it was terrible, a real problem. I was told that to get rid of them I had to use lemon peels. And they disappeared completely.

She was very happy to find a little studio on rue Chardon-Lagache.

Her work took her regularly to Sweden. She went to sell collections of jewelry and fashionable Parisian clothes to individual clients and to department stores . . . *a one-woman show.* The selling, and the scheduled meetings with her lover, were coordinated in a rhythm with hotels, travels, the complaints . . . It was unsettled, but I have the impression that it was a life that suited her.

The 1960s, the era of Charles de Gaulle in France, the period of other great figures. The Champs-Élysées was covered with the most interesting theater posters. Even the king of Jordan came to visit. He quickly grew tired of formal presidential dinners and made his departure from them as soon as he could. Someone had told him that in Paris there was a little cabaret called the Tsarévitch, where a pretty young woman sang very well. He decided to go there.

She liked to call herself the *enfant terrible,* and she took pleasure in recounting this story. She sang in several languages and ended by singing in Hebrew. It amused her that the proprietor of the club almost had a heart attack.

I threw "Lajla" at him, a lullaby, so that he would know I was Jewish. The king slightly pursed his lips trying not to smile. He apparently understood my irony, or my aggressiveness—who knows how he interpreted it. He listened till the very end, and then applauded. His bodyguards looked to see how he was taking

At the peak of her career, the 1960s, Vera was performing in Parisian cabarets and concert halls. At the Alhambra–Maurice Chevalier theater, she was photographed against large advertising kiosks featuring posters of her upcoming appearances. She could not believe it was all really happening.

it. He continued listening without taking his eyes off me. He came back every day.

She had experienced several triumphs. The great satisfaction of singing with Charles Aznavour at the Alhambra.

I can't remember who suggested that I appear with him. I

*was invited to a rehearsal, and then there was an interview. I
promised to get rid of my Slavic accent. I had begged, I wanted
to sound convincing. Then I heard: "If you lose your accent, don't
bother coming back." I couldn't believe it, I felt like falling on my
knees.*

They hired her. Photos of her, immense portraits, were plastered all over Paris on advertising kiosks; she was very happy.

She had numerous impresarios. She was proud of knowing the most influential, Leonid Leonidoff, thanks to whom she was able to perform in the most prestigious venues. She participated in galas given in the most elegant hotels in Paris, the George V and the Lutetia. She often sang at the annual ball of the Union of Jewish Combatants. She was afraid of the Jews of Poland, she always tried to avoid them. They didn't want her to forget.

*I have always been very difficult and it has served me very well
in life.*

She performed in what were called the "Russian" nightclubs, very elegant: the Dinarzade, the Étoile de Moscou . . . at the cabaret Novy and the Tsarévitch. At the time there were few clubs with orchestras, but in those you could listen to a real Gypsy orchestra with a violinist.

*I had started cutting records with Ducretet-Thomson, Azna-
vour's studio.*

Nothing falls from heaven.

She thought that she could have a major career in Paris, but her personality prevented it. She didn't know how to ask.

The Alliance Française, rehearsing her songs in French, looking for professional contacts. That's how she renewed her acquaintance with Ysrael Szumacher and Shimen Dżigan, her co-stars on the screen with Ida Kamińska in the prewar Yiddish film *The Homeless*. They proposed that she accompany them on their tour. She accepted. America and Canada, the centers of Polish immigration. They called her the pillar of the program. She kept the reviews of these performances. How was she able to travel with all that? So many years, so much baggage, all the time she spent cutting out, gathering, and minutely arranging all these papers.

In Paris she became friends with Albert Willemetz. He had written more than three thousand songs, including major hits for Maurice Chevalier, Mistinguett, Josephine Baker. She called him "my godfather," her counselor. She went to the office of the assistant prefect of the police to extend her residence visa. Again she applied for naturalization papers. She came up against a wall. A rumor originating in Venezuela accused her of having been an agent of the Gestapo.

She went on a new trip to Sweden. The showing of new collections was an activity that absorbed her more than singing. That is where the person named Tutu first makes his appearance in her diaries, a strange character she describes very precisely and who remains, however, an enigma. He does business with Russia, lives in Stockholm, is married, keeps a mistress, and Vera worked for him in Sweden. He lives with his wife, who—according to Vera—is losing her mind, taking drugs, and is suicidal (she had made four attempts at suicide), and is responsible for her husband's depressed state. Vera misses him, surreptitiously she prowls the street where his office is located. That's where he spends his days. With a racing heart, she reads his name on a visiting card. She takes in what he sees every day from his window. That's where he walks, here's where he lives. In love? Entranced when he is there, in despair when he leaves.

July 1963—on the road with the collection.

Tutu would greet her at the station with a bouquet of seven Baccarat roses in hand and take her to an expensive restaurant. Then they would retire to her hotel room. But never on weekends. *And then, like an automaton, I let myself be bedded—when he had done his little business, he kept glancing at his watch. I asked him how much time he deigned to grant me. He answered* to say that I was an idiot, and that at five o'clock (an hour later) he had to leave to walk his dog! Unbelievable! This went beyond all bounds of proper behavior! While keeping in her feelings of anger, she told him what she thought of his concept of "duty." He made a grimace, too bad, he would sacrifice the health of his dog for me. He granted me another hour during which he addressed me as if speaking to the armoire. He recovered a little of his liveliness again when he climbed into his car and was going home again, to this captivity that he preferred, by the side of his paralytic despot.

November 17. The snow is falling in gusts, the city is all white. I am not having much luck here with my collections, but I am rejoicing because I see him every day. After work—5:30—he came to see me; we remained in the hotel and made love until dinner time. Then we went to eat Chinese—tired, happy, and tender with each other. Afterward to the Bacchi Vapen for a drink. The Swedish performers—ultra-terrible—a great shame that there isn't a show worthy of the name in such a big city.

November 22. Malmö. Tutu: I am worried that I make love to you so rarely. Me: The interested party wishes that it is your only worry.

She fell in love with an Italian man relatively younger than she; he was a painter. A love that was as reciprocal as it was voracious. She was moved by his solicitude and his attachment. Doubts were not absent, but she tried to laugh them off. Until he introduced her to her replacement, she would fully enjoy this unhoped-for gift of fate.

That's when my inner censor sticks its tongue out at me and whispers, "It's not going to last!" I know very well that it won't last. And it made me think all the more that this adventure, this passion which right from the start made me lose all my bearings, would be ephemeral.

At first I was certain that it would be the end when I decided *to tell him that I was Jewish. He was delighted. My inner censor snickered and said: "You are in luck, he finds it amusing!"*

I then decided to put him through another even more difficult test. I confessed that my long hair that he liked so much was . . . gray. Almost without thinking he answered me that it was a shame that I dyed it because if I had gray hair, it wouldn't bother him at all.

It has lasted three years already! Three charming years when he gave me courage and happiness and, to the extent possible, met all my whims and my all-too-frequent bad moods.

Guido died at the age of forty-nine.

Warsaw, 1965

Of Warsaw she remembered the welcome in the airplane circling the city. It was the 20th of October. The stewardess announced that aboard was the great singer Vera Gran who was returning to her homeland for the first time after years of absence. She held in her arms her beloved little dog, Punia.

She wrote: *I received from Stołeczna Estrada* [the artistic agency of the capital] *five little yellow roses with their wishes for my success. Six big chrysanthemums from Stefania Grodzieńska, Jerzy Jurandot, and their daughter. Ten enormous and magnificent salmon-colored roses from the luxury caterer Blikle. A telegram from Irena Prusicka, my dance teacher before the war: "My darling, I welcome you to Warsaw with love, I kiss you with all my heart, greetings."*

She stayed several weeks. She had not imagined coming back. *I had to show that I was not afraid of being bad-mouthed by those who would constantly denigrate me.* She made a recording on which she sings Szpilman's composition "Her First Ball." He asked her to sing the lyrics by Bronisław Brok. Only Vera Gran knew the lyrics by Szlengel; after she left Poland, it was as if they had disappeared.

New York, 1969

March 22nd. She performed in Carnegie Hall, a two-hour concert. Eddy Courts, composer of the melody of her first hit, "The Letter," had taught Vera the English pronunciation of the lyrics of his songs and had translated them for her before the concert. He had sent her cassettes with explanations.

Her big suitcase of well-worn yellow leather bears several stickers from the Cunard Line. At the time of her triumphs it accompanied her on her tours. She made a trip to America on the British liner the *Queen Mary,* the suitcase followed her on a tour of several weeks, from Venezuela to Israel, passing through Mexico, and it certainly served on her European tours. Afterward Vera used it for her archives. In it she enclosed folders and little plastic bags where you would find photographs, press clippings in black and white and in color, French, Spanish, Polish, Hebrew, Swedish, English . . . There were also tickets. Small pink stacks. *VERA GRAN, recital de chansons.* January 24, 1970, Salle Pleyel, Paris.

14

They threatened to attend the performance wearing the striped pajamas of the camps

They threatened to attend the performance wearing the striped pajamas of the camps if she appeared on stage.

The place will be destroyed and the performer beaten up.

The organizers of Vera Gran's recitals in Israel were flooded with letters of this sort originating from the members of the World Association Against Nazi Criminals.

Why? She was a victim of the war. And they were as well. She couldn't even begin to understand.

She herself had left Poland. Israel, the homeland of the Jews, the Promised Land of her ancestors, had refused to give her asylum several times. The blows she received there hurt her the most.

Despite all the dire presentiments and the wounding aftermath of the "affair," she obstinately returned there. Roman Messing, Vera Gran's Israeli impresario, had planned ten concerts for the singer in May 1971.

The announcement of these performances, along with her

photograph, appeared on May 7th in the only popular newspaper in Israel for Polish Jews, *News Courier.* This resulted in a
great number of reservations.

However, during this time, the organizers of the concerts,
the directors of the theaters, and the managers of the concert
halls started receiving telephone calls to inform them out of
"good will" about the past of the star they had the temerity to
invite. Then the threats became more concrete. From Pesach
Burstajn, president of the International Union of Jewish
Combatants, Camp Prisoners, and Victims of the Nazis, came
threats that were categorical, clear. Adolf Berman, an underground activist in the Warsaw Ghetto, followed in his steps.

Her existence was tolerated. But it was unacceptable that
she perform in public or that she express herself on the subject of the war. Her honesty and her credibility were placed
in doubt again, and her behavior in the ghetto was subject to
moral judgment, continuing (how was it possible?) to be the
source of rumors. It was a deluge of sensational denunciations
and scandalous revelations.

She related the story of how someone had told her that in
the museum of Yad Vashem there was a poster from the ghetto
with her name on it. Why was it so important for her to see it?
She had fled the war and yet somehow she always returned to
it. She searched for it, within herself, in the world around her,
and in her memories.

Her reaction was enthusiastic when she was asked to record
a statement for the Institute of National Remembrance in Jerusalem. She believed that she should put her account at their
disposal. But under the blinding sun, and Israeli disregard
for privacy, the echoes of rumors and slander resurged with
astounding force. An avalanche of accusations, masses of accu-
satory telephone calls, explanations that were derided.

Seeing further problems looming ahead, Messing decided
for his own peace of mind, and that of his singer and perhaps
the nation itself, to cancel her tour.

This image—a black angel—was closest to her (Ducretet-Thomson)

Yad Vashem declined to record her statement, arguing, after a general consultation, that her account was of no interest to them.

Nothing happened as foreseen.

Bursztajn canceled a meeting with Vera, considering it useless. He himself did not know anything, he did not spend the Occupation in Warsaw, he was relying on the damning documents provided by Jonas Turkow, whom he trusted. Besides, he was acting officially in the name of the Union.

Berman left it up to Turkow, a curious thing, because when Vera was tried by the Central Committee of Jews in Poland, it was Berman himself who chaired the committee. It could mean that he had knowledge of new proofs, or until-then-undivulged proofs, of her guilt. They did not accuse her of informing, but that "it was public knowledge that she lived with Nazis." Despite the solicitations and the attempts of Vera Gran, Turkow would not let her cross the threshold of his house.

Spira, the director of the local radio station, wanting to help Vera as a friend, telephoned the legendary Antek Cukierman, an insurgent of the ghetto uprising. He had heard it said that Cukierman had also been opposed to her going on stage. He wanted to inquire further about what he knew about this "affair" and the veracity of the documents accusing her. He received the following answer: "Me, I have nothing on her, it's Turkow who knows."

All the accusations seemed to be based on the so-called compromising documents held by Turkow.

The café tables occupied by viper-tongued Polish Jews, and those are not lacking in Tel Aviv, Haifa, and Bat Yam, Vera wrote shortly afterward, *were used by these individuals to dissect me with slashes of the scalpel. I had become a monster.*

She wanted to act, to fight, to defend her innocence still. And if they claimed they had proofs she had decided to take it to court. Blackmail and summary judgments disgusted her and could also paralyze her. Let them take the "affair" before the courts and let them examine her. She was ready once again to submit to official jurisdiction. She waited for a public accusation.

None dared to do it, as if a war by ambush was more efficient. More devastating, more hurtful. Destructive. Painful qualities.

She tried once more to settle the case amicably. She sought the most judicious way of unraveling it, she wanted to come to a truce. She came up against a refusal.

The letters she sent everywhere throughout the world were heartrending cries. She shared her despair equally with Kazimierz Jezierski. They exchanged about ten letters then, and all of Kazik's tried to restrain Vera's bellicose instincts, which he considered under the present circumstances unreasonable and dangerous. Or self-destructive.

He wanted to convince her to give it up.

On May 26, 1971, he wrote:

The simple fact of your being over there has "created the affair." It is you alone who are paying the consequences for everybody. Some gain profit by it, others some emotions, and others still are having fun. It's you who's going to pay. You, only you, you have nothing to gain, because in the best of cases you would find yourself back at the starting point.

It's difficult to have friends in this affair, they will get tired or bored, and by contrast you will make enemies. All those who will feel "caught" will be your enemies.

I feel that you have to completely change your tactics. You cannot take on this "affair" alone, nor "defend" it by yourself. You have to "distance yourself from the enemy." Adopt a stance that is adapted to all investigations. Politely give information by correspondence, without leaving any arguments or key documents at their disposal. People's taste for this will quickly vanish, they will find other things to interest them. All the same it's the height of absurdity to allow yourself to be thus ridiculed and to allow a bunch of thick brutes to force you to carry this cross that comes straight from their sick imagination.

Vera did not think this way. Perhaps she had lost patience.

The pain perhaps was too intense and had become unbearable with the years. She tried to convince Kazik, who lived in America at the time, to come to Israel as a witness on her behalf. His refusal was gentle but definitive. According to him, she was making a mistake in believing that the key witness that she saw in him could neutralize anything whatever.

I don't want to get involved in something that could suddenly turn against you. The circumstances of this whole "affair" are so absurd that by following their imposed terms you risk not correcting their stupidity but giving it greater attention without gaining any benefit.

At great length, patiently, and several times—not as before— he asked her to "be reasonable" instead of to "be brave."

Perhaps they had two different concepts of common sense?

In the beginning of July 1971, an article by Aleksander Klugman was published in the Polish-language Israeli newspaper *News Courier* under the title "Old and New Scores to Settle." Thirty-eight years later I read it on microfilm in a library in Jerusalem.

The author of the article lived through the ghetto in Łódź, Auschwitz, and other camps in German territory. He left Poland in 1957.

A short while ago, a performer to whom severe reproaches were made for her behavior during the Occupation had the intention of performing in Israel. She claimed to have been rehabilitated and that a certain commission had recognized her as not guilty. Former prisoners of Hitlerian camps had, however, announced their intention of demonstrating in the theater where she was to perform her act. To visit Israel, fine, but to go on stage and receive the applause of the Israeli public was another thing.

Fortunately, all the parties concerned in this affair, even those who had come out in favor of this performer, withdrew. Because this affair does not deserve to be defended—we have more urgent, more burning agendas. Only the enemy could profit from such a conflict, and that's what he does.

I asked him what he meant by that.

He invited me to his apartment in Tel Aviv, filled with Polish and Hebrew books and dictionaries of which he was the author. He neither tried to go over what he had said nor to justify it. He had not changed opinion. Today as before, he is an Israeli patriot.

"I considered that the reputation of our country had to be taken into account. Israel could have suffered because of this 'affair.' What good would it have served, between terrible wars and right after the Eichmann trial, to have new quarrels tied to collaboration? I was not in favor of fueling or fanning the discussions about collaboration, the complicity, the accommodations with the Germans during the Occupation. It was difficult enough to judge the case of the heads of the Council of Elders (Judenrat): Adam Czerniakow in the Warsaw Ghetto and Chaim Rumkowski in the one in Łódź. We change opinions. We put things in perspective. To what measure does survival justify moral compromise? The application of the rule of the lesser evil perhaps can find a justification? It's in the Łódź Ghetto that the most Jews were saved. It was an idea difficult to admit at the time. It is still today.

"According to me, and I repeat it, it would not have been in the interest of our country that a person suspected of collaboration—either rightly or wrongly doesn't matter, the suspicion is enough—should be made public. Those who survived the Holocaust considered it inadmissible. And since the plaintiffs were themselves victims, their protest had to be taken into consideration. I was not in favor of maintaining quarrels; it would not have profited anyone, and the country would have largely suffered."

In Israel they said of the Hungarian Zionist Rudolf Kastner that he had sold his soul to the devil. When he thought that he would be welcomed as a hero, he was accused of treason and collaboration. Klugman remembered the circumstances of his assassination; he had come to this country some time earlier.

In the spring of 1944, Kastner had made an arrangement with Eichmann—as inconceivable as that might seem, this Jewish activist "bargained" with an officer of the SS—in order to spare nearly two thousand Jews. The price of this survival was heavy: diamonds, dollars, gold. Then he had to make the selection, choose those who could live. Do they have the right? If they have the money, they will live.

June 30, 1944, the famous "Kastner's Train," with 1,670 people on board, arrived in neutral Switzerland. The others were sent to Auschwitz.

He was reproached for not having intentionally informed the people of their approaching end. The selection of passengers spared was put in question. Not everyone had the means to pay for survival.

Kastner's daughter was called "the Nazi" in school, was spat upon, and stones were thrown at her.

In the summer of 1952, a certain Malchiel Grünwald, an Israeli Jew born in Hungary, hotel worker and amateur journalist, accused Kastner of collaboration and of being responsible for the death of 400,000 Hungarian Jews. He distributed in the cafés of Jerusalem a free pamphlet printed at home. Kastner brought a suit for defamation. A political game in which the judge took the facts and sided in a surprising way with the author of the pamphlet.

Kastner was murdered five years later "out of vengeance," by another survivor of the Holocaust, like him.

Years later the perspective on the past has changed in Israel. What had been the most painful right after the war, with time began to be viewed from another perspective.

He saved more Jews than all the partisans, all the fighters of the Warsaw Ghetto, and all the other heroes put together, wrote a survivor in 2008 in the correspondence section of the daily *Haaretz*.

Who saves a life saves the whole world, they say in Israel, in repeating the motto on the medal of the Righteous Among the Nations. Kastner had saved 1,670 worlds. No gratitude was ever shown him. Perhaps it was too soon?

Aleksander Klugman also said: "In the eyes of the Israelis, a dark mystery weighed on those who survived.

"I have just learned that you mustn't judge a person as long as you are not in his place.

"We were silent. Others had fallen silent, as if surviving was a fault. It was passivity that killed the Jews in the ghettos and the camps, they said. But we survived. How?

"I cannot read the history of the war objectively, because I was one of its subjects. A strange atmosphere has reigned here around us, those who lived through the war, the survivors. I don't know if Vera Gran was guilty. To expose her when rumors were circulating about her was in my opinion a mistake."

I had two meetings with the journalist Ran Kislew, who had always defended Vera Gran and the survivors. She considered him the only Just Person on this earth.

December 3, 1971, in the Friday supplement of *Haaretz,* he published an article headed: "Vera Gran Fights Against Shadows." He had been living in Israel for more than ten years. He had caught wind of what the survivors from Poland were saying in the cafés of Tel Aviv. They said she often gave concerts for the men from the Gestapo, she had been allowed to leave only so that she could give up the Jews in hiding. It seems that this information was published in a bulletin from the Polish Resistance. Nobody has ever found this document.

Nor did I. And yet I really searched for it.

Kislew continues to say:

"I have no doubt that Vera Gran was innocent. The Germans, despite appearances and the rumors, did not willingly sleep with Jewish women. They risked being punished for it. It could take place in the camps, but not in the ghettos. They had their own women, who suited them, and they did only sleep with Aryan women. And if there was anyone in the ghetto who would be asked to make an appearance for the Germans, it was Mrs. Turkow, Diana Blumenfeld, rather than Vera Gran."

He claimed that it was Szpilman, right after the war, who had railroaded her. It was difficult for him to say why. Perhaps he was afraid? Perhaps he had reasons to be afraid? In any case nothing can be proven. However, he stressed that it was not Szpilman who organized her persecution in Israel. It was Jonas Turkow.

"His wife was not a great shining moral example, and the dirt about her stuck on Vera. In fact, I think that Vera Gran attracted rumors more than anyone. Perhaps we should ask why.

"Turkow told his version of the facts to whoever would listen. He took his time. Pitiless. Efficient. It was his way of solving his problems. He was intractable. Invulnerable. In addition, he considered himself a specialist of the Holocaust."

I checked this.

Turkow's book *The Struggle for Life* was published in Yiddish by the Unión Central Israelita Polaca in Buenos Aires in 1949. He described with aversion the Café Sztuka, where Yiddish was banned and the Polish repertory reigned supreme.

It was only twenty years later that he revealed the information about the Mokka Café, Marszałkowska Street in Warsaw, where the Jewish Gestapo sympathizers gathered, among them Leon (Lolek) Skosowski, Adam Żurawin, Königel, Marek Rosenberg, Franciszka Mann, and the cabaret singer Vera Gran. The book *There Used to Be a Jewish Warsaw* was published in Hebrew in 1969. He also mentions the lists of collaborators published by the Polish Resistance in numerous issues of the *Home Army Information Bulletin* from 1942 to 1943.

Then Stefan Grajek, an active member of the Resistance in the ghetto, a Zionist and fighter, came to weigh in on the list of

Vera Gran accusers in Israel. The Polish historian and sociologist Michał Borwicz wrote him a letter:

This, then, is the purpose of this "International Union," to do the bidding of Turkow, like this Mr. Bursztajn who threatened to disguise himself in the pajamas of the camps as if it were the Purim holiday, and Grajek, not wanting to "bother about useless details," attempted the same thing in an "official way" under the auspices of the "International Union" . . . and so on? This is your concept of the "role" of these pathetic pajamas?

It disgusts me. It borders on Stalinism and Kafka, but above all it's the irresponsible behavior of people who drag the "Union" into miserable demonstrations of personal hatred and stubbornness, doubly reinforced by a total absence of even the most primitive notion of what is required by law.

On February 28, 1972, Vera received a letter from Simon Wiesenthal, the Jewish activist known to be the "Nazi Hunter":

Your name does not appear among those who have collaborated with the Germans.

At the end of June 1972 the Israeli newspapers reported that Vera Gran had initiated a case with the Tel Aviv District Court, an action for damages with interest for a sum of 250,000 pounds for defamation (*because they spread the rumor that she had given concerts in a café frequented by Gestapo sympathizers and their henchmen, that she had intimate relations with the Nazis, that her name was cited among the Jewish agents of the Gestapo*). These proceedings were instigated against Pesach Bursztajn, the president of the International Union of Jewish Combatants, Camp Prisoners, and Victims of the Nazis; Jonas Turkow; a member of the council of this union; and Dr. Adolf Berman. It also included the publishing firm of Mifalej Tarbut Wechinuch, 53 Weizman Street in Tel Aviv.

In 2009 I tried to find the records of the proceedings of this case.

In Israel, court records are burned after ten years unless they are forwarded to the Supreme Court of Justice or if they are of a certain importance for the state. My research in the Tel Aviv Civil Court led to no results. I did not even find a mention of the case being initiated in the records for 1972, which were neatly filed in alphabetical order.

I also addressed my inquiries to several legal firms. Lawyers have an obligation to keep records for a certain amount of time, which can vary. I checked under the names of the four defense lawyers hired for the case. The sons of two of the lawyers, Trunk and Cymerman, have their own offices. Trunk's son found the number of the file and case (filed under the name "Gran Mara," under the category: DEFAMATION— LASHON HA RA, *slander*), but when I checked the central files, it appeared that the papers had been destroyed. The trail ended there.

After several months, Turkow requested that the investigation be stopped because of the statute of limitations. Berman persisted in saying that the plaintiff entertained intimate relations with the Germans and their agents.

In October 1975 Vera found herself back in the courtroom of the tribunal in Tel Aviv. The case was judged in her presence, but in Hebrew—thus she could not understand it. The lawyer for Berman proposed a conciliation for "the benefit of Israel."

Gran's lawyers demanded that Turkow produce in court copies of the bulletins in which appeared the information concerning the activities of Vera Gran as well as the notes linking her name with those of other collaborators.

Turkow said he had searched for these bulletins in vain in the archives and the libraries across the world.

Neither could I find any proof of her guilt there.

On March 23, 1977, the Polish weekly *The Right and Life,* more commonly known as *The Right and the Fist,* published an article by Jacek E. Wilczur with the title "A Criminal Accuses." It was a pitiless and hateful attack on Vera Gran.

The person accused paid dearly for reading this article. She had a heart attack.

The language used in this article is reminiscent of the classic examples of Nazi propaganda:

In 1950, the cabaret singer guilty of the crime of treason against her own people and the crime of collaboration had left for Paris. It can be assumed that this was facilitated through the generosity of her powerful benefactors.

The truth on the subject of Vera Gran-Jezierska and the rest of the informers is well known in the West; besides, well-documented articles on the groups of Jewish Gestapo sympathizers Kohn, Heller, Gancwajch, Szternfeld, and Dawid Gertler (Łódź–Warsaw) have been widely distributed in Poland. The affair of the so-called Thirteen and of the organization known as the Torch (Żagiew), Jewish collaborators, was not a secret, and yet certain influential Zionist groups do not want to take sides on the subject of such a "shameful" affair.

It is for this reason that when Vera Gran's charges were brought before a judge in Tel Aviv, Jonas Turkow had to produce in court the proof of what he had claimed in his books and that he continues to affirm today.

In the autumn of 2008, I interviewed Jacek Wilczur, the author thirty years earlier of this virulent text. He explained why he had written the article then without the least doubt and with the conviction that he was right. In his youth, during the Occupation, he had been a member of the Home Army under the command of the legendary leader Jan Piwnik, nicknamed "Ponury" (the Sinister One). He had complete confidence in the spy network and the counterespionage of the Home Army. In their honesty and their reliability.

He also went over the circumstances around Vera Gran's departure from Poland. He explained that from what he knew, in 1950, people were not allowed to leave the country so easily. For him, it was a new aspect against Vera Gran. He suspected the Communist Secret Service of protecting her. I found no document that could confirm any of this.

At the top of his article he added a photocopy of the report from the counterespionage of the Resistance. Written on the typewriter: *Extract from the list of informers and collaborators of the Gestapo.*

Gran. Vera. No known address. Jewish origin. Profession: cabaret singer. Operates in the cabarets serving the Gestapo.

None of these documents were known at the time of her trial before the People's Tribunal of the Central Committee of Jews in Poland. They are kept in the folder "Vera Gran" in the Institute of National Remembrance.

Professor Andrzej Kunert, historian, advised using great caution in analyzing the contents. Not to accept this in any case as irrefutable proof of her guilt. Without confirmation from three different organizational levels of the Resistance, it is difficult to draw any conclusions. I believe this.

There are seven reports containing the name of Vera Gran. All date from 1943, the first from January, the last from September. Her name is misspelled twice (Grant, Grun), but there is no mistaking that it's about her. In the same way, she is mentioned twice as a dancer. She appears next to her friend the dancer Mann. No known residence.

January 9, 1943. This Jewish cabaret dancer before the war presently directs an office of informers for the Gestapo interested particularly in Jewish matters. This information comes from two different sources, from the ghetto and from the circle of Staszauer and Fichna.

(Józef Staszauer—Jewish, officer of the Home Army, informer for the Gestapo. Executed by the underground in the bar Behind the Curtain on Mazowiecka Street.)

April 6, 1943. Warning. Agents of the Gestapo . . . The sweets shop on the corner of Koszykowa and August 6th streets is the meeting place of the Skosowski gang, and it has also been estab-

lished to be the place of contact for the aforementioned Fokszański, Mirecki, Clondau, Grun Wira, Jews from cabaret and artistic milieu.

May 6, 1943, source "Karol." Grant Vera, former singer of the Polish Radio, lives with a certain Fuks, Jewish, owner of a pharmacy on Orla Street and proprietor of the Café Modern.

(Fuks/Piotrowski was mentioned several times for having maintained a relationship with Vera. She herself told how he furnished medicine and bandages and ointments for homeless children. They saw one another at the Sztuka. He was at least twenty years older than she. In 1950 she went to Israel with him and his wife.)

Author Henryk Grynberg, in his article "Survival Can Be a Nightmare" (in *Dziennik Polski,* August 8, 1981), believed that *The Right and Life,* which published Jacek Wilczur's attack, was the most anti-Semitic weekly in Europe since the fall of the Third Reich, and he thought that it was the unofficial organ of the Secret Service of the Communist regime.

Using the term "criminal" to describe Vera Gran, based on relatively undefined sources, is what could be termed a psychological assassination.

Correspondence of Vera Gran with the editors of *The Right and Life,* dated April 12, 1977.

Following this slanderous article concerning me . . . I request that you insert in your publication the following refutation.

Jonas Turkow was not a "pariah" in the ghetto during the war, that is false. What is true is that he earned a comfortable living as director of a concert booking agency, a position facilitated by his official status of the only censor serving the German authorities inside the ghetto until its liquidation. Turkow's wife, Diana Blumenfeld, performed three to five times a week at the private soirées that took place among well-known Jewish Gestapo sympathizers, as well as public evenings organized at their initiative by Turkow's agency. A double benefit, because his wife earned 500 zlotys per concert, which was confirmed by Turkow's secretary (to think this "pariah" had a secretary in the ghetto!), Elżbieta Neumark, at my trial before the Central Committee of Jews in Poland. With my 100 zlotys a day, I am not the one who could pass for a big deal compared with him.

My only "crime" during the war and even after, which Turkow has screamed about from the rooftops, was for ONLY ONE TIME to have been forced to sing for the Gestapo sympathizer Szymonowicz—Turkow was the first to learn about it, not only as the official censor but also because of the 500 zlotys that his wife wouldn't receive.

What is also true is that during the Occupation, Turkow was telling people of the artistic milieu to beware of Vera Gran, the collaborator. Yes, it's true. Turkow was spreading the virus of hatred that was infecting him. In mongering this accusation invented of whole cloth, he was avenging himself on me, because he had neither the popularity, nor the success, nor the enormous goodwill people showed me.

It is not true that the People's Court absolved me for "lack of proof," but . . . "for unfounded charges."

Dictionary of Usage of the Polish Language
by Stanisław Skorupka

JEALOUSY

Impotent, ferocious, egoistical, violent, human, small, petty, vindictive, relentless, intransigent, personal, intrusive, biased, secret, enraged, reciprocal, mean.

Jealousy against, toward, about someone.

Yes, but what is jealousy? A consuming envy. The inability to forgive others their successes and triumphs. Those who succeed awaken an ill will, a hatred even, as if they had taken away something from those still on the road. As if there were not enough room in the world for several stars. As if there existed only one summit, and it was already reached.

How is it possible after a quarter of a century that these feelings are still so alive? To such a violent extent that they still come into play against the people unjustly privileged?

But perhaps it is about other things? Perhaps I must return to the source, to the war? Go back over my calculations, look at the cost, the acceptable price of survival?

In a draft of an article concerning Vera Gran, kept in his archives, Jacek Wilczur wrote: *Her letter is a mixture of deceitfulness, lies, and falsehood.* For him there is no doubt: *It was destined to "catch people's imagination"!* He insinuates that *the former cabaret singer remembers perfectly to whom and to what she owes her survival, those days in May 1945. And how she avoided the gallows.*

He suggested that she preferred fleeing Poland, conscious that those loyal to her, *her powerful protectors* (followed by a whole litany of names of high functionaries of the Secret Service in the Communist regime: Józef Światło, Anatol Fejgin, Roman Romkowski, all three of Jewish origin), could weaken in their role as her shield. And it would be more difficult for her to make a deal with others. Wilczur tried to convince all his readers that in 1950 Gran knew very well that she had been protected.

He was pitiless: *She understood that it was better to distance herself as far as possible from the scene of the crime.*

In an interview with me, Jacek Wilczur is full of repentance. It is difficult to recognize in him the bloodthirsty person of thirty years earlier, avid to unmask traitors, urging passionately the pursuit of those who escaped justice and punishment.

"My knowledge of the subject has changed, it is larger and less blind. My experience has also changed. Today, I would not dare to formulate such accusations."

The case before the court in Tel Aviv came to an end in 1982 without a final verdict.

Ran Kislew wrote: *From society's point of view, Vera Gran, as such a person, did not exist; she was condemned to death by a lynch mob in which the principles of justice had no place.*

"Fate has made me pay dearly for having survived the Jewish Holocaust," she used to say.

She stopped singing.

15

It's the last letter

It's the last letter among more than a hundred written over a quarter-century.

Kazimierz Jezierski from Smithtown, New York State, written to Vera Gran in Paris, France, Europe. He had attached a twenty-six-cent stamp and had to pay an additional ninety-five cents to send it by registered mail. The cancellation indicates the date of October 17, 1975.

The envelope is rather pretty, long, pale blue, framed by a red-and-blue border. The air-mail designation *Par Avion* is also printed in English and in Spanish. Kazik's address is in a small box on the upper left, under "K.J. MD." He had typed Vera's address in the center. Across the whole length of the envelope Vera had written in capital letters with a red ballpoint pen and underlined twice in black ink and once more with a felt pen: *Another fake, a liar until death! For me, he is dead!* "Dead" written in bold letters. On the back of the envelope: *Actually, did he die in 1993 or in '96?*

The last exchange in a relationship between Vera Gran and Kazimierz Jezierski that had lasted thirty-six years.

In 1963 Kazimierz Jezierski left Poland to work in the Belgian Congo. Beforehand he had asked for an exemption from his service at the Ministry of Public Security. For a quarter century after their farewell he kept in touch with Vera's life through regular correspondence.

The war had united them and cemented their relationship. They didn't stay together for any longer than that.

It was she who decided to leave Poland and everything that was related to her: her husband and benefactor, the concerts, her public, her professional success. But also the graves. The memories.

She thought that perhaps leaving would settle everything, alleviate the suffering in her soul, the pain of loneliness, their disappointing life as a couple. Enable her to extricate herself from the network of slander. That it would be a remedy. She could think this, even if it might appear infantile.

Kazimierz Jezierski, still a young surgeon, after the war organized health services in different hospitals, and in time he donned a uniform. In his scale of values, work always came first. "The hospital . . . then, for a long, long time, nothing, and finally, Vera," said mean-spirited but perhaps well-informed people. Thanks to his profession and his courage, he brought Vera safely through the Occupation, the successive flights, the ghetto, and the necessary vigilance on the Aryan side. Perpetual dangers and their perpetual mutual presence. It must have been difficult for both of them.

I don't know if they discussed her decision to emigrate. She did not say if he tried to stop her, to persuade her, to explain to her that she was making a mistake or that she needed to think about it further. Nor if he tried to convince her to leave. Years later, it seems as if he did not play a key role in this step she took and which was perhaps the most important after having been spared.

My darling little fish!

"My darling little fish"—that is how he almost always addressed her, he said "darling," "dear," or "venerated." Sometimes he called her by her first name ("Verochka!") and he added in Russian: *Kak dela* (How are you?). It had been that way since the beginning, in the first letter written in small handwriting, almost lazy, of someone with an "indecisive temperament." That's how it was when he took the pain to settle things between them, but also later, when he had lost all hope and only wrote down a list of "practical things," which turned out in the end to be fairly exotic, considering Dr. Jezierski's departure to Africa.

He kept her in his thoughts, wherever she was, and no matter what was his situation. She scrupulously noted down on the envelope the day when she answered him. She never spoke to me about the place he had in her life. None. As a comfort. Benefactor. Correspondent, both by letter and by telephone. None.

I received your letter today and I am answering immediately, because if I don't do it right away, I am afraid of being hopelessly late.

At this time, here is the rhythm of my daily life—I work at the clinic three days and three nights in a row, I rest for two days, and again I work a twenty-four-hour shift.

Dr. Jezierski, sixty years old at the time, had been living in the United States for five years. And even if he complained about *having already used up, wasted, my given span in life,* he did not back away from this new challenge. Already no longer young, after years practicing in Africa, he successfully passed two medical board examinations as well as a medical licensing examination that would enable him to start a private practice, and he found work in his field. He changed country and language once more. He spent much time poring over his books, which he grumbled about a little, but he proudly sent as a present to Vera a dollar bill, a symbol of his first earnings on the other side of the ocean. He awaited her approval.

He worked very hard. On the one hand he complained about loneliness and on the other about the constant attention of his American women neighbors. He found it difficult to decipher the ways of dependent relationships between men and women in the particular world of New York State.

He had already traveled a great deal during the 1950s, in China, the Soviet Union, Czechoslovakia, and in the West within the context of the World Health Organization. He knew French and German. He was in possession of a working passport.

He left Poland finally in 1963 because of the hopeless prospects for his career, and the state of his health. He left his country convinced that he would never return there. In the questionnaire he had to fill out for his passport application he hid the departure of his "wife" for Israel, and the fact that his brother (Andrzej, born in 1925, an electrical engineer in South America) had lived abroad for a long time.

At the beginning of 1954 he had requested leave from his duties within the Ministry of Public Security. To support his request he mentioned his desire to find work again in research (thoracic surgery), and that he had a diseased liver. His request was accepted at the end of January.

How many of these workers were there, gray, disciplined, indistinguishable, and yet all participating in building the socialism for the people's Poland? *Politically active, socially passive,* commented one of his superiors. Ordinary.

The documents gathered in the cardboard files in the Institute of National Remembrance show him as a person full of contradictions. In the reports by his superiors I read: *Lacks flexibility and determination around the operating table. Calm, cynical, has a high opinion of his skills and of his experience. Insolent and nonchalant. Lacks discipline and punctuality. Not precise. Not methodical. Lacks organization and shows little initiative. Tolerant and weak in relation to the staff. Good rapport with patients. Poseur. Expresses his opinions with an artificial solemnity.*

In his letters to Vera he appeared romantic, yet not lighthearted. He liked to quote the verses of poets and sentimental songs from her repertory that echoed his mood at a given moment. He considered himself an expert on loyalty and empathy.

Remember that you can always count on me.

Remember that it is easier to live with expectations than together.

In the beginning right after his departure, it seemed he still tried to win her back. He pressed her, he declared his support, did his best to comfort her in her *difficult fate as a lonely immigrant.* As time passed, he spoke to her less and less of love.

He admired her valor but reproached her for being naive. He regretted not being able to take care of her as he should.

At the end of autumn 1972, I was in Paris and I fluttered like a moth at night around the ground floor of your building. The concierge told me that you were going to arrive, but you never came. I wanted to discuss with you all those matters which have no place in a letter.

It was not the first time that he had sought her in vain in Paris. He had traveled several times in Europe and tried many times to telephone her in the hope of seeing her. He had a camper, he wanted to invite her to travel with him. But the telephone wasn't answered. Later he sent her flowers, most often roses. From Geneva, Amsterdam, Munich . . .

Was there anything more between them than these letters? Telephone conversations, awaited, expensive, first in Israel, then in France, they had to be reserved in advance (international, "Please wait")—for him, *it was an upsetting experience. The voice was so close, and it was so difficult to understand one another.*

He had the impression he was her protector. Why he had taken on this mission, no one knows. I don't know, either, how this relationship started, in what circumstances he fell in love with her. And she? Was it the panic of September 1939 that provoked this union?

He wouldn't let her forget about him. He treated her like a high-flying bird. He wanted to find his own happiness in her success. *The most important is that you realize your ambitions and your needs. You must live intensely; that you have your public, your successes, your experience, is very important.*

Sometimes it seemed to him that she managed her titanic struggles in life like a moth going toward a flame. He felt sorry for her, all the while wondering if all great artists did not experience this need *if only for a moment to move the hearts of these blasé have-it-alls.* He tried as best he could to help her from a distance. He often asked her for the number of her bank account—to buy her a birthday present.

In the autumn of 1960, after a visit to France, he finally understood that she had hit a "catastrophic victory."

In a bitter letter he expressed the tragedy of his difficult and unsatisfied love. He reproached her for egoism and her total lack of interest in him. We don't know what happened. Nor what they said to one another, nor of what they convinced one another. Nor in what way.

I am almost afraid to ask you if I matter to you, because the answer could be shattering for me. I am aware that these words can be vexing for you, not because they are not true, but because you don't understand them.

He fell silent for three years.

When he left Europe, he sent her as a present an amber necklace and a Zorki camera. He resumed corresponding shortly after settling down in Luluabourg, a town in a southwestern province of the Belgian Congo, where he had succeeded in obtaining a contract.

He liked the place, where the seasons didn't exist and where nothing happened. Time was suspended. He told her about this "demoralizing" life in the condition of scorching heat. He did not complain about the climate, he was becoming tanned. *I have recovered financially and recuperated a little.*

In numerous places in his letters, he brought up the world of animals, in which they both apparently had a keen interest.

He had bottle-fed a little female monkey named Massina, very pretty and intelligent. She had a charming room with mosquito netting. He and the monkey often sent their mutual greetings to "Pańcia i Puńcia" (Punia and her mistress). I imagine that Vera enjoyed these stories very much. She always said that animals had reached a level of moral development superior to that of human beings. The feeling of jealousy was unknown to them, and if they were cruel, it was solely to satisfy their hunger.

He doesn't hide the fact that Vera's presence there would give a meaning to the exotic taste of the fruits and to the sunsets over Luluabourg, to the red-flooded land of the Kasai seen from the sky. He missed her fantasy and her *driven energy.*

They were united by a past that was inconceivable to many, unknown to others, but most profoundly shared by them.

After everything that they had gone through during the war, he was no longer afraid of anything; over there they called him the Intrepid One.

After what we lived through, he wrote to Vera, *the fears and difficulties encountered here are child's play, without taking into account that here I earn my living and have insurance.*

Your last letter gave me a shock. I was seriously ill—for the second time in my life [Vera's note: *Sic! What am I to understand from his previous letters? What a dirty liar!!! In the next one, he will tell me that he was never sick a day in his life*] *and that is why I feel all the more helpless at the idea of a probable, indeed necessary, journey in order to come testify. At the same time I am aware that the basis of the case is elsewhere. I almost have the impression that my presence and my testimony in Israel would work against you in your case.* [Vera's note: *???*] *I was afraid to write this because I was wondering if, so violently implicated, you would take my decision as an evasion on my part. I think that it is a bit of a shame you did not have the instinct to see what a risky maneuver it would be to have me come and put me in the spotlight.* [Vera's note: *a shameless coward.*]

In 1963 he declared: *Of course I can testify in your case, before God the Father himself. Think of me, and speak to me during your trip. I would love to hear your hearty laugh.*

In another letter: *It has become even more difficult for me that you are not giving me any signs. I understand that you hold a grudge or that you are angry with me. I have always thought, and I still think, that it is not in your interest to initiate these proceedings, but obviously I would like to be useful to you in all situations.* [Vera's note: *No, you little shit! You were afraid of the Jews, because they would have destroyed you if they had asked you to show your circumcised dick!*]

How is it that both of them had kept this secret for so many years? And why did they consider that it should be kept a secret? They were silent.

This subject was not part of their daily life or of their conversations. She knew. She had to know that he was Jewish. Since when? Would spending the war under his protection have been more dangerous with the knowledge of this?

His father, Jerzy Rubinsztejn, son of Lejba and Sima, née Jezierska, was confirmed in 1920 at the age of thirty-four. At that time Kazik's father changed his name to take Sima's maiden name, which he used as did his two sons.

Kazimierz Jezierski had traveled a great deal. He had gone everywhere in Europe, he had seen half of Africa, he considered going to Australia, even to settle there permanently, or to Vietnam, Yemen, or Lebanon. He had never shown any desire to go to Israel. Not when Vera lived there and gave her concerts, nor later. The land of the Jews was not for him synonymous with the Promised Land.

To return to the actual situation, I think that there is nothing more dangerous than to sidestep the truth [Vera's note: *For whom? There is only you who is avoiding it, and it frightens you! Me, I am afraid of nothing. It's little, but it's everything—I sang once! Poor darling, I am too big for you. Me, I would never have told that you are Jewish.*] *because unfortunately, since the beginning and by the momentum of events, this affair has been directed in such a way that they have almost nothing to lose and it is you who will suffer the consequences and who will have to swallow the bitter dregs. When a person brings a case before the court, she puts herself in a position where any thug can ask her insinuating questions that have nothing to do with the case but which can put her "credibility" in doubt; that is to say that if they can prove that she has lied, all the rest of her case can be considered false. If I understood your letter, you prefer to stay with the unvarnished truth, and I am in complete agreement with you. I will not refuse this "bitter cup," which is the price to pay to advance this case. I think that mine will be only a minute participation in your problems. Starting from this premise, all the decisions are in your hands.*

Of all the talents, I feel you are missing only one—understanding people.

It is necessary *to disengage—with moderation! And stifle your fighting instinct!*

He let himself have dreams: *I would love to take you to Santa Fe, as in one of your earliest songs. Perhaps you would remember that laughing at human folly is the only means of getting through the situation.*

He warned her that he could express opinions completely opposed to what she considered reasonable or appropriate. He considered his active life to be over, which enabled him to maintain his distance in relation to people and their frenzy, and to protect them from mistakes typical of the young, or those whose life is marked by everlasting youth. *I am speaking about you here.*

He was rational.

I don't have the impression that during the Occupation the formalities of marriage had a legal standing. Consequently, what you have written fortunately doesn't prove anything, because there was no Catholic religious marriage, nor any other. [Vera's note: *Sic! The marriage took place in Lwów, but it was a civil marriage. I was in no hurry to go to church, and already by that time I detested synagogues.*]

If they were married, it was before a civil servant who during the Soviet Occupation had validated their union for life. This union permitted them to become part of the communal life that was a means of survival during the war years. Perhaps a married woman could survive more easily? Certainly the wife of a man who was not condemned to die. Were they actually married? I don't know. I did not find any documents confirming it. They could still be hidden in the archives in Ukraine.

Until the end she spoke of him as "my husband," even if it seems more realistic when he said that there was no official stamp validating their union, either civil or religious, as he confirmed after the war in the statements made to the Ministry of Public Security.

Yet in their letters they seem closer to one another than to anyone else. He confided in her about his visa problems, but also his dental ailments; he discussed with her the problems of aging, she gave him the details of her menopause, asking his intimate advice about the soul and gynecology. Acts of exceptional closeness.

Growing old is not sad, he wrote, *but feeling young.*

I think that you are young, very simply, and it is torture for you to be confronted by the calendar.

In 1964, he celebrated his fiftieth birthday in the Congo. *In a way, my whole life is over: an interesting adventure although brief.* According to him, there remained only a short extension. To be confronted with new goals, new objectives, could only spoil your mood. However, he didn't see why he should stop playing. It was now that he could take full advantage of the things for which he didn't have time when he was young. He told her, proud and amused, that he was making progress in swimming, tennis, and that he was training for his pilot's license for civil aviation.

In 1974 he wrote:

I have to tell you that several months ago, Isia came to the United States and our marriage was celebrated here, in a civil service at town hall a short time afterward. I did everything— perhaps not—in any case a great deal, to dissuade her from taking such a disastrous step, but I didn't succeed.

I kiss you.

Kazik [manuscript, in fountain pen]

He married the girl who, in a photograph from before the war, was seated on the lap of his brother in the garden of Podkowa Leśna, near Warsaw. Isia Latoń was only a few years old back then; she had blond braids and a happy little face. A long friendship linked the Jezierski and Latoń families. When they married in 1975, she was a widow and the mother of two sons. She was seventeen years younger than her husband. When she lived with Kazik in America, she started sending packages of food to Poland. She was empathetic and liked to feel useful. She died young, surviving her second husband by only a few years.

Kazimierz Jezierski died in 1994, in Podkowa Leśna.

Vera did not get rid of their correspondence. Dozens of letters, postcards tied by a faded ribbon, as it should be. A largish package. New Year's and birthday wishes. In a black tea box, she kept the postage stamps separately. Her favorites were the stamps from Africa with plants and animals: chimpanzees, giraffes, peacocks and other exotic birds, colorful parrots, palm trees and cacti in bloom.

The postcards could be arranged in this order:

1956, Berlin, Strausberger Platz.

Liebling! Mein Herz las dich grussen, pamiętasz? My love! My heart, let me kiss you, do you remember?

1963, Geneva, view of the Mont Blanc.

I have just arrived, I don't know where I am going to live or where I will be working.

1966, Lisbon.

I have just arrived from America, I am passing through Lisbon to check on the authenticity of the local color in one of your songs.

1966, Montreal, on the front a little dog, a type of terrier, with enormous imploring eyes.

In the eyes on the front you can read all the intensity of my feelings during my Parisian stay. I won't write any more because I am an exhausted vagabond.

1968, on a card with a Sabena airplane.

Greetings from the road toward the unknown.

16

She's happy when I bring records of her singing

She's happy when I bring records of her singing. Or recordings taped from radio broadcasts or during her concerts.

She listens attentively. Sometimes applauds with joy.

"There, that's good, can you hear, this upper register, do you hear? Do you see the color?"

Most often—severe.

"Here it's not right. That's me, that also? It's horrible! I was drunk, with love . . . this coronal consonant *l,* can you hear it? I am a singer, it's morphological. But I am not going to sing anymore! Never again. I saw the famous Mistinguett on stage and I promised myself never to sing when I am an old lady."

She told me that once in Polish and repeated it in French. This statement echoes not only a decision, but despair as well. She shakes her head more and more emphatically.

Suddenly she becomes pensive. She is quiet. As if she is letting her memories resonate.

Then she is singing again: *The dance swept us up in its whirl . . .*

She waits for me to answer. Then she continues:

"I know, I knew it somewhat, but now there is no doubt, you and your ear are two separate things."

She enjoys tormenting her interlocutors. I rebel (by playing the same game she's playing). I try to compensate for myself, make up for it by remembering a version of a song that was popular during the Occupation—"A Hoe and a Saw"—with the lyrics by Szlengel:

A hoe and a saw and patterned slacks
They've gone away and won't come back
But next year you'll once again
Recall the Sztuka and Vera Gran . . .

"That's another life. The one before the nightmare," she said. "Perhaps it wasn't mine?"

The dressing table of a star, or rather its accessories, which are reflected in two mirrors—the bathroom one above the wash basin and the round one of crystal leaning against the wall.

A small red-and-yellow metal box, Transitol, for treatment of constipation (one teaspoon at bedtime).

Estée Lauder liquid foundation, Revlon powder box.

Silver shoe polish, long-lasting shine.

Cleansing cream.

Mascara for black lashes, green eye shadow, white concealer for tired eyes. False eyelashes.

A bottle of perfume, Audace by Rochas.

Tablets for migraines.

On the floor a pile of old posters. Tangible reminders of her glory. Folded across the face. Impassive eyes.

Among the scattered seashells a sheet of paper labeled "exercises for the face": *o, a, e, i, u,* while inhaling. A drawing of the forehead, two dots on the eyebrows above the eyes, exercise to stretch and tighten the wrinkles simultaneously. Lips form a fish mouth while trying to stretch them.

Wooden coat hangers with Vera Gran's monogram—VG.

Silver-colored eyeglass case with her four addresses in the lining: Warsaw, Tel Aviv, Caracas, and Paris.

She tried to convince me to take a little doll made of straw that someone had brought her from Poland.

"For some time now I have been subject to panic attacks at the prospect of departure. I anticipate the last voyage, the most distant, from which one does not return. I can't prepare for it by purchasing gifts, but by a great housecleaning in anticipation of this voyage. Besides, not only don't I feel like buying anything, but neither do I feel like giving away what I have. Because, in fact, there is no one who deserves it, or to whom I might give pleasure. More specifically, no one alive."

A wooden box fell down from a shelf. A small coffer, like those souvenirs from the Polish mountains. The contents scattered on the floor in the dust among old newspapers.

"Help me," she ordered, "and make sure you do not look at anything, put everything back quickly inside the box."

"Perhaps you'd rather I didn't touch anything," I shot back.

"Maybe," she answered, "if she manages . . ."

She sometimes spoke to me in the third person.

I try to gather the small pebbles spread under the table and the bed. She controls each of my gestures, she hurries me. She grumbles, thinking I am not taking enough pains. But when finally I hand her the little box, she puts on her nicest mask and shows me the contents.

"Topaz is a sacred stone, orange yellow like fire, it gives strength. Amethysts . . . you know that in Greek it means a cure for drunkenness? It takes care of all addictions. I have always kept some near me. Just in case. They free me from anguish. Jasper, malachite, agate . . ." With relative skill she juggles this lore of a princess from the realm of darkness.

"And this little jar?"

It's a jam jar, the German brand, Zentis. Traditional. A miniature strawberry jam jar from a hotel. With a metal cover.

"She can open it."

Visible through the thick glass are pieces of amber with sharp angles like cubes, or rounded, different sizes. There are many of them. Some crumbs also. On a bed of blue cotton.

I unscrew the cover. On top, a small sheet of paper folded in four with writing in an elegant hand. In printed letters. *Sum of gallstones extracted from my gallbladder at the Wolski Hospital in Warsaw, 1949,* and her signature: *Vera Gran.* On the back: *My Wisdom Teeth, extracted in Paris in 1979.* Signed: same as above.

"I have to take my medication. For my nerves.

"In 1942 I was attacked by the Germans, they beat me horribly. I have a scar on my forehead and one on my jaw. I had a miscarriage and I lost my fetus. I was sick for a long time, my hair turned white, I started losing my hair. I also stopped having my periods. I was almost blind after the war because of my nerves. It was also because of my nerves that I had diarrhea for years, I had palpitations and the shakes. I also often had pains in my tongue. The father of my child was killed in the ghetto."

"The father of my child was killed in the ghetto"—this information came to me late. It surprised me. Then she was pregnant in the ghetto? Of her own free will or despite it? Did she feel proud or ashamed? Happy or raped? Was she afraid? And of what? Of being criticized, of the pain, of rejection, of the lost? Or perhaps it was a source of joy, and hope? She felt life growing within her.

She searches for her medicines. Groping around on the table, blindly. She extracts the little phials, bottles, containers, sachets with a dexterity I hadn't suspected in her. She must have been as skillful when she composed her floral ornaments and her herbariums.

There's a pause in our intellectual work.

Silence.

On the subject of Christmas:

"I have so many needles in my head I don't need a Christmas tree."

In fact, what's the use? Of what use is it to the Jews to have a crèche and a newborn Christ? She celebrated his birth only once, during the war. Something she never wanted to admit.

Her shoes. Not large, a small foot but rather wide. All with heels, except for a pair of slippers for the house, blue with pom-poms. Suitable for a lady. Pointy flat shoes, with slightly rounded tips. In good taste. Worn. Brand names. Most in good-quality leather.

Tired, worn too often. Still elegant, but a little out of shape. Most have the tips stuffed with newspaper. The lightest are noticeably dirty, some have sweat marks at the heel. Well maintained. Resoled. But the years of wear are visible.

Black patent leather with silver edges, open heels, closed by a little strap. Clear, cream, woven, sling-back, close-toed, with a pink strap. In satin, salmon with a little knot. Brown imitation snakeskin. Silver, imitation fish scales, without heel or toe.

They showed off her ankles, enhanced her figure. They had traveled the world, the sidewalks, the boards, the floors of cafés and hotels. The waiting rooms.

They could be placed end to end to trace a path. The path of a stroll or of a flight. Toward the stage.

Do they add up to the sum of the paths of her fate? Where did they take her?

The book she wrote at the end of the seventies was titled *The Messengers of Slander*. She sometimes called it this "reservoir of blood." It was the voice of despair, the ultimate attempt to proclaim her own truth.

"The writing of it was a healing therapy. It kept me from turning on the gas. Several times I almost did it. It absorbed me completely. I was almost in a feverish state of excitement.

"I could not tell the whole truth. I had to silence a portion of it, or else they would have stoned me to death. But I will never forget and I will never forgive.

"It's not the first time that in response to my clearly fixed opinions, I hear people say that I am crazy. If expressing the truth, saying what I think and what I feel, is a proof of madness—I willingly accept this label."

She wasn't sleeping, didn't eat, smoked cigarettes . . . she wrote. She published her memoir in 1980 at her own expense and devoted herself to promoting it in the following years. Not only did it have to come into being, but it had to be read. Be the subject of discussion. Visible. She did not give up the struggle, energized by the need to convince the world of her innocence.

She made several efforts to offer her book to French and American publishers. She met translators and she asked, she implored. She made an enormous effort, without success.

She recalled her visit in 1993 to the Warsaw office of the Association of Authors and Composers (ZAiKS). Antoni Marianowicz, the president, listened to her attentively. She told him about the thirties, and the stories about the Occupation. A prudent man, he did not believe her judgments that fell like blows, nor her various pictures of the ghetto.

"Are you sure that it was HIM? Was it he you saw wearing a Jewish policeman's cap in the ghetto?"

She repeated it to me several times.

"I screamed," she said, "I screamed: 'Sure, one hundred percent sure! I saw him with my own eyes.' President Marianowicz turned away, and he didn't shake hands with me. He left."

They never spoke to each other again.

She told this story to numerous people. Sylwia Karchmar, whose parents had taken her to Vera Gran performances when she was a little girl, and with whom she stayed during her visits to New York, was moved when she heard this story years ago in Manhattan.

"Vera played it like a stage actress from the Jewish Theater. She screamed: 'I saw him, it was him, it was him!' Followed by, 'I have the documents!! Have the proofs! It was those hands, I saw him as he crammed people into the cars. I remember the hands of the pianist! I had been looking at them for so many months in the ghetto, they were very near me, I only had to extend my arm . . .' "

I listened to Vera all the time. Always Vera.

"The lie is the seed of crime. Its ferment, its reason, its temptation. Do you agree with me? I am accurate to the point of recklessness, with each word; it's difficult to catch me in a lie. I cannot tolerate this seed, none, but especially not that of the lie! I live constantly with the pain of suspicion."

To get to the kitchen, she had to lean on several things—a pile of paper beside the table, cartons, the wall, the door frame. To go, as she liked to say, fondle the kettle. "Kettles have a certain weakness for me." She spoke nicely to the electric plugs that were sticking out, and if she chose the right words, at the end of a quarter of an hour, you could hope to have some hot water. Like now.

She wanted absolutely to serve some jam she had made herself. At one time, she liked having guests. Some Earl Grey tea and candied fruits in crystal glasses.

"I have never made preserves like that—in any case I don't have the tools to cut the carrots, or the idea to mix them with cherries. The jar has remained at the bottom of the cupboard above the kitchen door, which usually stays closed with a little padlock. This was done when it was placed there, pure as crystal. But I have every reason to think that this sticky substance is full of poison."

She did not eat any of it. Me either, even if it smelled good. She was complaining that the Brute or his gang had come during the night and they had dripped the honey everywhere.

The Brute, him, this loathsome enemy. The one spying on her life. The imaginary persecutor.

"Now I stick to the wall everywhere like a trapped fly, frantic (and poor). I have just blubbered in the bathroom."

She had gotten ready to attend the premiere of *The Pianist* by Polański. No, she could not attend, but she wanted to know where and when it was. A good place. The Palais de Chaillot.

"The Jews are going to talk about me. They will rejoice to see me gagged. But perhaps I will recover enough to succeed in giving Polanski a slap.

"I am Jewish, they are Jewish. I was in the ghetto, and they also. We have the same rights. And the bastards will always be bastards.

"That's my sickness, I throw the truth full in the face, right in the eyes. For me, lying is the worst thing in the world. You receive blows if you tell the truth. And me, I get it full in the face. I receive blows from everywhere. Until I bleed."

Several days later, she greets me dryly. I am late; my baguette is no good. Nor the color of the grapes. She will eat some, even though it was not such a long time ago that she had to spit out the poppy-seed cake brought from Poland, and even the honey, which was supposed to be buckwheat but had the taste of dishwater.

I feel the anguish rising in her, I feel reality becoming distorted. The daily forms and images separating from their frames. The imaginary world becomes stronger.

She doesn't wait, done with all niceties. She hurries to tell me.

"I threw out Fatma, who was my housemaid, because I couldn't bear to see her hatred and contempt: she immediately picked out the posters in Hebrew on the wall (*nota bene,* as if this filthy Arab did not know that in Israel there are performers of all persuasions and of all nationalities!). Thus, as she knew that I wouldn't prove anything, she really had no compunction about robbing me."

Vera grumbled out loud that I was all soaked, that I had to dry my hair. Next she was going to cut it because I continued touching it, and it got on her nerves. It was magnanimous on her part, it would spare me from getting pneumonia, but I had to remain with her when they showed THAT (*The Pianist*) on television.

That's why he came, the sorcerer for the TV. He turned a thing, did marvels, and it came on. No matter if he is mixed up with THEM. She didn't remove her eyes from him, he was never alone for a moment.

She is waiting to see the neighborhood behind the wall, occupied Warsaw, and the sound of the piano from the Café Sztuka at the end of autumn 1941. She is waiting for her own voice, one of her hit songs, perhaps "Her First Ball" . . . ?

The walls of Vera's tiny Paris apartment (ceiling included) were hung with her portraits. She liked looking at them.

Waiting for herself. Without results. Suppressed from the film, erased from the past, without value.

The star who resembled her never existed behind the walls of the ghetto.

Her feeling of injustice was even stronger after the world-wide success of Polański's film.

The star of the film, Adrien Brody, wept on receiving the statuette. He thanked the eponymous pianist, the model, the real survivor, whose fate was the basis of the film. He dedicated the award to him, his success on the screen. He wept for all the wars and their tragedies. The audience gave him a standing ovation.

Władysław Szpilman attained the honor of beatification over there, he became the symbol of heroic survival in time of war. She was boiling.

She constantly worried about her naturalization papers. *I don't have a homeland.* Between the old newspapers and the written proofs by her various employers she worked with in Paris, there is her residency card (*carte de séjour*), the only document of identity that she possessed. She didn't have a passport from any country. All that she had to show was this piece of paper folded in half, written in French. It described the bearer as *apatride d'origine polonaise,* "having no nationality, of Polish extraction." She belonged nowhere. She lived for more than half a century as an individual deprived of country in a place where it is not easy to be a foreigner.

In 1993, in an insurance questionnaire, under the heading "Family Situation" she wrote *enfant mort*—dead child.

She tires me out more and more. She is growing more and more alienating. Her little notes, her mirrors, her gloves, her cuffs, the photos and the buttons scattered everywhere, collections of postage stamps and hotel matchbooks.

Her old glasses. The first, the oldest, those from the fifties and sixties, are coquettish. Pointed like cat's eyes, spotted, decorative. And with passing time, larger, bigger, heavier. Less and less stylish. Another look on the world. Many pairs of sunglasses, which resemble one another like reproductions.

Her records, her dictionaries, her inscribed books about the war. *Stars never dim . . .* Vera's comment: *But they fall to earth . . .*

Dozens of turbans, toques, berets, hoods. Not one hat.

A Basque beret, yellow with red lining.

A sealskin hood.

A little velvet toque with silver appliqués.

A black turban of crushed silk, ornamented with a knot on the left side.

She, everywhere.

17

It was to Lailly-en-Val, in the vicinity of Orléans

I t was to Lailly-en-Val, in the vicinity of Orléans, she was transferred at the end of the year 2006 after a long stay in the hospital. She was too weak to live alone. This chateau, a former residence of nobility located in the Loire Valley, was granted to Polish refugees in the second half of the last century. From her window she could see the leafy plane trees and an old dovecote, a heavy and imposing structure topped with a pointed roof.

"The dovecote over there is a large death house for birds. Whole generations in superimposed layers—a record of death. They have been lured there for years, I don't know how. They arrive one after another, attracted by the smell of their own kind. They don't sense a trap. They gather there. And then they alight on top of one another. Bodies, wings, bones.

"Others come. Multitudes of them. They are shut in there without air. Only at night are the latches opened, allowing them to fly. For a moment. I don't know what happens next to bring them back. Perhaps they return by themselves, to be together, next to one another, in the communal warmth, with their children, their families, half dead, nothing matters, together, nothing bad can happen. The walls are airtight. The sentry box well guarded. Nothing green. No trees. The door shut on the ebb and flow of life.

"The hospice for people is below. The birds die smothered, closer to the sky. It's easier for them."

At Lailly-en-Val we dance the waltz. To a record from before the war. She sang the same songs in the ghetto. She's diverting attention from death. She knew how to wrestle with ghosts. A sensual voice, a dress with a low back, applause. The echoes of a colorful past in the context of a curfew.

She is in her pink dressing gown closed with safety pins, I'm in black. She comes up to my chest. She holds on to me with a clenched hand so as not to fall, but at the same time she attempts to lead, to set the tempo. She tries. She rolls her eyes coquettishly, she wants to be seductive, and she weeps because she bears half a century on her shoulders and walking is difficult, like finding the rhythm and not getting dizzy. She mumbles each step of the dance. A smile, wide, joy, she is dancing, we dance.

A small room. The stifling smell of an old lady. Like other old women, nothing in particular. Without the reek of perfume. Rather, a humidity. A mixture of sweat, bodily secretions, and resignation. The shutters have remained closed since the night before. Twilight. A semi-darkness not natural for this early afternoon transformed by this change of scene from day into night. A bed and a table, the basic accessories, only the indispensable ones when the end is near. A sink and a chair with a chamber pot that she cheerfully invites me to use.

She won't allow herself to be photographed. She hides her face in her hands. I do the same thing. We are seated facing each other for a moment, looking through our fingers. Vera spreads her fingers wider and wider. She is the first to burst out laughing.

"I am a clown. I am obliged to be one. To get myself through it. Otherwise, life is too hard. It's hell. You know what hell is? No, you don't know, you haven't any idea, the same for the ghetto."

At Lailly, they remember Vera as a colorful character, and a woman of class. Apparently she had the right to use the familiar form of address with everybody. She arrived there as the wicked witch, screaming, with hair tousled. She calmed down in time, although she always liked making insults. "Have you finished, stupid?" she would say to a young nurse who was wiping her posterior. "It's bitterness," they explained. "She's extreme, perhaps, but she has the soul of an artist. Life has treated her badly." She refused to take meals in common. She didn't participate in group activities, did not go to gymnastics, nor to exercises in memory, nor classes in painting or writing poetry. She did not sing. She didn't want to hear about it. Sometimes she hummed in her room.

She despised her companions in misfortune. She didn't want to look at old people. "A hundred misshapen degenerates! What did I ever do to deserve this?"

It wasn't unusual to see her in the grounds, lifting the skirt of her dressing gown to show off. What? Her legs, her panties, the secret of her youth? "Why are you doing all these things to me?" She was affected, sniveled, screamed out loud, and repeated with delight, "Holy blood of Christ!" She enjoyed the scandal provoked by these words coming from the mouth of a Jew.

She screamed at cameramen: "Get out of here, get away from my window, damned paparazzi! And they came all the way here to find me!"

Soon a new place, March 27, 2007.

The Saint-Casimir nursing home, 119 rue Chevaleret. A small room in the house of the Polish Sisters of Charity, where the Romantic poet Cyprian Kamil Norwid had died.

Her hair is gathered with a pink elastic band, her gray pony-tail is spread out on the pillow. I immediately notice that her right hand is inert. I stroke it. She squeezes.

"*Mamochka, gde ty?* Where are you? They have taken her away, he has taken her, he dragged her by the hair. He was hunting them down. I know that it was him. Do you know that it is possible to scream only once and that afterward it's silence?

"*Geld, geld . . .* You had to see him on the hunt. That evil look in his eyes and his way of being careful of his hands. Irreproachable. Nothing must happen to those hands, they would still play Chopin one day.

"He was in love with me. He composed 'Her First Ball' for me, and afterward . . . what a price I've had to pay for that!

"He took my heart. My mother was everything to me. Vera, Wierozhka, I only had to extend my hand to be given her breast.

"*Teper zabyla*—now, I've forgotten. Ah, yes, he wanted to sell me to a bordello. I wouldn't agree. To tell the truth, I was never tempted by this sort of work.

"Besides, I can't be had for nothing. I've never sold myself cheap.

"Now begins my catastrophe, the real catastrophe . . . " she murmured. "There are some small birds. They flew away. They'll come back." She smiled, calm.

"I am alive. Alive and not among these . . . corpses. I can't remember the faces anymore. Not that of Mother or that of my little boy. It's as if they were in a bank of fog. Unreal. They are fading. I am incapable of summoning up a familiar image. And I don't recognize those who appear in the fog.

"*S uma eshchë ne soshla, no uzhe nedaleko,* I haven't become crazy yet . . . but it won't be much longer."

"And you intend to do it?"

She laughs. "And you, *swołotcz* (scum)!

"*A little street in Barcelona . . . Everything in life comes to an end,*" she sings. "The crazy lady has to be put behind bars. I think your visit has come to an end."

I feel Vera's growing weakness. She still rebels, she continues to play at being independent. She is protecting herself against the feelings of affection she would like to express on seeing me. It's only when I leave that she calls to me at the door. She becomes cajoling, she wants to stop me. She thanks me in a tender voice. In every language that she knows. *Toda raba, merci, dziękuję, muchas gracias.* She is quieter now. A pink terry-cloth band holds her hair in a neatly done chignon, a shriveled Barbie, a doll, artificially elegant. It awaits us all, the inevitability of this condition intensifies the sense of pity.

Six months later.

Another face, mute. Her mouth is sunken, because her dentures are missing. She continuously moves her tongue. She grinds, verifies, finds. She speaks in a murmur; from outside the window comes an aggressive sound—the clatter of passing trains. You feel that everything is loud, even the tick-tock of a watch.

"No, I am not crazy. And it's a shame."

Her hands are still. The right one is dead, heavy, gnarled. But the left hand is also weak; she doesn't make her little "butterflies" in the air. I try to cheer her up. I tell her it's a boo-boo.

Turned against the wall, she wears a diaper. "Poor Wieroczka." She speaks of herself as a little girl. "Poor little hands, my poor little hand. *Imeła kogda-to chest' i chvału, a teper mnogo govna imieet so vsekh storon!* Before, I had honor and glory, and now I'm covered with excrement from everywhere!"

She hums, half-humming. She laments. *My drawer that I locked.*

"One of my hits, do you remember? The stage, the burst of spotlight. That was my daily bread. But you can make do without bread.

"Me, I don't throw anything away, not the least thing. I have everything in a drawer. In there, there are many pages black with writing. Many black letters. You have to know how to experience them. The black letters. You have to have them engraved on your skin."

Written, inscribed, branded with iron.

"Why this room exactly, this hospice and the Umschlagplatz, and Treblinka, the trains, the monotonous rolling, exhausting . . . I hear little footsteps, boo-boo, boo-boo, *merde,* yes, I am the one preparing dinner, I am going to make a tzimmes. I haven't cooked for a long time."

Not only is she growing weak, but also her thinking is disconnected, words are missing, she croons an old nursery rhyme: *a train is rolling, rolling, going far away,* toward an unknown destination, like over there, like before, the trains in the direction of death. She doesn't smile, *train be nice,* monotonous rumbling, *nice, be nice to the little girl from Warsaw.* The RER interurban express train in Paris is approaching the station Bibliothèque Nationale François Mitterrand. She is becoming a child again. With gray hair. She hugs her striped pillow tightly.

An old little girl who wears diapers. Spunky, no, not any longer now, only her hair tied up like going to play jump rope, like going into the fields on a summer afternoon when she didn't know the taste of ashes. Afterward, everything had this bitter aftertaste: "The kikes are burning, Mrs. Doctor—look, madame, there the kikes are burning."

Pussy willows in bloom, little gray catkins, nature, silent, still, unaware. She looks out the window open onto a field, she sees the bushes, the trees, she doesn't want to see anything else. Not the somber glow on the horizon, not the horizon, not the smoke, she doesn't see the fire. Nor does she see them jumping from the open windows, or burning. She doesn't see the human torches.

Nor the carousel. She doesn't hear it, doesn't see it going

around. The rustling of blue polka-dotted dresses, the excited whirl of the world in its verve and dash, because spring has opened the eyes, because the sun brings hope, and not everything is lost, since the seasons continue turning.

A mechanical song, a scratched record, the music goes on and on, sibilant syllables, rhymed, the faithless one, he abandoned her, some popular hits. Not hers, unknown hits. Forbidden to sing. She doesn't know the tune. She has nothing to do with all that. She has no voice. She can't manage to make it come out. Bring it out.

"Mrs. Doctor, you are so pale . . ."

"They are burning, burning."

She raises her hand, her whole arm with difficulty, only as far as her forehead, in a slow gesture imitating the movement on stage, rehearsed. Studied, anchored for years in this body, less and less obedient. This gesture that in the past was fascinating, attractive, seductive, is now only the expression of fear. She wants to hide, protect herself from the world.

"When will I see you again? *Wozmożna czto nikogda—* perhaps never."

Only the whites of her eyes are visible, her skin so diaphanous that you can see through it, the corridors, the canals, the spider webs. *Wieroczka, idi spat', idi w kibini matier*—go to bed, go to hell. She sucks on some chocolate like a nipple, Liba's little girl. She falls asleep.

I went to see her. She recognized me by my voice. Or rather, that's the impression I had. I bent over her. I hugged her.

I held her hands. The right hand, swollen and clenched. Decrepit. Close to me, nearer the bed. I raised it gently within both my hands, like a nest; gently I extended her fingers. She made a face. They wouldn't easily allow themselves to be handled. "Squeeze my hand hard." I wrapped my hand around hers. I raised it up and down, up and down. The pain was eased. She let her hand be moved. I tried again to open it. It barely unfolded. In a cone.

Her eyes. They stop the light and images and sink more and more deeply, more and more hermetically. They block the brightness that comes from beyond the world. Abandoned.

Photograph old age. Photograph death. They have the same resigned face.

Sister Aniela, who remained by Vera's side when she was dying, said that she was not afraid. She was ready to die. She believed in God, the sister was sure of it. Perhaps in her own way, in the Israeli way, but she was a believer.

The Sisters of Charity prayed in her name and for her, by her side. It seemed to them that she knew the Our Father. To me, in my presence, perhaps it was for herself, she spoke of liberty in the face of the ultimate truth that was death. "If you were God," she murmured without her dentures—they were afraid she might choke on them—"If you were God . . . you would not have done this to me. And since . . . and since it happened like this, it means that you are not God.

"I have never gone to a funeral in my life. What do you do at a funeral? It's absurd. Hug the earth? What for?"

She didn't remember the death of her father. She was not present at the departure of her mother. Vera doesn't know where she was caught—in the street or at home—nor how and on which day she was loaded onto the train in Umschlagplatz. The fate of her sisters has neither form nor closure. She saw them for the last time together the morning of August 2, 1942, when she was leaving the ghetto. She remembered that it was a very hot day.

Her little boy, three months old, died of hunger. She never mentioned accompanying him to the cemetery.

The men also left her, and the dogs. All slipped away unnoticed.

Never any tears at the mention of all these deaths. Except that of her mother.

"Incinerate me, scatter me around the base of a tree, let the dogs piss on me. It will warm my soul. And there you have it."

She withdrew within herself, without any self-consciousness, at the same time with exhaustion and relief. Within her. Her last hiding place. A bunker where for the first time in half a century fear would not leave its stigmata.

December 12, 2007:
The Burial Place

December 12, 2007, the Cemetery of Pantin in the Paris suburbs. Three weeks after the burial.

There is nothing, not a plaque, nor flowers, not even a sign. The brown clayish earth clings to shoes sinking into it, sucking them in. Lost, I try to identify the grave. I count the numbers according to the instructions of the cemetery worker specializing in the dead: 122-20-24. Several times. I can't find it.

I can't hear her breathe an indication to me, not a voice, not an echo.

I finally find myself standing before her plot. Bare. Not the least trace of anything, no name. Basically, what's the difference? Her relatives also have no graves.

Acknowledgments

I spent several years with Vera. The last years of her life. Not every day; there were pauses, for long or short stretches of time, sometimes for several months. However, during all that time she never ceased being present. Just as after she passed away, she remained with me. It will soon be five years.

Our relationship was incredibly strong and emotionally heavy. Full of affection and reserve at the same time. Full of this imperious need that Vera had to protect herself against her enemies, real or imagined, and against herself.

It was often difficult for me to bear this.

I admired her combativeness and her determination. I tried to listen to her, to reassure her. Without the participation of Vera Gran this book would not have existed. Without her permission, her presence, her conversations of hours on end, her monologues, I would not have been able to get near her world and its secrets.

I am grateful to fate for having granted me this possibility.

Vera's sole heir, Andrew Green, her half-nephew, the son of her half-brother from her father's first marriage, gave me unlimited access after her death to all the documents that she had left. He authorized me to use them and to select everything that I considered important (books, scores, records, photographs, correspondence) that would give a better understanding of her.

I did not write a biography. I wanted to tell her story so that it would be put to the test by someone—like me—who did not live through the war, but who by family ties has still "never left the ghetto" for years. This is not a monograph about Vera Gran's artistic successes; these are my meetings with her, her personal account of the period during the Holocaust, which I have not experienced but which is invariably present in each of the choices I make in life.

I began by searching for the witnesses of her life. To get closer to her, to know her differently. I attempted at numerous periods in time, at different stages, and in many countries.

It was a difficult challenge. Often complicated because—paradoxically—for Vera and others like her, the end of the war was not completely synonymous with the termination of hell. The survivors, the victims of Hitler, have never stopped struggling. They were caught up in a chain of mutual accusations from which it was difficult to find a way out toward clarity.

I constantly had the feeling of going forward through the quagmire of her memory, vacillating and changing, often called back to life in contradictory contexts, and for different ends. The interpretations of past events changed form according to an unknown plan and unconscious needs.

Several times I did not know if I was in the presence of the truth or one of its latest incarnations.

In Warsaw, I again had the opportunity to meet one of Vera's friends from the Irena Prusicka Dance School, the dancer and satiric writer Stefania Grodzieńska (now deceased). She knew her the longest, they were friends in their youth and several years after the war. They still remained in contact even after Vera's departure from Poland. It was an important testimony about the path they shared together.

It was the great actress Nina Andrycz who told me about the very young and phenomenal Vera of the Paradis before the war.

Marcel Reich Ranicki, at the time a young translator for the community and critic for the *Jewish Gazette,* saw her in the ghetto. I met with him and his wife in their apartment in Frankfurt am Main. The late Teofila Langnas also remembered seeing Vera in the performances she gave at the Café Sztuka in the ghetto. We evoked daily life in the sealed-off quarters and the choices it necessarily imposed. And the thirst for art, despite everything.

The participants in the Warsaw Uprising of the ghetto and its inhabitants knew Vera Gran, but not everyone remembered her willingly. For the time and the attention they gave me, I want to thank the late

Ala Edelman, the late Marek Edelman, Kazik Simha Rotem (Ratajzer), Israel Gutman, and the late Jerzy Szapiro.

Vera was a character who very rarely left people indifferent. She was as loved as she was hated. A woman of character, she provoked extreme feelings ranging from admiration to hostility. I spoke about her to people who had met her all through her life as well as with people who knew her only by reputation. In addition to the people mentioned above:

In Warsaw: Olga Johan.

In Katowice: Jerzy Płaczkiewicz.

In Paris: the late Jerzy Giedroyc, the late Bronisław Horowitz, Maria Sartowa, Sister Aniela of the Sisters of Charity of the Saint-Casimir nursing home.

At Lailly-en-Val: Marek Szypulski.

In Tel Aviv: the late Natan Gross, Henryk Weksler (Ran Kislev), Aleksander Klugman.

In New York: Sylwia Karchmar.

These meetings were as different as the testimonies that were elicited. More or less positive, more or less understanding, revealing, full of enthusiasm, admiration or irritation, embarrassment, or further questions.

To all those who spoke with me, keepers of memories, creators of my memories and my pieced-together past—THANK YOU.

For their precision and their invaluable contributions, I want to express my gratitude to the following historians: Marian Fuks, Andrzej Kunert, Jacek Leociak, Dariusz Libionka, Anna Mieszkowska, Paweł Szapiro, Piotr Wróbel.

I want to thank Professor Barbara Engelking for having accompanied me in this project from its inception, for all those long conversations and her generous solicitude concerning this book.

I have equally received very generous moral support from my friends. They remained understanding and concerned about my obsession with Vera Gran's fate. They stinted neither their time nor words; they tried to search with me for the answers to the most important questions.

Without them, my task would have been much more difficult.

For their encouragement and their show of support during these years of working on the book I especially want to thank Magda Bosakirska, Elżbieta Bugajska, Annick Jakobowicz, Ewa Junczyk-Ziomecka, Sharon Kanach, Joanna Lassere, the late Irena Majchrzak, Ewa and Zbyszek Stachniak, Mirosław Supruniuk.

ACKNOWLEDGMENTS

For their thoughtful reading of sections and their valuable commentaries: Justyna Jancewicz, Marta Ruszecka, and Jerzy Żurek.

Anna Wróbel and Małgorzata Smorąg-Goldberg demonstrated an angelic patience during the ten months and more that we have spent together committed to this work, and a generosity that made the existence of this project possible on the French and American markets.

I want to thank Karolina Dzięciołowska for her help with the documentation.

My publishers, Wydawnictwo Literackie in Cracow and Grasset in Paris, have displayed nerves of steel and an unfailing support in all the difficult situations. For their encouragement, their motivation, and their confidence I want to thank in particular Małgorzata Nycz and Ariane Fasquelle, as well as my New York agent, Carol Mann.

Heartfelt thanks to Victoria Wilson, my American editor at Knopf, and my translator, Charles Ruas, for patience and continued support. I really enjoyed working with them. Joellyn Ausanka and Weronika Ruszecka were invaluable in preparing the final version of the English edition of this book.

For her unfailing presence in the course of these last months of work, which were the most difficult, I especially want to thank Angelika Kuźniak.

Without these people this book would never have been completed.

I thank all those closest to me for their understanding.

I especially want to express my gratitude to the places that welcomed me in the course of the writing of this book. In order:

The Villa Montnoir—the Foundation Marguerite Yourcenar; Pink Soda (Danuta and Andrzej Pawłowski, Canada); Herzliya Artists' Residence (Israel); the Villa Hellebosch (Vollezele, Belgium).

January 1, 2012

PHOTOGRAPHIC CREDITS

Archiwum Ośrodka KARTA: 58, 72, 110
Archiwum Żydowskiego Instytutu Historycznego: 68, 77
Narodowe Archiwum Cyfrowe: 27, 30, 32, 43, 48
Polska Agencja Prasowa: 192
Zwiazek Artystów Fotografikow Polskich: 16

All other images are courtesy of the author.

A NOTE ON THE TYPE

This book was set in Adobe Garamond. Designed for the Adobe Corporation by Robert Slimbach, the fonts are based on types first cut by Claude Garamond (c. 1480–1561). Garamond was a pupil of Geoffroy Tory and is believed to have followed the Venetian models, although he introduced a number of important differences, and it is to him that we owe the letter we now know as "old style." He gave to his letters a certain elegance and feeling of movement that won their creator an immediate reputation and the patronage of Francis I of France.

COMPOSED BY

North Market Street Graphics, Lancaster, Pennsylvania

PRINTED AND BOUND BY

Berryville Graphics, Berryville, Virginia

DESIGNED BY

Iris Weinstein